Locating Irish Folklore
Tradition, Modernity, Identity

Locating Irish Folklore

Tradition, Modernity, Identity

Diarmuid Ó Giolláin

CORK UNIVERSITY PRESS

First published in 2000 by
Cork University Press
University College
Cork
Ireland
and in the United States by
Stylus

Reprinted 2004, 2007

British Library Cataloguing in Publication Data
A CIP catalogue record for this book is available from
the British Library

Library of Congress Cataloging in Publication Data
Gio'lláin, Diarmuid Ó., 1955–
    Locating Irish folklore : tradition, modernity, identity / Diarmuid Ó Gio'lláin.
       p. cm.
    Includes bibliographical references and index.
    ISBN 1-85918-168-6 (alk. paper) – ISBN 1-85918-169-4 (pbk. : alk. paper)
       1. Folklore–Ireland–History and criticism. 2. Folk literature, Irish–History and
    criticism. I. Title.

GR153.5 .G56 2000
398'.09417–de21   00-022739

ISBN 1-85918-168-6   hardcover
ISBN 1-85918-169-4 paperback

Typeset by Tower Books, Ballincollig, Co. Cork

Printed and bound in Great Britain by
CPI Antony Rowe, Chippenham and Eastbourne

For Nora Gillan
And in memory of Leo Gillan

Contents

Acknowledgements

Many debts have been incurred in the writing of this book, to family, friends and colleagues (and to any combinations of the three). Naturally, I wish to implicate no one in any of the errors of fact or interpretation that may be in the book. I would like to thank Nora Gillan, Mary Gillan and Simeon and Elisabeth Gillan for their unstinting moral support. Mícheál Briody painstakingly read through several chapters, weeded out many errors and added various illuminating points of information. Mary Gillan, Ethel Crowley and Neil Buttimer gave me valuable feedback on individual chapters. Maeve Conrick tracked down a particularly thorny quotation (the Weinreich one) for me. An anonymous reader provided an extremely useful and detailed report on an earlier draft of the book. Séamus Mac Philib gave me useful advice and information. Maeve Conrick and Frank Martin, Ethel Crowley and Jim Mac Laughlin, Pól Ruiséal, Mary Donnelly and John Mee, Siobhán Mullally and Pat Crowley, Patrick O'Flanagan, Linda Connolly and Andy Bielenberg all gave sound practical advice, encouragement and lashings of optimism. Above all, I would like to express my gratitude to Gearóid Ó Crualaoich, who in many ways made this book possible through pioneering many of the topics in it, through the creation of a departmental culture that encouraged openness to new ideas, and for being a generous friend and colleague. I thank my departmental colleagues Marie-Annick Desplanques and Stiofán Ó Cadhla and Colin Rynne for their help, friendship and forbearance; and Colin too for bringing the cover photograph to my attention, and Christopher and Amy Ramsden for permission to use it; An Léann Dúchais and Folklore students, who are a constant source of inspiration and who make the job worthwhile; Veronica Fraser for her good humoured help at every step of this project; Dónal Sugrue and the Northside Folklore Project. Being in, if not of, the History department has allowed me to benefit from the proximity of many dynamic scholars. Tom Dunne, Dermot Keogh and Donnchadh Ó Corráin have been particularly supportive. Sharing the seminar, 'Culture, nationalism and identity', with Joe Lee taught me a lot. A couple of years of attendance at Sociology department seminars and the influence of Ethel Crowley, Jim Mac Laughlin and the late Vincent Tucker opened my eyes to ideas I am only gradually coming to grips with. And I have always benefited from the friendship and kindness of the members of the Irish departments in UCC.

The book has depended a lot on information acquired over a long period of time in various places and through various institutions, and directly or indirectly, through the friendship, inspiration or assistance of various individuals. Hence I wish to acknowledge my indebtedness to the Department of Irish Folklore in University College Dublin; the Ulster Folk and Transport Museum, particularly Jonathan Bell and Mervyn Watson; the Department of Anthropology in NUI Maynooth; Anders Ahlqvist; Garrett Barden; Angela Bourke; Eva Buchwald and Matti Eerola; Linda Cardinal; Emer Crean; Síle de Cléir; Joe Enright; Jaak Johanson; Jaak and Aigi Jürisson; Tuula Lehtonen and Jussi Klemola; Jocelyn Létourneau; Eric Long; Sylvie Muller; Grace Neville; Úna Ní Chaoimh; Tony O'Brien; Paddy O'Carroll; Carme Penyalver Quesada and Esteve Bartomeus; Grazia Reati; Giancarlo Rizzardi; Celia Roose; Tuula Sakaranaho; John Sheehan; Declan Smith; Fionnuala Sweeney; Laurier Turgeon; Ríonach Uí Ógáin.

The UCC travel grant helped me to visit Argentina and Chile in 1997, and I am grateful for the help given to me by Martha Blache and Alicia Martín of the University of Buenos Aires and by Carlos Ossandón of Universidad Arcis in Santiago. I would like to acknowledge the help of the Arts Faculty Research Fund in UCC in enabling me to visit Brazil in 1998, and I am grateful to Renata Leite de Menezes in PUC-Rio de Janeiro and Liv Sovik in the Federal University of Bahia for sharing their knowledge with me. During my sabbatical in Buenos Aires in 1999, Martha Blache, Armando Scalise, Stella Accorinti and Alejandra Cragnolini were excellent research guides. I am grateful to Diego Alconchel, Teresa Jiménez and Víctor Goytía in other ways. I am grateful to Anna-Leena Siikala, Lauri Harvilahti and Pauliina Latvala for the invitation to me to lecture at the Folklore Fellows' Summer School in Lammi, Finland in 1997. I learnt a lot from lectures, presentations and conversations and also produced early drafts of some of the material for this book. I owe much to what I have learnt in Finland over the years to folklorists in the universities of Helsinki and in the Finnish Literature Society. I would particularly like to thank H.P. Huttunen, Annikki Kaivola-Bregenhøj, and Carsten Bregenhøj, Leea Virtanen, Urpo Vento and Pertti Anttonen. The Finnish Literature Society's generosity has constantly kept me in touch with Finnish research. Among its staff I would particularly like to thank Jukka Saarinen. Mícheál Briody has always been a great guide to Finnish (and Irish) scholarship. Across the Gulf of Finland, I have been privileged to receive the friendship and cooperation of Estonian colleagues, especially in the Kreutzwald Literary Museum and in the Folklore department of Tartu University. I am particularly grateful to Külli Tamkivi, Ülo Valk, Mare Kõiva, Ants Johanson, Ingrid Rüütel, and also to Krista Kaer. In Sweden, a period spent at the Department of Ethnology in Stockholm University introduced me to many of the themes and approaches which are central to this book. I am particularly grateful to Jan Garnert, Georg Drakos and Barbo Klein, Bo Nilsson of the Nordic Museum, and also to Mark Comerford. In visits to Catalonia I benefited from conversations with Josefina Romà Riu of the University of Barcelona and Dolors Llopart of the Museu d'Arts, Indústries i Tradicions Populars in Barcelona.

I am grateful to Charlotte Holland, the staff of the Boole Library, the Computer Centre University College Cork, Ark Scientific, and Caroline Jeffrey and her staff in USIT. And I would especially like to thank Winifred Power for the dextrous copy editing and Cork University Press for taking on this project and bringing it to a happy conclusion.

Diarmuid Ó Giolláin
February, 2000

Introduction 7 pp. r

'Folklore' is both subject matter and critical discourse, amateur enthusiasm and academic discipline, residual agrarian culture and the popular urban culture of the present; it is both conservative anti-modernist and radical counter-culture, the sphere of dilettantish provincial intellectuals and of committed nation-builders, transmitted by word of mouth in intimate settings and negotiated electronically in the public domain.

Writing in the early 1930s, Antonio Gramsci observed that folklore was usually studied as a picturesque element.[1] *Folklore* in French (the word borrowed in 1877) means 'picturesque aspect but without importance or without deep significance', while the familiar locution '*c'est du folklore*' indicates something that is not serious.[2] The word has developed the connotation of 'element of local colour', usually appreciated by tourists in set-piece displays put on by semi-professional or professional performers. It may be considered a perfectly legitimate term for colourful cultural phenomena such as folk song, regional costume and festival, which can be considered national even if not belonging to high culture. As part of the national or regional heritage, folklore is of ideological importance and has often provided a reservoir of symbols for identity politics.

Borrowed by many languages, the foreign-sounding word also has a scholarly connotation – as a branch of learning devoted to the study of residual peasant culture, to popular culture in general, or to the verbal art of small groups. The very homeliness and vagueness of the term folklore, quite unlike the arcane names for scholarly disciplines like anthropology or sociology, has helped to give it – in contrast to those disciplines – a life independent of the academy. It never became the exclusive preserve of specialists. On the contrary, the specialists continued to share it with the intellectual descendants of those *amateurs* who pioneered the concept. Neither monopolized nor mystified by specialists with a professional training, it is comparable in this sense to the position of history, the study of which has been enriched by

1

a great number of local and other non-academic historians. But folklore has not been de-mystified by specialists either and, in Ireland, and analogously in other countries, it has come to resemble de Valera's projected nation, to a large extent 'continuous with an imagined Irish, Gaelic, Catholic and communal past' in Tom Garvin's phrase.[3] History is an ancient word, unambiguous and relatively low in real or potential ideological weight. 'Nationalist', 'revisionist' and 'post-revisionist' histories do not fundamentally question the meaning of 'history' itself. 'Folklore', however, is a word bulging with ideological weight, a relatively new addition to the English language, describing a phenomenon that was only visible from above, to members of the elite. Scholars have constantly questioned its definitions and indeed the very usefulness of the concept itself.

Folklore escapes clear definition, but its aura gives it an immediate emotional resonance. It seems to have to do with the past, or at least the residual. It has to do with the countryside, in Ireland particularly with the West and even more so with the Irish-speaking West. Perhaps most of all with places like the Aran Islands or the abandoned Blaskets. It has to do with old people rather than young people. If it plays music it is pipes or fiddle rather than electric guitar. If it tells stories it is orally and in intimate settings. It belongs more under a thatched than a slated roof, by a turf fire rather than a radiator, in a humble kitchen as opposed to elegant drawing-room. If it travels on land it is by donkey, bicycle, or – perhaps – Morris Minor. If it travels by sea it is by *currach* rather than by yacht. If it travels by air it is on its way to a folk festival.

Yet if we look more closely, we find that these apparent truisms are not valid any more – if they ever were. The *currach* is having a revival, but for leisure and especially for racing. Thatching is making a comeback, with the help of a heterogeneous clientele (many of whom already have a house in the city) and a state grant for a thatched roof. Storytelling has been revived, with international festivals and frequent sessions in pubs and other venues. Irish folk music is thriving in Ireland and abroad – has gone beyond its ethnic roots – and has a strong place in the culture industries (recording companies, broadcasting, concert promotion). Having its origins in the countryside and for long specifically identified with it, today folk music is mostly found in the cities. It is heard on the radio, television, in concerts, pubs, advertising jingles, hotel lobbies and shopping centres; just like country and western, rock and roll, jazz and classical music. (Another Irish popular music derives from post-Second World War American influences and their British imitations and has been assimilated into Irish culture. Irish rock has little to do with Irish folk music but it speaks from a transnational – and no less Irish – experience of urban youth culture.)

Are these folk culture or are they not? If not, is it because they are not authentic? What is authentic? Can folklore be other than residual? Can it be emergent? Can it move to the towns, like Irish music or storytelling sessions? Or was it always in the towns? Or is folklore a term that represents something fixed and static, or if, in motion, only towards its own extinction?

Where is Irish folk culture today? Where is the Irish folk? The majority of the population lives in cities and towns, a small and dwindling minority depends wholly on agriculture. The same culture industries serve town and country. The largest political parties in the Irish Republic still defer to traditional values, understood as rural, but it is crystal clear that these are far from the experience of the majority of the population. There is a significant proportion of the married population living in second relationships and a high proportion of children is born to single mothers. There has been a rapid decline in church attendance, particularly among Catholics, and arguably a gradual de-linking of religion and ethnicity in the Republic. The received wisdom of Ireland as a poor, oppressed emigrant country famed for its hospitality has been turned on its head as a growing prosperity has attracted small numbers of refugees, asylum seekers and illegal immigrants (who have been treated with a considerable degree of official and popular hostility). Two important icons of Irish popular culture in recent decades have been black, Phil Lynott of the band Thin Lizzy, and the soccer player Paul McGrath.

What of the most picturesque and most folkloric region of the West, the Gaeltacht, first identified a century ago as the repository of traditional rural and Catholic values, as a reservoir of Irishness? Consisting of small dispersed rural communities whose land has extremely limited agricultural potential, can its future be any different to that of thousands of other rural communities throughout Europe which are losing populations and traditional livelihoods while at the same time becoming more and more the playgrounds of urban professionals? The writer Máirtín Ó Cadhain was one of the few to point out another Gaeltacht – of national politics and of new songs – that is very much alive, in Connemara above all, though this vitality does not lessen the real problems of sustainability of rural communities and minority languages. The Connemara Gaeltacht today is 'a living progressive modern community' with reasonably good employment prospects, according to Gearóid Denvir.[4] There has been a renaissance of traditional boats since the 1970s, but now for pleasure and for racing. 'Patterns' (patron day) and other local festivals are also having a revival. Traditional ('*sean-nós*') singing has widened its audience and practitioners beyond Connemara, traditional music in general is thriving and there has been a revival of set dancing (as elsewhere in the country). New songs are strongly influenced both by country and western and by '*sean-nós*'. Micheál Ó Conghaile estimated that forty people were composing songs in Connemara in the early 1990s and that upwards of a hundred songs had been composed in ten years.[5] The songs were heard on the radio (especially Radio na Gaeltachta) and television, from cassettes and records, in public houses, concerts, competitions and at the meetings of local cultural organizations.[6]

Are these the uncomfortable compromises with modernity that an ancient folk culture has to make in order to survive in an unsentimental world? Or are they part and parcel of the unavoidable and necessary engagement that every living tradition makes with change? The point is that the continuity of traditional cultural elements is not necessarily compromised by embracing, rather than resisting, modernity, even if the resulting 'second life' (see Chapter 7) may not satisfy the purist. There is no alternative since the continued embrace of cultural features that have outlived the pragmatic functions of their 'first life' – thatch in addition to slate or galvanized tin, tarred canvas as well as fibreglass boats, the Irish language along with English outside of the Gaeltacht – is due to their developing a 'second life' over and beyond their original pragmatic function. The examples from Connemara show the unavoidable compromises of the 'folk' with modernity and, because there is nothing particularly modern about these particular instances, they problematize the separation of a 'folk' experience from the general in the modern world.

Locating Irish folklore is the task of situating folklore within Ireland's history, geography and research traditions. Of necessity, the perspective is comparative. The concept of folklore developed partly as a 'nationalist' reaction to a metropolitan culture with universal pretensions. Intellectually the notion is traced in this book through the history of eighteenth- and nineteenth-century European ideas and contextualized by looking at other countries in addition to Ireland. The same ideas varied in their ideological potency. In England or France, 'folklore' was primarily a regional interest, meriting scant mention in national histories, whereas in Germany, Finland or Ireland, it was a key element of modern history and national identity. Metropolitan countries had old, long-established and legitimated high cultures. Peripheral countries (we use 'metropolitan' and 'peripheral' in terms of a power relationship) aspired to their own high cultures, which could not come from the cities, where a metropolitan one was already firmly established. Romanticism greeted the industrial world with horror, seeing the destruction of agrarian culture and the creation of an exploited, alienated and degraded urban proletariat, and at the same time valorizing cultural difference. The idealization of the countryside and its inhabitants then opposed both metropolitan culture and industrialization, limiting the concept of folklore to the countryside, and viewing it as the basis for a national culture.

The institutionalization of folklore research in universities came late to metropolitan countries, if at all, since the idea of a scientific discipline devoted to the study of declining elements of culture without a legitimate status in society made little sense. On the other hand, the outward ethnographic gaze of the discipline of anthropology had practical applications as colonial empires were being consolidated. If folklore could be construed as national culture then it deserved a place among the other scientific disciplines whose implicit task was to benefit the state, which towards the end of the nineteenth century increasingly provided their financial basis. If a rough distinction can be established between folklore and folklife, the former tended to encompass more the intangible aspects of agrarian popular culture – beliefs, narratives, music, customs – and the latter the more tangible aspects – material culture specifically, even if this went against the usage in Sweden, where the term originated. Romantic nationalism tended to identify the former with earlier, often medieval, elite traditions, thus allowing the establishment of a greater historical depth or continuity to the nation. Folklife, then, almost by default, dealt with the more obviously prosaic and pragmatic aspects of rural life and was usually less ideologically productive, and not as likely to be carried away on flights of Romantic fancy. It was thus less central to the folkloric discourse which is one of the main themes of this book.

Folklore, folklife, folk culture, popular culture and subaltern culture can be more or less synonymous, though on a sliding scale which goes from the philological towards the sociological and from the conservative towards the radical. The same applies to folk, peasantry, (common) people, masses, popular and subaltern strata or classes. All of these terms will be discussed and used, partly because the variety of sources used makes it difficult to be fully consistent and also because the terms are useful evidence of the perspective that informs them. The discussions here are in a broad comparative context, and the variety of international comparison is a deliberate strategy to contextualize the Irish case, not just in terms of the experience of other countries, but in terms of other countries' research perspectives, less known in Ireland.

This book is neither a history of Irish folklore nor of Irish folklore scholarship. It is mainly the historical and socio-political contexts which colour the text. While recent developments in popular culture and its study are mentioned, the focus is not primarily on the present, though it is emphasized that the ideas that are plotted and studied throughout the text continue to inform scholarship, ethno-political identities and various aspects of culture in general. The focus is on folkloristic discourse, its origins and its applications. Those who interested themselves in folklore in Ireland in the past represented traditions which either opposed the political status quo or accepted it. Thus there have been in the most general terms two orientations, the former nationalist by implication, the latter unionist, even if its focus was regionalist. To some extent this has influenced the subsequent institutionalization of research, with the one focusing more on folklore and the other on folklife. The focus in this book is primarily on the former. Anthropologists have long worked parallel to folklorists in Ireland and have left a number of invaluable monographs on Irish rural communities, mostly in the West. Their projects were not informed by the dominant concerns of Irish intellectual life and were not part of a national discourse as that of the folklorists undoubtedly was. Hence they are somewhat marginal to the focus of this book.

The first chapter sets the parameters for the discussion that follows, in general terms and in terms of the Irish implications, in the transition from tradition to modernity and the responses to it in European thought. The debate between universalism and cultural relativism that developed from the Enlightenment project of a modern society and the reactions against it in Romanticism and its precursors established the conditions for the development of a notion of folklore. The second chapter traces the gradual crystallization of this notion through antecedents in literature, church writings on 'popular errors', antiquarianism, travel accounts and enlightened enquiry, to the development of scientific theory, methods and institutions in the nineteenth and early twentieth centuries. The third chapter discusses the relationship between folklore and nation, and looks at the circumstances under which folklore was interpreted as a key element of national identity and thus acquired optimal conditions to develop as a research field. The role of ethnicity, of intellectuals and of national movements is crucial. Folklore could be a nation-building resource, an endangered national monument the saving of which mobilized and in a sense 'nationalized' significant numbers of individuals, or a tool for nationalism. In other circumstances it could be an obstacle to the consolidation of the nation. For comparison, there is a brief discussion of the use of folklore in several European countries and in Brazil. The fourth chapter is the first to focus specifically on Ireland, outlining the antecedents and the historical and intellectual background to the notion of Irish folklore. The focus is continued in the fifth chapter, which takes over the story of the development of Irish folklore study at the point when, already informed by cultural nationalism, it converges with the project of reviving the Irish language. The sixth chapter looks in an international context at the relationship between folklore and poverty, whether idealized in a Romantic anti-capitalist perspective which saw a lack of materialism rather than misery in folk communities, or set in a more radical position that idealized the people as an authentically national stratum which needed to be removed from its isolation in order to fully contribute to national life. Thus two dominant perspectives in the approach to the study of folklore and popular culture are debated. The seventh and concluding chapter looks at the relationship between folklore and modern culture, whether through the transformation of rural life by capitalism, rural migration to the city, the influence of mass media, the decline of the urban proletariat, globalization and the growth of an international popular culture. It evaluates the usefulness of the notion of folklore in an era where folk, popular, mass and elite culture are no longer where they used to be.

I have used a wide range of sources from many different countries and intellectual traditions, and have tried to make my sources as transparent as possible, referring frequently to authors and making copious citations. This is in part a deliberate tactic, to encourage an engagement with these works which, I think, offer fresh perspectives that may not be particularly well known in an Irish context. The vast majority of the sources are secondary as a result of the comparative and synthesizing purpose of this work. Many of the citations are from languages other than English and the translations, if my own, make no great claims to elegance. When the quotation is in English and the reference is to a work that is not in English, then the translation is mine. When I use a published English translation, I give the translator's name after the citation of the title of the work.

1. The End of Tradition?

Folklore is predicated on the death of tradition. Since the word first appeared it has carried an aura which has been a burden to the study of popular culture. 'Folklore' appeared as it was disappearing, it was discovered as it was being lost, it was recovered as it ceased to be. 'Folklore' was tradition, or at least it was traditional, and tradition helped to legitimize identity. Hence the loss of tradition had negative implications for the maintenance of identity. It has been taken for granted for generations that modern society dooms traditional ways of life. The question preoccupied the Romantics as well as the classic sociological thinkers. The notion of tradition is important, with its strong emotional connotations, and it has tended to dominate definitions of folklore to the present.

The word tradition is noted in English from the fourteenth century. While all four senses of the Latin original – delivery, the handing down of knowledge, the passing on of a doctrine and surrender or betrayal – have been recorded in English, it is the sense of something handed down with 'a very strong and often predominant sense of this entailing respect and duty' which has come to the fore. The meaning of the word 'tends to move towards *age-old* and towards ceremony, duty and respect'. In that sense the word has often taken on a dismissive tone, with the derivative traditionalism 'becoming specialized to a description of habits or beliefs inconvenient to virtually any innovation . . .'[1] This has been part of the problem that engages us here: the development of modern societies which saw a break with the 'dead weight' of tradition as the reason for their dynamism.

 There is a prescriptive and authoritative aspect to tradition and in the same way tradition legitimates authority. The criteria for authenticity in tradition, according to David Gross, are the linking of a minimum of three generations, the carrying of spiritual or moral prestige and the communication of a sense of continuity between past and present, 'this feeling of consecutiveness'.[2] Tradition is imagined as a thread linking us to our shared

8

trad legitimates

past as we move forward and at the same time it legitimates what we do in the present. Going back to the origins for regeneration is a part of all mythical worldviews. Christians are constantly put in touch with their origins through ritual, with the creation of the world on the Sabbath, with the passion and death of Christ every Easter. But what if the link is broken? How then can people go back to reorient themselves, to renew their purpose?

Undermining Tradition

The societies best known to us through the work of nineteenth- and early twentieth-century folklorists and anthropologists were small-scale, adaptations to specific ecological and economic niches and with limited social and occupational differentiation. To an extent these societies were unified by traditions shared more or less by everyone, which in the case of European peasant communities was part of their attraction for Romantic folklorists in search of utopian 'classless' models for nation building. Complex highly differentiated societies have a greater variety of traditions, specific to and limited to status, class or occupation, or to town or country. Gross argues that the greater variety of traditions offers a choice that conversely subverts the prescription of tradition in general. The latter kind of society developed in Europe in a process which seems to have been complete in most places in the period between the fifteenth and the seventeenth centuries and was undoubtedly helped by the development of print.[3]

Both the Renaissance and the Reformation (and the Counter-Reformation) impinged on tradition, but by arguing that we had lost sight of the genuine tradition. Empiricism, by maintaining that truth is only that which can be tested by observation and experience, and rationalism, by claiming that truth could be discovered by reasoning, undermined the claims of tradition and saw it as a hindrance to rational thought.[4] Another blow to tradition was the idea of breaking with the past and beginning again. This was different to the mythical sense of re-beginning known to all cosmologies through ritual. The establishment of European societies in America was a new beginning on 'virgin territory' removed from the obsolete debris of the past. The naming of places as 'new' in the Americas of the sixteenth to eighteenth centuries, according to Benedict Anderson, was different to the previous naming of places as 'new', where the new place was seen as a successor to or inheritor of a place that no longer existed. The new place in the American case existed contemporaneously with the old and in competition to it: Vizcaya and Nueva Vizcaya, London and New London.[5] The present was legitimated on the basis of its newness and originality rather than on its continuity with the past. The idea of the present as better than the past, the desire for novelty and the development of the notion of progress, coincided with the development of capitalism which, by the sixteenth and seventeenth centuries, exercised a strong influence for change in Western societies.

Medieval European society with its closed economy and hierarchical organization rejected novelty, and hence 'progress', as a threat to the established order.[6] The kind of individual who characterized capitalism was distinguished by a variety of novel traits: a tendency to instrumentalize persons and things, to see productivity as the criterion for evaluating an endeavour, to look to the consequences of actions rather than to their legitimation from precedence, to base economic activity on rational criteria, and to reorganize all available resources in order to maximize profit. At the same time a dominant notion of interest as the accumulation of capital through the rational pursuit of economic advantage came to the fore. Through the internalization of these ideas and values by the bourgeoisie, rationality came to be incorporated into life-styles and attitudes to life.[7] At the same time the division of labour derived from capitalism led to a sharp compartmentalization of traditions between an 'upper' and a 'lower' social class who had previously lived side by side and shared many cultural traditions.[8]

Centralization hardly existed in the ancient and medieval state that was in a sense a 'federation of social groups', in which subordinate groups could have autonomous institutions that sometimes had state functions. The absolutist state, from the seventeenth and eighteenth centuries on, downgraded the intermediary governing role of the estates, regional assemblies and corporate bodies and at the same time co-opted regional elites. An unprecedented push towards centralization developed, helped by a rising national consciousness. Inevitably the aggressive extension, with church support, of rational state control into more and more domains of life had profound implications for traditional values and customs.[9] Various writers have commented on this. Mikhail Bakhtin notes a contraction of the field of French popular culture, particularly of its festive and spectacular forms, from the seventeenth century onwards, during which period it retreated from the public domain.[10] Robert Muchembled observes that around 1550 French writers constantly used popular culture to enrich their work. This lessened in the course of the following two centuries, as a growing gap appeared between the supposedly uncultured masses and the culture of the court, the nobility and the bourgeoisie.[11] By 1800, according to Peter Burke, the upper classes in Europe had withdrawn from popular culture, leaving it to the lower classes. Correspondingly, the meaning of the word 'people', previously carrying connotations of 'respectable people' or 'everyone', came to acquire the sense of 'the common people'. This withdrawal from popular culture was a result of the demand for a learned clergy made by the Reformation and the Counter-Reformation and of the new aristocratic interest in refinement since the Renaissance – a reflection of the decline of the traditional military role of the aristocracy and the attendant need for new strategies of distinction.[12] The lessening of elite support for tradition helped to undermine its integrative role for society as a whole. Henceforth popular traditions lacked a wider authority in the social system.

The Enlightenment was based above all on a heterogeneous group of eighteenth-century Parisian intellectuals often called the *philosophes* but with important contributions from others (the most important figures included Montesquieu, Diderot, Voltaire, Rousseau, Hume, Adam Smith, Ferguson and Kant). Their project was to create a modern society and they were explicitly hostile to tradition. The philosophical basis of this is clear, but there was also a political dimension to this hostility since opposing tradition was by implication to oppose aristocratic rule, itself normalized by tradition. Significantly, while the Enlightenment championed myriad communities and peoples – 'the rights of citizens, the rights of slaves, Jews, Indians, and children' – it reasserted the traditional subordination and the rational and moral inferiority of women to men.[13]

Modernity – variously dated in its beginnings from the European encounter with America, from the Renaissance and the Reformation, or, above all, from the Enlightenment – is understood as involving a number of characteristics, all antithetical to tradition. These include the decline of the old social order with its rigid hierarchies and religious worldviews, and the secularization and rationalization of power and of social and political life. It involved the establishment of a money economy of exchange based on large-scale production, circulation and consumption of goods as well as capital accumulation and the extensive ownership of private property. This led to a social and sexual division of labour, involving the rise of new social classes and new forms of patriarchal relations. The promotion of scientific investigation, a conception of nature as subject to human will and agency, and trust in the diffusion of education and high culture to bring about moral development were characteristic traits of modernity. The notion arose of a self-sufficient self, disembedded from tradition and achieving a status, not through ascription, but through the application of reason and industry. There was an orientation towards the future rather than the past, and an understanding of the modern age as unprecedented, superseding everything that had gone before, and thus regulated only according to its own internally generated – rather than inherited – values.[14] Modern ideas spread gradually, but arguably by the middle of the nineteenth century, they had been internalized by large sections of European and American society.

Traditional life was traumatically affected by the Industrial Revolution: the mechanization and rationalization of agriculture drove millions of peasants away from their traditional world to the factory system of the burgeoning industrial towns at home and abroad.* Karl Polanyi – writing of nineteenth-

---

* From 1850, Britain's population was 55 per cent urban (Germany's was 35 per cent and France's 25 per cent); 34 per cent of the working population was employed in industry and 22 per cent in agriculture. Between 1858 and 1862, Britain produced 53 per cent of the world's iron and 49 per cent of its textiles. See Emmanuel Todd, *L'Invention de l'Europe*, new edition (Paris: Seuil, 1996), pp. 179–80.

century England – demonstrated that if the Industrial Revolution involved 'an almost miraculous improvement in the tools of production', then it was also 'accompanied by a catastrophic dislocation of the lives of the common people'. Machines for specialized production required the constant availability of labour and raw materials, without which the investment was too risky. Thus all transactions became money transactions and the motive of gain took over from that of subsistence. Until the end of the Feudal Era in Western Europe, economic systems had been based on the principle of reciprocity, redistribution or householding (production for one's own use), while the motive of gain was not significant. The development of a market economy brought together 'all elements of industry, including labour, land, and money', each of which had to be organized in its own market.

> But labour and land are no other than the human beings themselves of which every society consists and the natural surroundings in which it exists. To include them in the market mechanism means to subordinate the substance of society itself to the laws of the market.[15]

The bourgeois world was consolidated in the closing decades of the nineteenth and the early decades of the twentieth centuries. The state and the economy now came together as capital came to depend on the protection and regulation of the state, and as the state financed itself to a much greater extent from borrowed private capital. Industrialization and urbanization intensified while consumer capitalism penetrated everyday life. Cheap mass-produced goods replaced traditional goods and a break with the past was facilitated in various domains of daily experience. Rationality proceeded to extend its reach into the state bureaucracy, the factory, the school, the prison, the hospital, the home.[16] Many contemporary observers were certain of the unprecedented nature of the changes about them. Eugen Weber writes of that period in France:

> Traditional attitudes and traditional practices crumbled, but they had done so before. What happened after 1880 was that they were not replaced by new ones spun out of the experience of local community. The decay and abandonment of words, ceremonies, and patterns of behavior were scarcely new. What was new and startling, said [André] Varagnac [the French ethnologist], was the absence of homemade replacements: the death of tradition itself.[17]

The modern age is inherently destructive of traditions. To an extent this is implicit in the word 'modern' itself which, in the course of the nineteenth and twentieth centuries, took on the connotation of 'improved' from the older – though surviving – connotation of 'belonging to the present', as opposed to 'ancient'. 'Modernization' originally referred to the alteration of buildings and of spelling, but it came to mean something undoubtedly desirable.[18] A key implication of modernization is that tradition prevents societies from achieving progress. Hence to be modern is to turn one's back on tradition, to live in the present and be orientated only towards the future. According to the post-Second World War 'modernization paradigm', development was to be understood in an evolutionary sense and its absence explained in terms of the economic, political and socio-cultural disparities between poor and rich countries. It has been pointed out by Björn Hettne that 'the modernization paradigm took it for granted that the societies characterized by industrial capitalism are universally desired, but in fact no people ever voted for capital accumulation and industrialization, processes which have usually implied a substantial amount of coercion'.[19] Sociology was the main contributor to modernization theory, with its concern – reflected in the work of the classic theorists – with the transition from tradition to modernity. This concern was also fundamental to folklore research and to anthropology, the traditional being understood through the category of the peasant from the beginning to folklorists and somewhat later to anthropologists, as a replacement for the primitive.[20]

Karl Marx (1818–1883) and Friedrich Engels (1820–1895) famously described the turbulence of the modern world in *The Communist Manifesto* (1872):

> The bourgeoisie cannot exist without constantly revolutionising the instruments of production, and thereby the relations of production, and with them the whole relations of society. Conservation of the old modes of production in unaltered form, was, on the contrary, the first condition of existence for all earlier industrial classes. Constant revolutionising of production, uninterrupted disturbance of all social conditions, everlasting uncertainty and agitation distinguish the bourgeois epoch from all earlier ones. All fixed, fast-frozen relations, with their train of ancient and venerable prejudices and opinions, are swept away, all new-formed ones become antiquated before they can ossify. All that is solid melts into air, all that is holy is profaned, and man is at last compelled to face with sober senses, his real conditions of life, and his relations with his kind.

Marx and Engels argued that 'the history of all hitherto existing society is the history of class struggles'. Echoing the Romantics, they saw the division of labour in modern industry and mechanization as the source of alienation of the proletarian, who becomes a commodity and whose work 'has lost all individual character, and, consequently, all charm for the workman', who 'becomes an appendage of the machine'. Only the proletariat is a revolutionary class: '[t]he other classes decay and finally disappear in the face of modern industry; the proletariat is its special and essential product'.[21] This is the fate of the peasant: to join the ranks of the urban working class.

Émile Durkheim (1858–1917) saw the division of labour as the motive force of modern societies. It derived from progressive occupational differentiation, and gradually took over from religion as the basis of social cohesion since individuals became dependent on each other for the provision of basic goods and services. This represented a shift from the 'mechanical solidarity' of simple societies with a rudimentary division of labour and a social control based on shared beliefs and norms to the 'organic solidarity' of complex societies, deriving from specialization of production and based on relationships of exchange and cooperation. At the same time the individual became freer in a large complex society than in a small one, where social control was more easily applied. Individual differences then appeared more obviously in a complex society, individualism became established, and in time it was converted into a right. The state in turn became the developer of the individual and the guarantor of individual liberties, overruling the secondary groups such as those based on kinship or locality which at the same time had to continue to exist as a counterweight to the state's power: indeed the conflict between the two is a precondition of individual freedom. Durkheim observed that change in the modern world can be so rapid and intense that traditional social control and morality no longer relate to the lived world and can break down. Communal solidarity disappears, leaving individuals feeling a lack of purpose and moral control of the will: an anomalous and transitory state of 'social pathology' he termed *anomie*. While not exclusive to modern societies, it is endemic in them.[22]

Ferdinand Tönnies (1855–1936) established an influential distinction between the notions of *Gemeinschaft* ('community') and *Gesellschaft* ('society'). He saw the passing from the traditional world to modernity in terms of a move from the customary affective, intimate, direct, reciprocal and unavoidable relationships of community towards those relationships which are rational, abstract, objective, formal and instrumental in the society of the modern state. While accepting that 'society' freed human relationships from the traditional bonds to which they were subjected, Tönnies saw this gain at the expense of the destruction of all fundamental forms of solidarity and their replacement by the contract, the market and intense competition. Modern European society could not have been formed without the destruction of previous forms of social organization based on the family, kinship and land. Tönnies' critique of contemporary society sought to recuperate 'community', not through a return to the feudal past, but through a coming-together of 'community' and 'society'. The relationship between 'community' and 'society' was evolutive, the seeds of the latter growing from the former, and culminating in socialism, whose logic was present in 'society'. Some have argued that Tönnies' vision was a Romantic and conservative one. Rafael Farfán argues, however, that the context of his work in the contradictory modernization of Germany, where the economic structure was radically altered while leaving intact the conservative political and social structure, shows his sociology to be a critique of German society and culture. Tönnies was an active Social Democrat, and was driven from his chair in the University of Kiel by the Nazis in 1933.[23]

Max Weber (1864–1920) linked modern capitalism and the nascent modern state. He contrasted the 'spirit of capitalism' with 'traditionalism'.

> A man does not 'by nature' wish to earn more and more money, but simply to live as he is accustomed to live and to earn as much as is necessary for that purpose. Wherever modern capitalism has begun its work of increasing the productivity of human labour by increasing its intensity, it has encountered the immensely stubborn resistance of this leading trait of pre-capitalistic labour.

He saw the rationalization of production and the development of bureaucracies whose remit covers much of social life as distinguishing modern from traditional societies. Private capital, a party political system and political leadership appeared as counterweights to the power of a rational bureaucratic administration. If justice and equality were gains from rational bureaucracies, there was a negative side to modernity in the loss of shared meanings. The growing rationalization of modern life and the decay of traditional society and of a magico-religious worldview led to a 'disenchantment' of the world. The modern state has the monopoly of legitimate violence over a given territory, with which it maintains order. But the state itself rests on a legal legitimation, based on rational rules. Weber saw an ascetic Protestant ethic of hard work, planning, thrift and reinvestment of profits closely linked with the development of capitalism, thus linking capitalism to religious rather than, as Marx argued, economic values.[24]

The Decay of Irish Tradition

The above outline of the decline of the traditional world and the development of modern societies, based largely on Gross's framework, applies to the Western world in general terms. How did all of this affect Ireland? The seventeenth-century English conquest had profound implications for traditional political autonomies and for the religion of the country, which was proscribed. The resulting divide between conqueror and conquered, settler and native, over time normalized into the broad ethnic categories of 'Protestant' and 'Catholic', was to nuance all subsequent political and economic developments. The dispossession of the native secular and religious elite, the appropriation of its wealth and the plundering or destruction of much of its material culture, legitimated by the law and by the religious ideology of the conquerors, had a profound impact on native culture. Specifically it impacted on the relationship between the colonial and the déclassé native elite cultures on the one hand and that of both with popular culture on the other. These developments had a profound impact on Gaelic traditions, leading to the beginning of the decay of all native learned traditions and of a slower decline of the Irish language and of popular Gaelic traditions.

From the second half of the eighteenth century the Tridentine reform of the Catholic Church began to make inroads into popular religion and social life and had largely achieved its aims in the decades after the Great Famine. This involved the suppression of much of the earlier popular religion and the internalization of new religious forms.[25] Towards the end of the eighteenth century enlightened ideas were championed by the politically disadvantaged Ulster Presbyterian bourgeoisie who made common cause with their oppressed Catholic compatriots against a government and an Anglican elite for whom these ideas, at least those with direct political implications, were subversive of and threatening to the latter's privileges. The enlightened attitude to tradition was more ambiguous in Ireland than elsewhere: the first 'Gaelic revival' took place in the enlightened and incipiently industrial milieu of late eighteenth-century Belfast (see Chapter 4).

Intensive industrialization took place in only the North East of Ireland but the Irish experience of industrial modernity came as much through Irish emigrants forming a large part of the proletariat of North America and Britain. The land-owning system derived from the seventeenth-century conquest condemned a large proportion of the population to abject poverty in the nineteenth century. The emigration which became endemic from early in the century helped to undermine tradition by creating an awareness of traditional culture's inability to achieve worthwhile goals in the individual's life. Indeed the choice of emigration itself reflected a conscious rejection of the inherited world and, as has been argued by J.J. Lee, was motivated more by the 'modernisation of Irish mentalities' than by purely economic reasons.[26] The Great Famine of the 1840s, through death and emigration, dealt a near fatal blow to the still powerful Gaelic culture and particularly to that of the largest and most traditional social grouping, the rural proletariat, who disappeared almost completely from the face of the land within a couple of generations. The relative decline of the Irish language had long preceded the Famine but was partly masked by the rapid rise in population.* In the decades after the Famine the decline in the proportion of Irish speakers was much faster than the decline of the population as a whole. The loss of the language involved the acquisition of English and a greater likelihood of literacy, with the direct loss of Gaelic oral traditions, traditional knowledge in general, and the attendant opening to modern ideas. The demand for literacy – invariably in English – increased from the eighteenth century, for various reasons. They included, according to Niall Ó Ciosáin, the growing commercialization of the rural economy and the attendant need for paper

---

* The first attempt to enumerate Irish speakers was in the census of 1851, which recorded 1,524,286 out of a population of 6,552,365. The census of 1841 had recorded a total population of 8,175,124 of which Anderson estimated 4,100,000 Irish speakers. See Reg Hindley, *The Death of the Irish Language. A Qualified Obituary* (London: Routledge, 1990), p. 15.

transactions; widening contact with politics and civic affairs, as witnessed by the widespread use of political propaganda in the 1790s; recruitment in the British army; dealings with the legal system; and the reading of religious texts, emphasized by reformers.[27]

Writing just after the Great Famine Sir William Wilde lamented the decline of traditional culture. The 'discursive introduction, written in 1849, and to be skipped by those who feel no present interest in Ireland' argued that the recent 'great convulsion' – 'the failure of the potato crop, pestilence, famine, and a most unparalleled extent of emigration, together with bankrupt land-lords, pauperizing poor-laws, grinding officials, and decimating workhouses' had 'broken up the very foundations of social intercourse . . .' He observed that '[t]he old forms and customs . . . are becoming obliterated; the festivals are unobserved; and the rustic festivities neglected or forgotten . . .' He feared for the future.

> In this state of things, with depopulation the most terrific which any country ever experienced, on the one hand, and the spread of education, and the introduction of railroads, colleges, industrial and other educational schools, on the other, – together with the rapid decay of our Irish vernacular, in which most of our legends, romantic tales, ballads, and bardic annals, the vestiges of Pagan rites, and the relics of fairy charms were preserved, – can superstition, or if superstitious belief, can superstitious practices continue to exist?[28]

Douglas Hyde's seminal address to the National Literary Society in 1892 was informed by a similar concern. He argued that the Irish had 'at last broken the continuity of Irish life' and were 'cut off from the past yet scarcely in touch with the present'. They had 'lost all that they had' – language, traditions, music, genius and ideas'.[29] Listing the different Irish traditions which were being lost – language, Gaelic personal names and surnames, place names, music, dress, games – he derided their anglicized replacements. However, he had a revolutionary proposal to reverse this decline, which was to leave an enduring imprint on subsequent Irish life (see Chapter 4).

The death – and the protection – of tradition has been a common theme in Irish cultural life up to the present day. The death of traditions in general cannot be doubted, any more than the birth of new traditions. But the unprecedented losses of the modern age have called the whole notion of tradition into question. The loss of cultural continuity has involved the loss of the shared past which is a foundation of identity. This aspect of the death of tradition is behind the development of concepts such as Durkheim's *anomie*. As we will see, the loss of identity had profoundly political implications, and indeed as old as modernity is a counter-current of thought has defended tradition – for political reasons certainly – but also for ethical reasons. The defence of tradition took many forms, some reactionary, but it also left an enduring legacy. A part of that legacy is the scholarly discipline of folklore.

Re-evaluating Tradition

The European encounter in America with a race of people unforeseen by the writers of antiquity helped to relativize traditional sources of knowledge and to establish the myth of the noble savage. This cultural relativism, made possible by the idealization of cultures which had no relationship with classical European models, helped to clear the way towards the later valorization of the European peasant. Pietro Martire, Jean de Léry and Bartolomé de las Casas were among those writers who defended and idealized the Indians, exalting their virtues, which they saw as deriving from their lack of civility.[30] Montaigne, strongly influenced by such writings, remarked that 'everyone calls barbarism that which is not according to his own custom'. The abbé Raynal, a precursor of anti-colonialism, wrote in an influential eighteenth-century work that it was not in the depths of the forest but in the heart of civilized societies that one learned to disdain and to distrust humanity.[31]

Travel, to America or within Europe, whether it led to overtly ethnocentric accounts or to more empathetic observations, involved the unavoidable encounter with cultural difference and laid the foundation for speculation. The most important conclusion Montaigne drew from his journey to Italy and part of Germany (from 1580) was the role of experience in human knowledge. The first edition of the *Essais* appeared six months before his departure but significant differences appeared between the first and third editions, and these have been put down to his travelling experiences.[32] In that sense travel was a precondition of 'ethnography' – the description of other peoples; and indeed there is an undoubted ethnographic dimension to the writings of many classical authors, for example, Herodotus in particular (called 'the father of history' by Cicero).[33] The voyage became one of the key influences in the development of the 'cultural relativist' approach to popular culture, from the notion of the noble savage, founded on American travel writings, to the nineteenth-century Romantic journey to the sublime, of which the folklorist's expedition was to be an important example.[34] Until the twentieth century, 'nothing guaranteed, a priori, the ethnographer's status as the best interpreter of native life' since travellers, and above all missionaries and colonial administrators, were likely to know the appropriate languages and to have a much deeper knowledge of the culture.[35]

Cultural relativism was a useful weapon in criticizing the European feudal and absolutist order. The universalistic principles of the Enlightenment implied a single route to human happiness. In the middle of the eighteenth century Jean-Jacques Rousseau (1712–1778) was already reacting against this. The 'founder of the sciences of man', according to Lévi-Strauss, Rousseau posed the problem of the relationship between nature and culture in *Discours sur l'origine et les fondements de l'inégalité parmi les hommes* (1755). In it 'one can see the first treatise of general ethnology'. Rousseau made a clear distinction between what would later be called the ethnologist on the one hand and the historian and the moralist on the other: 'When one wants to study men, one learns to look around oneself; but to study man, one must first learn to look into the distance; one must first see differences in order to discover characteristics'.[36] Rousseau reinvented the idea of nature. Opposing 'nature' to 'culture', he saw human nature as the state of nature, and thus defined a variety of social phenomena not associated with – that is not corrupted by – 'culture' as forms of nature, from childhood to the 'primitive'.[37]

He was not the first to be taken by the myth of the primitive, but he was particularly influential in its spread throughout Europe. In primitive peoples he found a state of grace, the 'youth of the world'. This condition had been corrupted by civilization in Europe, where all subsequent movement ostensibly towards the perfection of the individual was in reality towards the degeneration of humanity.[38] The primitive world for Rousseau was a yardstick by which contemporary European society could be measured: he made a 'philosophical' use of the Indians, 'without worrying himself too much about knowing whether what he said about them was true or false'.[39] Indeed in *Discours sur l'inégalité*, Rousseau cautions that the state of nature in which he places his primitives 'does not exist any more' or perhaps 'has never existed'. But he argues for the necessity of the notion in order to properly judge the present. The noble savage was not only in distant lands, however, but even among the European peasantry. Rousseau, a Genevese, disliked the corruption of Paris, had an enthusiasm for country festivals and encouraged his compatriots to be true to their own traditional customs. His famous letter to the Poles encouraged them to resist the Russians by remaining true to their own traditions.[40]

In 1760 the Scotsman James Macpherson (1736–1796) anonymously published *Fragments of Ancient Poetry collected in the Highlands of Scotland and translated from the Gaelic or Erse language*. The 'fragments' consisted of the poetry of an ancient Scottish poet, Ossian, and won immediate success with the reading public. In 1762, Macpherson, emboldened to give his own name as the editor and translator, published *Fingal*, an ancient poem in six books along with the beginning of *Temora*, which was to appear separately in its entirety in 1763. The poems excited controversy from the beginning, not least in Ireland, over the question of Macpherson's sources and scandal when it was shown that the poems were Macpherson's own composition. In fact they were very loosely based on the Fianna tradition of Gaelic Scotland, which was shared with Ireland and had been equally popular in the oral and literary tradition from medieval times, surviving in oral tradition to the present (the 'Fionn', or 'Fenian', or 'Ossianic Cycle'; *fiannaíocht* in Modern Irish). Fingal and Ossian were none other than the Fionn Mac Cumhaill and

Oisín of Irish tradition. Fionn was the chief of a band of warriors, the Fianna, whose exploits were conventionally set in the third century, and Oisín was his son who supposedly survived into Christian times, meeting St Patrick and engaging in dispute with him, a popular literary theme from the twelfth century. An important part of the controversy was the old Irish–Scottish rivalry: Macpherson's own contention on the Scottishness of Ossian and on the priority of the Scottish Gaelic tradition over the Irish (thus going against the received wisdom) was greeted with outrage by Irish scholars.

The Ossianic poems had an enormous influence in contemporary Europe; were translated into several languages, and were greatly admired by Herder, Goethe, Napoleon and others.[41] One reason for their success was that

> the intellectual world of the larger society became interested in the primitive at a time when the Highlander was peculiarly suited for the role, in a way that neither, say, the Lothian peasantry, who were too close, nor the South Sea Islander, who was too far away, could approach. The conceptual boundaries of civilization were expanding fast, following on the great exploratory periods of the 16th and 17th centuries, and the strange and exotic were becoming elusive enough to merit lament for their absence.[42]

Ossian can be placed in the spirit of this time, an age of enlightened investigation, that wished 'to clarify the problems inherent to the origin of ideas, poetry, society, religions, customs'. Ossian, the 'Homer of the North' in Madame de Staël's phrase, became 'the minstrel of a patrimony which has poetic but above all national value', and through Ossian the Middle Ages were confirmed as an heroic epoch. Cesarotti, the Italian translator of *Ossian* (1801), encapsulated his contemporary significance: 'Ossian is the genius of wild nature: his poems resemble the sacred groves of his ancient Celts: they inspire horror but here is felt at every step the divinity that inhabits them'. *Ossian*'s importance hardly rests on its poetic value, but also on what it mediated from contemporary poetry, feeding 'not only the taste for a new poetry, but also the taste for popular poetry'.[43] Much of the reason for *Ossian*'s success was, according to Malcolm Chapman, Macpherson's 'loosely structured blank verse style, [where] emotionally laden, atmospheric and apparently casually organised images succeeded one another effortlessly'.

> This was in complete contrast to the formal, tightly structured intellectual verse of his contemporaries, and this was a major feature in his success. He broke all the rules, and this was perceived, as at rare moments it is, not as mere confusion, perversity and violence, but as a bid for a larger freedom – a freedom that in this case was not only poetical, but moral.[44]

The 'revolt of poetry' encouraged a more positive evaluation of tradition by calling on popular poetry to 'revitalize and to renew that poetry which is not popular'.[45] The importance of the English bishop Thomas Percy (1729–1811) is, along with Macpherson, in helping to initiate this new sensibility and to rehabilitating the 'Gothic' and the 'Celtic', previously synonymous with barbarism but gradually coming to represent a heroic medieval era, when this literature was formed.[46] Percy published *Reliques of Ancient English Poetry* in 1765, and in his preface emphasized both the originality of this folk poetry, the remnants of the forgotten art of the ancient poets, and its national character, that it was the voice of the English people from earlier centuries. He pointed out that in the contemporary enlightened age, many of those relics of antiquity needed to be treated with some indulgence, but that they were nevertheless graced with a spontaneity and a lack of artifice which compensated for their defects and touched the heart. *Reliques* influenced poets as well as scholars, not least in Ireland, where Charlotte Brooke's pioneering anthology (see Chapter 4) was published on Percy's advice and reflected its indebtedness to him in its choice of title: *Reliques of Irish Poetry* (1789).

The reaction against the abstract universalism of the Enlightenment found a champion in Johann Gottfried von Herder (1744–1803). His battle was on two fronts: against the perspective of the Enlightenment that saw the force of tradition as synonymous with ignorance, and against contemporary German literature and art which was based on foreign, and especially French, models.[47] Central and Northern Europe in Herder's time resembled Italy a couple of centuries earlier, but the Italian kind of renaissance was not achievable there because of the relative absence of a documented ancient culture, despite the vogue for Germanic, and specifically Scandinavian, mythology. Italy, France and England on the other hand had long had national literatures and literary languages. They had embraced classicism and the Enlightenment and had less reason to abandon them.[48] A German renaissance, then, would be of a different order, and in this and in its wider implications is where the importance of Herder lies. His fame, according to Isaiah Berlin,

> rests on the fact that he is the father of the related notions of nationalism, historicism and the *Volksgeist*, one of the leaders of the Romantic revolt against classicism, rationalism and faith in the omnipotence of scientific method – in short, the most formidable of the adversaries of the French *philosophes* and their German disciples.[49]

Berlin outlines the originality of Herder's thought in certain ideas that were 'incompatible with the central moral, historical, and aesthetic doctrines of the Enlightenment'. Firstly, his belief in the value of belonging to a group or to a culture, but emphatically not in any political or nationalistic sense. Secondly, 'the doctrine that human activity in general, and art in particular, express the entire personality of the individual or the group, and are intelligible only to the degree to which they do so'. Thus they are part of a process of inter-personal communication and have no existence

culture =
process + dev.

independent of their creators. Thirdly, 'the belief not merely in the multiplicity, but in the incommensurability, of the values of different cultures and societies and . . . that the classical notions of an ideal man and of an ideal society are intrinsically incoherent and meaningless'. Herder rejected the notion of inexorable progress and the idea of the superiority of a culture; every culture had to be admired for what it was and according to its own terms of reference.[50]

The word 'culture' in its early uses indicated process, in particular the *tending* of something, and from the sixteenth century was also applied to human development. In French it gradually shifted from the notion of 'formation', of 'education', of the mind to an indication of the consequential state, that of the cultivated mind or the 'cultured' individual. The opposition between nature and culture was fundamental to the thinkers of the Enlightenment, who saw culture as the definitive mark of the human species. Culture was singular, reflecting the universalism of the Enlightenment. It came to be more or less synonymous with *civilisation*, another term used in the singular, though the former tended to indicate individual, the latter collective, progress. The notion of progress is central. Some peoples were civilized, but all could become so. Indeed the term *ethnologie*, coined by Alexandre de Chavannes in 1787, was understood as the history of the progress of peoples towards civilization.[51]

The notion of culture today owes much to eighteenth century German intellectual debate, where *Kultur* came to be opposed to *Zivilisation*. Norbert Elias argues that the English or French notion of civilization to a degree minimizes differences between peoples since 'it emphasizes what is common to all human beings – or in the view of its bearers – should be'. It 'expresses the self-assurance of peoples whose national boundaries and national identity have for centuries been so fully established that they have ceased to be the subject of any particular discussion, peoples which have long expanded beyond their borders and colonized beyond them'. On the other hand, the German notion of *Kultur* stresses differences between peoples. It comes from a nation which was consolidated very late: it 'mirrors the self-consciousness of a nation which had constantly to seek out and constitute its boundaries anew . . . and again and again had to ask itself: "What is really our identity?"' The *Kultur–Zivilisation* opposition derived from the social contrast in the German states between the German-speaking bourgeois intelligentsia, whose position rested on its intellectual or artistic achievements, and the French-speaking nobility who were distinguished by a particular mode of behaviour governed by refinement and etiquette: 'On the one hand, superficiality, ceremony, formal conversation; on the other, inwardness, depth of feeling, immersion in books, development of the individual personality'. The bourgeois intelligentsia were excluded from political power, but they could be independent in what they wrote, and they more or less monopolized the cultivation of the German

Enl.   culture ≈ civilization

language, literature and philosophy. They became the chief bearers of the German national ideal, and when they became the dominant class in Germany, the *Kultur–Zivilisation* opposition took on a national flavour with the attributes of *Kultur* coming to be national characteristics.[52]

Herder seems to have been the first to use the word culture in the plural.[53] Each culture to him was beyond value, to its own society and to humanity as a whole. But he considered chauvinism 'the stupidest form of boastfulness'. He saw the Roman Empire in negative terms, because it had destroyed the cultures it conquered.[54] His concern for the Slavs, the interest in them is revealed in his works – including examples of their folk songs – and his predictions of their great future had a major impact among them. His earliest Slavic follower was the poet Jan Kollár, the founder of Panslavism.[55] Herder argued that the contemporary period was no longer the 'original time' but was 'under the clouds' in the 'cold light of evening'. Every period, he maintained, contained the foundations of its own happiness in itself and at the same time sought to regenerate itself. This way passed through the *Volkseele*,* 'the soul of the people', which was unique and as old as the nation.[56] Thus the people offered the means of renewing the nation.

To Herder human groups were the products of climate, geography, physical and biological needs and were unified by common traditions and memories and above all by language, 'the most precious possession of a nation, which expressed the group's collective experience'.[57] The ambiguity of the word *Volk* was especially productive since it brought together connotations both of the nation and of the people. In the 1930s Gramsci was to point out the lack of equivalence in Italian, using his coinage *nazionale-popolare*§ as an ideological equivalent, a term which encompasses both connotations of the German word.[58] The 'people' in Herder's writings carries suggestions of the rural lower classes but at the same time the notion remains vague. This allowed Herder to include Goethe, and other celebrated writers who were true to the *Volksgeist*, in his collection of 'folk' (*Volk*) songs. *Volkspoesie*, which he opposed to the artifice of *Kunstdichtung* ('art poetry') was *Naturpoesie*, 'nature poetry', and he argued that it best reflected the character of a people. Hence he lamented the decay of popular traditions.[59] As Jennifer Fox points out, tradition to him was inherently masculine in its transmission, in its inculcation and in its source: the forefathers.[60]

Folk songs to Herder were 'the archives of the people'. His interest in song, nevertheless, was not ethnological but aesthetic: Hermann Bausinger

---

* As Berlin points out, Herder expressed the notion in various forms: *Geist des Volkes, Seele des Volkes, Geist der Nation*, etc.

§ He found that the cognate French word *national* carried this connotation which the Italian lacked. *National* 'has a significance in which the term "popular" is already more politically elaborated, because linked to the concept of "sovereignty": national sovereignty and popular sovereignty have or have had equal value'.

notes 'popular poetry is not treated as a fact of oral tradition, but as a creative fiction making "popular" and "artistic" coincide'.[61] Macpherson's *Ossian* (on which Herder wrote an essay) and Bishop Percy's *Reliques* were shining examples of folk poetry.[62] *Volkslieder* appeared between 1778 and 1779 – *Volkslied*, 'folk song', is his own coinage, replacing '*Nationalgesänge*' ('national songs'), which is how he first rendered the English 'popular songs'.[63] Here too, in these two terms, we see the ambiguous relationship between the national and the popular.[64]

The Gothic novel and Gothic architecture, 'a cult of sensibility and senti-ment, a taste for the exotic, a search for the primitive in time and in space' are among the features of a pre-Romantic period which coexisted with the Age of Enlightenment and has been dated from the 1730s.[65] Romanticism had its beginnings close to the time of the French Revolution and flourished in the first half of the nineteenth century among the aristocracy and the middle classes. It 'is still the most recent European-wide spiritual and intel-lectual movement'.[66] It was a reaction to the dogmatic rationalism of the Enlightenment and more specifically to the role of the French and the Indus-trial revolutions in transforming contemporary European society.[67] Anti-rationalism was a key characteristic of Romanticism, allowing in turn a fascination with imagination and the unconscious mind. The optimistic Enlightenment belief in history as the onward and universal march of progress had been challenged by Rousseau and Herder. One of the concomitants of progress was political and social equality, but the implica-tions of political, social and cultural uniformity were rejected by the Romantics who warned against the vulgarization of culture, and in this they prefigured later elitist concern about the masses. They emphasized the singularity and specificity of individuals and communities – hence a fashion for the exotic – and the aesthetic implication of this was to reject the classi-cal canon. Thus one of the key Romantic notions, already associated with Herder, was that of the *Volksgeist*.[68]

Bourgeois society disillusioned the Romantics. The industrial city with its spiritual emptiness horrified many of them, and they considered agriculture and a happy rural population as the best basis of the economy. Nature worship was a hallmark of Romanticism (although less so in Ireland, where nature, while celebrated for its picturesque qualities in the writings of the Anglo-Irish Romantics, had been repeatedly haunted by the threatening figures of dispossessed natives and rebels). The Romantics saw the indus-trial division of labour as turning the worker into an instrument – the young Marx, incidentally, had been strongly influenced by Romantic ideas. The Romantic movement, H.G. Schenk argues, opposed capitalism much more vehemently than did the materialist ideologies of socialism or communism.[69]

The Romantic nostalgia for the past had differing forms. The interest in and the example of the Christian Middle Ages offered encouragement in an era of spiritual insecurity. Demoralized or downtrodden nations could look back with pride on their golden ages. And the end of a feudal and aristocratic age could be lamented. Progress for one social class meant decline for another and in periods of such transition 'apocalyptic visions or jeremiads about the end of the world or the decadence of humanity' inevitably occurred.[70] The medieval period was idealized too for its decentralized political structures.[71] The idealization of barbarian and primitive peoples

> made the European barbarians of the ancient world an ideal location of romantic sentiment. They too had revolted against classicism in the most tangible way, and had lived beyond the bounds of self-defining civilisation. They were also suitable locations of irrationality and disorder, for they had been perceived as such by their more settled neighbours for as long as we have records.

In Northern Europe, Chapman points out, there were two such peoples known to the classical world: 'the Celts, who had resisted the Roman Empire in its growth, and the Goths (or Germans) who had brought about its fall'. Both peoples became fashionable in the early Romantic period, in the form of the Gothic novel, Macpherson's Ossian and 'the rehabilitation of the Arthurian theme'.[72]

Celticism in its formulation was strongly influenced by Ernest Renan (1823–1892) and Matthew Arnold (1822–1888), who exoticized the 'Celtic' and removed it from the here and now both in time and space to backward and desolate regions, proudly surviving from ancient and more noble times. 'Once identified', Joep Leerssen argues, 'this chronotope appears to be operative in almost all descriptions of outlying Celtic-language areas during the nineteenth and twentieth centuries, even in twentieth century cinema . . .'[73] An appreciation of the Celticness of Ireland – and all that it entailed – only became possible with the development of comparative philology, when it could be shown that the language indigenous to Ireland was a Celtic language. This was generally established with the work of Edward Lhuyd, *Archaeologia Britannica* (1707). Lhuyd definitively demonstrated the affinity of Welsh and Irish and thus that of Irish and the European languages.[74] With Romanticism the ancient Celts were idealized as were the landscapes inhabited by the modern speakers of Celtic languages: Macpherson takes much credit here. The Celts were thus seen as bearing the virtues so prized by the Romantics.

Ernest Renan's essay, 'la Poésie des races celtiques' – published in 1854 – was a key influence for the Romanticization of the Celts and directly, as well as by extension, the Gaels. It expressed notions that later became familiar in the influential writings of W.B. Yeats, Robin Flower and Séamus Ó Duilearga on Irish folklore (see Chapters 3 and 4). Renan wrote of 'an ancient race living, until our days and almost under our eyes, its own life in some obscure islands and peninsulas in the West'. This race had been increasingly subject to external influences, but was 'still faithful to its own tongue, to its own memories, to its own customs, and to its own genius'. This 'little people, now concentrated on the very confines of the world, in the midst of rocks and mountains whence its enemies have been powerless to force it' possesses a literature which in the Middle Ages 'changed the current of European civilisation, and imposed its poetical motives on nearly the whole of Christendom'. The Gaels had their 'own original manner of feeling and thinking'. Nowhere 'has the eternal illusion clad itself in more seductive hues' and 'no race equals this for penetrative notes that go to the very heart'. But it is 'doomed to disappear, this emerald set in the Western seas'.

> Arthur will return no more from his isle of faery, and St. Patrick was right when he said to Ossian, 'The heroes that thou weepest are dead; can they be born again?' It is high time to note, before they shall have passed away, the divine tones thus expiring on the horizon before the growing tumult of uniform civilisation.[75]

The surviving Celts are distinguished by 'the purity of their blood and the inviolability of their national character'; '[n]ever has a human family lived more apart from the world, and been purer from all alien admixture'. The Celtic race 'has worn itself out in resistance to its time, and in the defence of desperate causes'. Indeed, the Celtic peoples are not 'by themselves susceptible to progress'.[76]

Arnold, in *On the Study of Celtic Literature* (1867), similarly saw a Celtic failing in 'the outward and visible world of material life':

> . . . his want of sanity and steadfastness has kept the Celt back from the highest success. If his rebellion against fact has thus lamed the Celt in spiritual work, how much more must it have lamed him in the world of business and politics! The skilful and resolute appliance of means to ends which is needed both to make progress in material civilisation, and also to form powerful states, is just what the Celt has least turn for.

The Celt's nature, 'undisciplinable, anarchical, and turbulent', and at the same time susceptible to demagoguery, is bad for politics in contrast to the Anglo-Saxon's, 'disciplinable and steadily obedient within certain limits, but retaining an inalienable part of freedom and self-dependence'.[77] Renan and Matthew Arnold helped to develop some of the characteristic traits of the Celt: sensitive, spiritual, feminine, imaginative, poetic, passionate, impractical. They were as a result instrumental in establishing a long-lasting opposition between the Celt and the Anglo-Saxon, characterized as restrained, predictable, rational, materialistic and impassive.[78]

Romanticism reaffirmed the supernatural in the face of enlightened rationalism, and this also took the form of a turn towards Catholicism and against the supposed individualism and lack of ritual in Protestantism. An aspect of

Romantic nostalgia was the heightened appeal of ruins, representing 'the desire for withdrawal from the *malaise* of the present age, and a vague, semi-religious sense of timelessness beyond'.[79] The idolization of the people was another Romantic characteristic. This people was vaguely defined and was 'credited with such virtues as innocence, courage, faith, love and readiness for self-sacrifice'. The enthusiastic use of folk song and folk music by the Romantic composers was inspired by nostalgia, patriotism and 'the desire to penetrate into . . . the subconscious regions, of a nation's personality'.[80]

The notion of the popular in culture that emerged from Romanticism cannot be understood without appreciating the conception of the people as political actor which emerged from the Enlightenment, and according to which sovereignty was vested in the people. The people thus legitimized government in the social contract with the ruler, and, according to Jesús Martín-Barbero, 'are considered to be the founders of a democracy not as the collective population but as a category that provided the necessary endorse-ment for the birth of the modern state'. But in tandem with the idea of the people as legitimating civil government was a negative notion of the people in culture: to the enlightened thinker, '[o]ne must oppose tyranny in the name of the people while at the same time one opposes the people in the name of reason'.[81] While the Enlightenment recognized the right of the people to be politically incorporated into the state, this evidently implied their assimilation into the dominant culture. It did not recognize the right of the people to define the state. This is the case that the Romantics made, but on an idealis-tic level, while refusing to engage with the people socially, as a class.

The importance of Romanticism was in its transformation of the negative attitude to the popular. Henceforth the popular was associated with sensitiv-ity and spontaneity, but as 'qualities diluted in the anonymity of creation', as Renato Ortiz puts it. Romantic writers reacted against the Enlightenment's rationalism, its cosmopolitanism and its universalism. They 'turned towards particular situations, privileging the multiplicity of sentiments and of experi-ences', made picturesque journeys to distant places, and they cultivated an interest in the exotic and in peasants. Sensitivity, spontaneity, historicism, difference and distance are key notions in Romanticism and in the antiquar-ian was someone particularly receptive to these qualities, someone always 'more tied to a local history of that which was properly universal', whose 'particularism contrasted with the Enlightenment universalism'.[82]

Romanticism had political implications in a fragmented Germany, weak and overshadowed by a powerful France. The present was unattractive, all too clearly the result of a historical process of decline from a Golden Age which for long could only be imagined. The only link between the past and the present was a Germanness, not to be found in a Frenchified elite culture, but in the culture of the common people of the countryside. This showed continuity and was unchanging. It allowed a glimpse of that period

local rather than universal

before the Fall. To illustrate the notion of the 'folk', Martín-Barbero imagines a 'geological' structure of society:

> The superficial external level is in full view. It is formed by diversity, dispersion and inauthenticity resulting from historical changes. The internal level is below, in the depths. It is formed by the unchanging and organic unity of ethnicity and race.

The recourse to the mystique of the past obfuscated the historical nature of social development, and made the 'folk' into something transhistorical, 'impossible to analyse socially, supposedly without divisions and conflicts, both beneath and above any social movement'.[83] So 'the supreme good is no longer from this on the rousseauist individual, but the nation in its totality'. Julia Kristeva argues that Herder's *Volksgeist* was neither biological, scientific nor political, 'but [was] essentially moral'. Only after 1806 was the cultural concept of the nation politicized when the revolutionary wars forced a reaction against universalist values exported by French armies and encouraged a nationalist politics that took strength from the regenerating powers of a mystical past and the national genius.[84]

Romanticism had very different histories in the various European countries. It is linked to the reaction to French expansionism in Germany. In France, on the other hand, it did not appear until the 1820s due to the continued classicism of the Napoleonic period and at first took the form of nostalgia for the pre-Revolutionary past before later taking on a liberal colouring.[85] France did not share the intense interest in vernacular culture that characterized German Romanticism; indeed revolutionary France set out to destroy local languages and dialects and insisted on the universality of the French language.[86] Once the Académie celtique, itself inspired by enlightened principles (see Chapter 2), published the last volume of its *Mémoires* in 1812, ethnographic interest was insignificant until the end of the century. The closure to Romanticism can be explained by the long periods of instability from which France suffered and by the lateness of intensive industrialization and urbanization. In the United Kingdom, on the other hand, after 'the last mainland [sic] threat to the security of the establishment' ended at Culloden in 1746, there was 'a close relationship between the final incorporation of an entire island into subdued civility, and the appearance of an idealisation of difference', argues Chapman: 'romanticism of internal ethnic variety is a British invention'.[87] Romanticism, 'amateur de celtisme', made Ireland a fashionable subject. In large countries Romanticism, with its idealization of the past, represented a return to the *ancien régime*, but for small countries, 'past and freedom become synonymous'.[88]

European Romantic influences came to Ireland mostly through England. Irish Romanticism was mainly Anglo-Irish, strongly conservative and its works written for an English readership with a view to explaining Ireland to them. The nature of its audience along with its treatment of the major themes – 'the historical past, conflict over the land or religious settlements, Irish lawlessness and alienation' – are evidence of its colonial character, contends Tom Dunne.[89] Irish Romanticism's assimilation of elements of the Gaelic tradition and in particular its 'perceptions of the lost but lingering Gaelic world' are key characteristics which, by the end of the nineteenth century, were to become central to the Anglo-Irish tradition. For Anglo-Irish writers (with a residual fear of the native) the Gaelic theme could serve as a warning but also act as 'the basis for creating new cultural foundations for an eroding social and political hegemony'; for Catholic writers 'a vehicle for their burgeoning self-confidence, but also a necessary sublimation of trauma and loss'. The sources for information on the Gaelic world were the recent translations of Irish Gaelic poetry, the accounts of earlier colonial writers, antiquarian writings and more scholarly contemporary investigation.[90]

The Anglo-Irish Romantics portrayed their Irish characters as living 'in remote glens, on islands in lakes, on the shore or even off-shore, in crumbling ruins that are leftovers from the past, almost as if they do not really belong to the same time-scale as the other characters', in a procedure that Joep Leerssen calls auto-exoticism. It established the subsequent convention which represents Ireland 'primarily in terms of an anomaly, a riddle, a question, a mystery'.

> To put it crudely: Ireland, if it cannot be a nation in its own right is reduced to a province, is increasingly described in the discourse of marginality and in terms of its being different or picturesque. The implied audience for Irish literature is English rather than Irish, and the choice of an Irish setting shifts increasingly to the wilder, more peripheral and distant parts of the country. Paradoxically, the most peripheral areas of Ireland are canonized as the most representative and characteristic ones.

There was a temporal as much as a spatial distancing in the representation of Gaelic Ireland. Antiquarians had characterized Gaelic culture by its pastness since 'the most genuine and least adulturated form of Gaelic culture was that of the past, before the contamination of the English presence in Ireland'. So it was understood as 'a survival of bygone ages, a living fossil of older times, existing only in those places where it had not yet been adulturated by the influence of contemporary European civilization . . .'[91]

It was not until the Young Ireland nationalist movement that Romantic ideas coloured Irish political agendas. The visit of Thomas Davis (1814–1845), leading ideologue of the movement, to Germany in 1839–40 and his exposure to German Romantic thought made a great impact on him.[92] His writings give evidence of the Romantic idealization of the spiritual Celt who is contrasted with the materialistic Anglo-Saxon: 'where an Irish peasant is gay and gallant, an English boor is sullen and sensual'. He wrote of 'this thing, call it Yankeeism or Englishism, which measures prosperity by

romanticism of internal ethnic variety is a British invention exchangeable value, measures duty by gain, and limits desire to clothes, food, and respectability'. Davis considered a nation to have a unique character, which was defined by its culture and above all by its language – the expression of the national spirit and genius. Hence, a people without its own language was 'only half a nation' and 'Ireland must be unsaxonized before it can be pure and strong'. At the same time Davis, a Protestant of mainly English origin, emphasized the coming-together of a historic ethnic diversity in the unity of the people of Ireland, a product essentially of the Irish environment. It was through cultural regeneration that Young Ireland intended to realize the Irish nation.

> [Ireland] was to find its salvation, not in a modern industrial state, but in those parts of Ireland which had remained, as Davis put it, 'faithful and romantic'. The Young Irelanders . . . looked to the 'lower classes' for the hope of the future; and the concept of the Irish peasant, who typified all that was best and noble in the Irish character, indeed all that was essentially Irish, was born.[93]

Young Ireland pointed the way to the turn of the century cultural nationalism of the Gaelic League and the literary revival which arguably represented the apotheosis of Romanticism in Ireland, 'but by then', as Dunne puts it, 'it was a Romanticism permeated by Social Darwinism and modernist literary trends . . .'[94]

Different ideological tendencies opposed modernity, or certain aspects of it, because of its destructiveness. The Romantics stressed its negative ethical and aesthetic dimensions and the problem of alienation was treated by a variety of social theorists. Utopian socialism and anarchism reacted against industrialization and proletarianization. The anarchists 'favoured a decentralized and multifaceted social structure which made individual self-realization possible'.[95] The Russian Slavophiles – inspired by Herder – saw the backwardness of Russia as advantaging it over the corrupt West and they opposed autocracy and the Orthodox religion to rationalism, science and democracy:[96] demonstrating how modernity could be rejected for *national* reasons. The ideas that emerged from the Enlightenment issued from specific national contexts, in particular from the most powerful country in continental Europe at the time, and in that sense any claims made from the same quarter for their universal application could be dismissed as national chauvinism. Militant support for progress was the expression of a bourgeoisie in revolt against feudalism, absolutism and everything else which obstructed the full development of capitalism, but in countries such as Germany, which had not yet managed to constitute itself as a modern nation, and Russia and Spain, which like Germany lacked a democratic bourgeoisie and were economically backward compared to

France and England, the idea could have less resonance.[97] The specific national context is central to the subsequent development of the scholarly fields of folklore and ethnology, which were both national and popular. Folklore study was institutionalized above all in countries where Romanticism had the greatest influence, countries which had been marginalized in relation to the dominant political, economic and cultural powers of Europe and where any reiteration of the onward march of progress only served to underline their second-rate position.

cultural nationalism of the G. L.

2. Towards a Concept of Folklore

'Folklore' was conceptualized towards the end of the eighteenth century, coined as a word in 1846 and institutionalized from the end of the nineteenth century on. To speak of antecedents, then, is to some extent a contradiction, since folklore did not exist until it was named. 'Folklore' was more an ideological than a scientific concept. To seek antecedents is an ambiguous task: primarily it is to look for early evidence of interest in the cultural elements which were later called folklore. These cultural elements have been variously known as 'popular errors', 'popular superstitions', 'popular tradition', 'popular antiquities', 'folklore', 'survivals', 'popular culture' or 'subaltern culture'.

Popular culture has been defined by Jacques Revel as 'that mass of practices which do not have a legitimate status in the culture of the traditional [i.e. the established dominant] society'. In France in the middle of the seventeenth century, popular practices were identified through a series of oppositions to the established culture on the basis of their claim to truth, to rationality and to social acceptability. It was the concern of those whose authority in the matter derived from their professional status. These professionals were theologians especially, but also doctors, jurists and astronomers. The situation changed from the early eighteenth century so that popular culture, instead of being the object of study of a particular group of professionals, came to be generally and commonly understood 'as a distinct socio-cultural phenomenon'. However, from the middle of the eighteenth century the development of a more systematic and methodological approach to the question of popular culture led to a new professional competence, eventually leading to the establishment of new disciplines.[1]

In the terms themselves – 'popular errors', 'popular antiquities', 'folklore', etc. – a gradual shift in attitude towards the observed phenomena is clear, and this trajectory parallels the different understandings of folklore and popular culture. All of the terms were based on distance between the observer and the observed – distance in time ('antiquities', 'survivals') or distance in social class ('folk', 'popular'). Distance in space is not implicit in these terms so that, for present purposes, the observer of proximate cultural difference we may consider to be the antecedent of the folklorist. This is not particularly useful since the notion of folklore that later crystallized was strongly influenced in its gestation by the cultural relativism that was a reaction to the encounter with exotic cultures. Nevertheless, we will limit our 'antecedents to folklore' to observations within a European context of the culture of non-elite groups (which we will variously refer to as 'the common people', 'the people' and 'the folk', terms which will later be discussed). Ideally, bearing in mind the subsequent history of the notion of folklore, these observers should come from within the same national societies or states as those observed. In practice, this was not always the case. In multiethnic polities in which there was ethnic stratification as a result of recent or ancient conquest, ethnic distance was a subtext of the observations. The less the cultural distance between elites and people in a particular society, the less the difference there was to observe. Hence the richest observations were often those of outsiders. Those observations can be fitted into various categories: the 'literature of confutation',[2] antiquarianism, travel writing and enlightened enquiry into 'the people'. The examples given are from a number of European countries and attempt to show the pan-European nature of these developments.

Folklore in Literature

Before considering these, brief mention should be made of the use of popular material in literature. The study of the folktale took pride of place in international folklore scholarship from its nineteenth-century beginnings until the mid-twentieth century, based on the comparative scholarly framework established by the Grimm brothers. The diffusionist approach which was to become dominant – the Finnish historical–geographical method – of necessity had to use written evidence for the earlier existence of folktales, and usually this was in the form of folktales incorporated into or establishing the basis for a work of literature. The writers who used folklore in this manner were legion: from Chaucer, Boccaccio, Dante, Rabelais and Shakespeare and the writers of the Irish literary revival to Angela Carter's re-workings of well-known folktales.* Shakespeare's *Cymbeline*, for example, is based on the folktale known as 'The Wager on the Wife's Chastity'.[§] *The Taming of the*

---

* *The Bloody Chamber and Other Stories* (1979). 'The Company of Wolves', for example, is her version of 'Puss-in-Boots, and was the basis for Neil Jordan's film of the same name (1984).

§ It has been recorded from the oral tradition of Finns, Estonians, Livonians, Lithuanians, Lapps, Swedes, Norwegians, Danes, Irish (the largest single number of recorded versions), Basques, French, Spanish, Catalans, Germans, Austrians, Italians, Czechs,

Shrew was also used by the Spanish writer Juan Manuel in his fourteenth century collection of exempla, *El Conde Lucanor*, and by the Italian Ginafrancesco Straparola in his *Piacevoli notti* in the first half of the sixteenth century.* Literature has always been enriched by folklore, and the history of narratives passes from the oral to the literary and back again, and, in the twentieth century, includes narratives mediated by new technologies such as radio, cinema, television, sound recordings, the Internet, and so forth.

In his history of folklore in Italy, Giuseppe Cocchiara denies the place of the sixteenth- and seventeenth-century writers Straparola and Basile, who are conventionally mentioned in general historical overviews. He points out that they, like their French contemporary Charles Perrault (whose version of Cinderella is the best known today), were not 'popular storytellers' but 'storytellers who used, for literary purposes, popular motives and themes'.[3] This is very true, but it does not reduce the importance of these works for the historical study of popular culture. Indeed, Perrault's *Contes de ma mère l'Oye* (1697) was part of a wider contemporary interest in popular and regional culture, expressed in many other collections, of proverbs as well as of folktales.[4] In many cases the literary work in its turn influenced the oral tradition: for example, *Aesop's Fables*, the *Gesta Romanorum* and the great oriental storybooks, the *Arabian Nights*, rendered into a European language for the first time by Antoine Galland as *Contes arabes* between 1704 and 1717, and the Sanskrit tale collection, the *Panchatantra*, translated into German by Theodor Benfey in 1859.[5]

The Literature of Confutation

Before the seventeenth century, acts of councils and synods of the church often condemned *errores* and *consuetudines non laudabiles* as pagan survivals.[6] There are many Irish examples in the seventeenth century of the opposition of the churches to diverse aspects of popular religion, such as decrees which 'required priests to hide sheela-na-gigs, prohibit invocations to the devil, prevent the gathering of "magical" herbs, and stop the preparation of virility potions'.[7] Wake 'abuses' were condemned regularly at synods or by various statutes and regulations from the early seventeenth to the early

---

Serbocroats, Russians, Greeks, Turks, Arabs, Indians, Indonesians, Franco-Americans, Spanish-Americans, Cape Verdians and West Indians. Antti Aarne and Stith Thompson, *The Types of the Folktale: A Classification and Bibliography*. FF Communications No. 184 (Helsinki: Academia Scientiarum Fennica, 1973), pp. 299–300. I follow the nomenclature of the text. The type number of the tale is 882.

* Type 901. It has been recorded from Finnish, Finnish-Swedish, Estonian, Lithuanian, Swedish, Danish, Icelandic, Scottish, Irish (about half of all the recorded versions), Spanish, Dutch, German, Austrian, Hungarian, Slovenian, Serbo-Croatian, Russian, Indian, Franco-American, English-American, Spanish-American American Indian (Zuñi) oral tradition.

twentieth centuries.[8] 'Patterns' (patron day festivals) were also commonly condemned.[9] In Paris in 1679, the abbé Jean-Baptiste Thiers published his *Traité des superstitions selon l'Écriture Sainte* and in 1703–4 *Traité des superstitions qui regardent tous les sacrements*. His aim was to expurgate superstition, as was that of Fr Le Brun, who published his *Histoire critique des pratiques superstitieuses* in Rouen in 1702. Thiers seems to have been among the first to use the phrase 'popular tradition'.[10]

From the middle of the eighteenth century, 'popular customs' came to be of interest for various purposes, the Société royale de Médecine and the clergy exemplifying those who took an interest in them in France.[11] There are German pamphlets from the sixteenth and seventeenth centuries mocking papist customs. Scientific and semi-scientific works of the seventeenth century, which censured superstition from the perspective of religious faith and of rational understanding, are of particular interest. Towards the middle of the century more strictly scientific, demystifying, and partly legitimating works on superstition became more frequent.[12] This is part of a shift in attitude towards 'errors', visible in the Italian Michelangelo Carmeli's pioneering *Storia di vari costumi sacri e profani degli antichi sino a noi pervenuti* (1750), where he wrote 'I do not wish here to chide such an abuse, because that is not anything of my purpose . . . To me it suffices to have tracked down the origin of such a custom'.[13] This more questioning attitude is reflected in the works of the Swede Jakob Fredrik Neikter, who, in the last quarter of the eighteenth century, attempted a rational explanation of popular belief. Neikter saw folk poetry as history, proverbs as a society's values, and his comment that 'We paint God and the good angels white and shining, but Negroes paint God black and Satan as white as a European slave-trader', showed a critical awareness of cultural difference.[14]

Antiquarianism

Antiquarian interest came to see the 'errors' of the people in a new light, but it did not replace the corrective inventories of errors, which continued. The antiquarian and the historical approach came to be opposed. The former, as Leerssen outlines, saw the past 'as a storehouse of facts and curiosities' belonging to an undifferentiated 'long ago but not forgotten'. It dealt with the artefacts of the past and tried to explain them, in the absence of reliable historical information from early medieval or pre-Christian times for the north of Europe, through the Bible and the work of ancient writers. In contrast, the historical approach saw the past as a succession of events and took note of the various changes. Antiquarianism was undermined by the growth of scientific knowledge and was gradually relegated to the amateur, who became a figure of fun, while new scientific disciplines such as archaeology, history and linguistics divided out the former field of antiquities.[15]

The antiquarian impulse had various motivations. The rise of Sweden to the status of a great power in the seventeenth century led to a new national self-assurance and the desire both to find evidence for the country's greatness in the distant past and to prove, as King Gustav Adolph II asserted, 'that our forefathers have not been barbarians, as foreigners want to call us . . .' The phenomenon of Gothicism (*göticism*) saw the Goths as a great conquering people of the distant past and as the ancestors of the Swedes. The search for past glories then led to the establishment in 1603 of the State Antiquarian Archives, and of a Collegium of Antiquities in 1666. The clergy were exhorted to collect antiquities from the common people, and in 1674 the clergy in the Finnish part of the kingdom were asked to record 'old heroic and historical songs, which have been in the country since ancient times . . ., because they contain much truth about the heroic deeds of the forefathers'. The results were scanty, probably in good part because the clergy were trying at the same time to extirpate superstition.[16]

William Camden's *Britannia* (1586) was the British landmark in antiquarian researches. For this book, and for *Remaines of a Greater Worke, concerning Britaine* (1607), Camden (1551–1623) went on walking tours, involving observation and interviews with local inhabitants. John Aubrey (1626–1697), in his various antiquarian researches (including 'Monumenta Britannica or a Miscellanie of British Antiquities' and 'Remaines of Gentilisme and Judaisme'), proved to be a perspicacious observer of cultural change.

> Before Printing, Old-wives Tales were ingeniose, and since Printing came in fashion, till a little before the Civill-warres, the ordinary sort of People were not taught to reade. Now-a-dayes Bookes are common, and most of the poor people understand letters; and the many good Bookes, and variety of Turnes of Affaires, have putt all the old Fables out of doors: and the divine art of Printing and Gunpowder have frightened away Robin-goodfellow and the Fayries.

Aubrey acknowledged that many of his contemporaries denigrated popular culture, but argued for its scholarly value as antiquity. His work was to be highly valued by the nineteenth-century folklorists.[17]

Better roads early in the eighteenth century facilitated tours of England, and the contemporary classical interest led to a number of books on British and Roman antiquities. In 1718 the Society of Antiquaries was founded. Henry Bourne (1694–1733), an antiquarian clergyman, is best known for a work published in 1725, *Antiquitiates Vulgares: or, the Antiquities of the Common People. Giving an Account of several of their Opinions and Ceremonies. With proper Reflections upon each of them; shewing which may be retain'd, and which ought to be laid aside.* Bourne saw popular culture as 'heathen errors renewed and enlarged by the medieval church' – the linking of pagan and papist being part of the contemporary religious climate. In

1777, John Brand published *Observations on Popular Antiquities*, effectively Bourne's book, but with Brand's own commentaries. He used the notion of oral tradition as opposed to the written word, but by and large agreed with Bourne as to the origins of the antiquities. An edition of the *Observations* by Sir Henry Ellis, published in 1813, was very popular with intellectuals, writers and scholars and became 'an automatic reference and authority on antique custom and odd superstition'.[18]

Travel Accounts

Travel accounts have long been an important source for reflection on human diversity. In sixteenth- and seventeenth-century Europe, members of the elite, educated, versed in Latin and other foreign languages, and fond of travelling, met individuals like themselves on their tours and felt a degree of transnational community. This raised the question of the specific character of the population of a place, the understanding of which had rested on stereotypes deriving from classical times and from dissertations written for this purpose, which influenced the travellers' own accounts. Many accounts portrayed the character of the different classes in the region visited. The laziness of the local inhabitants was a favourite topic of interest, particularly for visitors to Ireland and Spain. So was the virtue of the local women or its supposed lack. Descriptions of superstitions and of the use of magic and witchcraft were commonplace, Protestant visitors frequently treating the subject in a more negative way when in Catholic countries. Many writers drew conclusions from the prices in different countries. The well-travelled Fynes Moryson viewed the low prices in both Poland and Ireland as evidence of the poverty and weakness of the state. As Antoni Mączak points out, the great number of accounts by travellers in Europe helped to create a sense of an inter-related continent, stimulating an interest in foreign parts and the publication of books on the subject, as well as the desire to see foreign countries.[19]

Foreign travellers often gave the most interesting proto-ethnographic accounts. For example, Goethe, in his travel journal of 1788–9 in Italy, gave a celebrated account of the Roman carnival, and of Venetian and Roman melodies, one of which he transcribed in musical notation.[20] French travellers of the seventeenth and the first part of the eighteenth centuries visited cities and historical monuments. By the end of the eighteenth century, they ventured deeper into the country's interior, to mountains and to islands: to places whose history was unknown. According to the account of J.M. De Gérando, published in 1800, the traveller-*philosophe* in his voyages explored different historical eras: '[t]he unknown islands which he finds are for him the cradle of human society'.[21] Such travellers in the eighteenth and early nineteenth centuries, visiting distant provinces of France, wrote accounts in which much exotic information of ethnographic interest was given, usually explained in terms of its antiquity.[22] In Germany, late eighteenth-century travel literature brought together the dominant objectives and topographies which would prevail in the future field of folklore research. Noteworthy in this literature were the more spectacular festivals and 'popular entertainments'. Descriptions of journeys and scientific literature came to cross-reference each other significantly.[23]

The accounts of travellers and colonists are an important source of knowledge for popular culture in early modern Ireland. Sixteenth- and seventeenth-century accounts are notoriously unsympathetic, 'pervaded by comparisons between the Irish and uncivilized races in other historical and geographical contexts, whether the barbarians of classical antiquity, the savage American "Indians" of the New World, or the Britons before the Roman invasion'.[24] Edmund Spenser, for example, while a colonial official and landowner who urged the total submission and anglicization of the Irish, was interested in Irish antiquities and left detailed descriptions of Irish society and culture. Fynes Moryson also held colonial office in Ireland and was present in the English party at the submission of Hugh O'Neill in 1603. He had travelled widely before coming to Ireland in 1600, staying three years. His *Itinerary*, describing the people and living conditions, gives a similarly negative view of the Irish.[25] Such accounts are of a society in the making. Spenser, for example, was burned out of his recently acquired estates in 1598 during the rebellion which only ended with O'Neill's submission.

Eighteenth- and nineteenth-century accounts depict Irish popular culture slotted in at the bottom of a troubled social order where the elite culture of the seventeenth-century colonists was at the top. Spenser and Moryson, recently arrived functionaries in a colonial apparatus which had not yet rooted itself, described *Irish* culture whereas eighteenth- and nineteenth-century accounts are much more informative on *popular* culture. From the second half of the eighteenth century, tours became relatively frequent, and the first half of the following century was noteworthy in this respect. The *Tour in Ireland* (1780), by the English agriculturalist Arthur Young, is an acknowledged authority on contemporary Irish social history. It is also informative on and sympathetic to the life and character of the peasantry, and empathic towards their grievances. Similarly sympathetic is the Chevalier de la Tocnaye, a Breton émigré who made a tour of Ireland on foot in 1796, and knew peasants at first hand. Impressed by their piety, intelligence and hospitality, he was horrified at their poverty and oppression. His book, *Promenade d'un Français en Irlande*, includes accounts of wake customs and 'patterns'.[26] These customs were a constant source of fascination to travellers, and are described in numerous accounts. The wit and good humour of the peasant was another constant theme, as was poverty. The novelist William Makepeace Thackeray, himself the author of an Irish tour published in 1843, described a foreign friend visiting the United Kingdom.

> He was going to Ireland. What to do? To see the grand misére. He went,
> and came back not in the least disappointed. He visited Scotland for its
> romantic recollections and beauty – England for the wonders of its wealth
> – Ireland for the wonders of its poverty. For poverty and misery have, it
> seems, their sublime, and that sublime is to be found in Ireland. What a
> flattering homage to England's constitutional rule over a sister country.[27]

Mr and Mrs Hall's *Ireland: Its Scenery and Character* (1842) is particularly
informative on popular custom and can be considered a kind of source book,
but most of the nineteenth-century tours are of interest for students of
popular culture.[28]

Enlightened Enquiry

Enlightened enquiry is another source for popular culture and with it we are
already touching on one of the functions of the modern state. As the state
developed and was consolidated, such enquiries became commonplace. The
word *Volkskunde* ('knowledge about the people', 'folklore') is first found in
statistical enquiry, in a work from 1787 by Josef Mader, a professor in Prague,
entitled *Verzeichniss einiger gedruckten Hilfsmittel zu einer pragmatischen
Landes-, Volks- und Staatskunde Böhmens*. The aim of such works was to
provide information to facilitate more rational government.[29] In his *Abriss der
Statistik*, Christian Heinrich Niemann, who taught statistics in Kiel and edited
ethnographic works on Lower Germany, distinguished *Landeskunde*
(regional sciences) from *Staatskunde* (state sciences). The latter included
Nationalkunde (national sciences) which concerned both commerce and the
economy as well as customs and culture, and it is here that *Volkskunde* fitted
in.[30] The extension of scientific knowledge had many applications – including
the people, and rational enquiry on various populations accumulated much
information. The statistical enquiries carried out throughout the German
lands – enlightened projects whose aim was rational administration –
belonged to one of the currents from which German folklore scholarship
emerged, the other being the Romantic one, associated with the project of
creating a national literature (see Chapter 1).[31]

The French Académie celtique was the result of the interest of three men
who met in 1804 in order to establish a research project on their favoured
subject of Celtic and Gaulish antiquities. Its inaugural meeting took place
early in 1805 and the first volume of the Académie's *Mémoires* was published
in 1807 (to be followed by five more, the last in 1812). The task was to collect
'the traditions, customs, usages, local languages' of the country for scientific
purposes and in view of their supposedly imminent demise. The principal
method was the use of a questionnaire, published as a tool in the first

volume of the *Mémoires*, and which was to be sent to 'the most enlightened persons' of each *département* of France, though fieldwork was carried out as well. The list of questions began with the preamble:

> To make up for the shortcoming of history, to turn new light on the darkness which covers the cradle of the Gauls; to gather together the materials that can finally elucidate national antiquities, and serve to recompose the Celtic language, history and mythology, the Academy has resolved to associate observers, national and foreign learned men, with its work, and to invite them to respond to the following questions. It points out to them that the practices there specified have been or are still in use in the French Empire which by a series of glittering victories has retaken, and more, all the ancient extension of the Gauls.

The questionnaire included sections on calendar customs (sixteen numbered topics), rites of passage (six), ancient monuments (five) and 'other beliefs and superstitions' (twenty-four). The following are a few examples, one from each section:

> 11. Does one go on St John's Eve at midnight to pick herbs to which are attributed supernatural properties? Does one go on the same night to roll in the dew?
>
> 20. Do barren wives invoke certain saints or give themselves to certain superstitious practices in order to become fertile? What names and what attributes do these saints have? What are these practices?
>
> 27. In the interior of places consecrated to worship, or elsewhere, are there stones to which the vulgar attribute the faculty of making miracles; what is the name and the form of these stones; what are these miracles?
>
> 30. What are the stories of fairies, of spirits? What are the places, the monuments consecrated to the fairies, or which carry their name? Are there fairies to which one gives particular names?

The great ethnologist Arnold Van Gennep considered the Académie's questionnaire to have been of great scholarly merit. One of the memoirs composed in response to it, that of Jean-François Le Gonidec, 'Notice sur les Cérémonies des mariages dans la partie de la Bretagne connue sous le nom de Bas-Léon', was of such a high scholarly standard that Van Gennep considered it to have few equivalents in the subsequent scholarly literature.

Nicole Belmont asks how it is possible to explain this interest among men formed by the spirit of the Enlightenment, 'itself incapable of surmounting the absurdity of popular beliefs and practices'.

> Reading their texts it appears that the irrationality of the traditions they compile becomes admissible on condition that they are removed not in geographical space, but in time, that they are attributed to a remote history. It suffices to proclaim that these 'singular', 'bizarre', 'absurd', and even 'grotesque' beliefs and customs are the fragments of the antiquity of France, the remains of Celtic civilization.[32]

The project of the Académie, then, was to demonstrate the cultural unity of France at the moment when its political unity had been achieved, and to prove that all these vestiges had their meaning within that unity.[33] The proud Celtic origins of the French were a part of the contemporary assertion of French nationalism, and this was why the term 'monument' appeared so frequently in the texts of the Académie, meaning customs, beliefs and language, as well as archaeological remains. Ultimately the Celtic hypothesis was to be the institution's undoing since its scholars found it more and more difficult to sustain. The year 1812 saw the last volume of the *Mémoires* published, though some of the members of the Académie founded the Société royale des Antiquaires de France in 1814. With the Académie gone, memoirs concerning traditional culture had more or less ceased to appear by about 1830.[34]

There were some noteworthy public enquiries of the same order carried out during Napoleon's domination of Italy. The first was the *Statistica di tutte le comunità componenti il circondario della Sotto Prefettura di Arezzo*, carried out in 1809 by the French government, in the form of a thirty-five-point questionnaire, with questions on the character of the inhabitants, the work of women and children, and festivals and rites of passage. The most famous was that carried out in 1811 in the twenty-four departments of the Kingdom of Italy. It took the form of three circulars from the director general of public education to teachers of design (the first and the third) and to teachers of literature and to prefects (the second), enquiring about costume, rites of passage, calendar customs, songs associated with calendar festivals, dialects and housing. The questionnaire was based on that of the Académie celtique and received a good number of replies. In the same year, Joachim Murat, then king of Naples, undertook a similar enquiry. These were not Italian initiatives; 'they carry clearly the imprint of the innovative spirit that Napoleonic rule introduced in . . . [Italian] administrative life, with its effort to establish a more immediate contact with the real conditions of life of the population'. The fall of Napoleon and the restoration precluded any further development of this kind of investigation for a long time.[35]

The second half of the eighteenth and first half of the nineteenth century witnessed an interest in the compiling of regional surveys of the physical and human environments of Britain and Ireland. These included county agricultural surveys of England and the Scottish Statistical Survey, carried out by Sir John Sinclair and compiled on a parish basis, and to be repeated in the 1840s with the New Statistical Account. In the early nineteenth century an incomplete series of county Statistical Surveys was carried out in Ireland by the Royal Dublin Society (founded in 1731 with the aim of agricultural and industrial improvement). The Ordnance Survey was established in 1791 to accurately map Britain in order to anticipate the feared French invasion. It came to Ireland in 1824 to map the names, boundaries and size

taxation

of the townlands for taxation purposes. Using an unprecedentedly detailed scale of six inches to the mile, it mapped all of the counties between 1825 and 1841, the last (Kerry) published in 1846. At its height some two thousand staff were employed, including noted Irish scholars such as John O'Donovan, Eugene O'Curry and George Petrie. In addition to mapping, information was gathered on antiquities, toponymy, geology and industry. It was envisaged that a detailed physical, historical and environmental survey should be carried out on the basis of the civil parishes. Fears over the cost of publishing all such information led to only one memoir being published, for the parish of Templemore in Co. Derry, though manuscript memoirs were prepared for most of the province of Ulster.[36] The work of scholars such as O'Donovan and O'Curry, sympathetic to the native tradition, helped to record the original placenames of Ireland in transliterations approximating their original form, rather than as translations into English, and noted much traditional knowledge and learning 'from communities which would fifteen years later be swept away by the famine'.[37]

The categories of information recorded by the surveyors included the social and economic conditions of the parish. The directors of the Survey sought very comprehensive information, and Thomas Larcom, who directed it from Dublin, prepared a pamphlet which inquired, for example, about the following:

> Habits of the people. Note the general style of the cottages, as stone, mud, slated, glass, windows, one story or two, number of rooms, comfort and cleanliness. Food; fuel; dress; longevity; usual number in a family; early marriages; any remarkable instances on any of these heads? What are their amusements and recreations; Patrons and patrons' days; and traditions respecting them? What local customs prevail, as Beal tinne, or fire on St John's Eve? Driving the cattle through fire, and through water? Peculiar games? Any legendary tales or poems recited around the fireside? Any ancient music, as clan marches or funeral cries? They differ in different districts, collect them if you can. Any peculiarity of customs? Nothing more indicates the state of civilisation and intercourse.[38]

The interest of the memoirs as a source for popular culture varies very much in quality.[39] There is information on alcohol and illicit distillation, on music, wake customs, weddings, quiltings, fairs and the amusements at them. On dancing, faction-fighting, hunting, horse-racing, cock-fighting, bull-baiting, ball-playing, shooting competitions at Christmas and other seasonal activities, the lighting of bonfires and housing. On agricultural matters – farm labourers, methods, draught animals, landlord-sponsored improvements, threshing machines, spade mills – as well as information on the belief in fairies and transcriptions of a few oral narratives.[40]

Another valuable source from roughly the same period was the result of another state initiative. In 1835 the *First Report of his Majesty's Commissioner for Inquiring into the Condition of the Poorer Classes in Ireland* was published.

State intervention in social affairs in Ireland in the nineteenth century was much greater than in Britain and was 'in response to what was seen as acute economic crisis and continuing violence and disorder . . .' The Poor Law of 1838 created a nationwide system of workhouses for the indigent and destitute poor, to be financed by poor rates. The 1835 enquiry gathered information at hearings which, remarkably, took oral evidence from members of all social classes, in one parish per barony in seventeen counties. For example, the witnesses in Kilkee, Co. Clare, 'included two landlords, two Catholic priests, an Anglican minister, a doctor, two large farmers, one middling farmer, two small farmers, a cottier with two acres, a labourer, a nailer, a widow "lately evicted", two beggars "and several other farmers, labourers and tradesmen"'. The inquiry sought the cultural reasons for Irish poverty and, as Ó Ciosáin has demonstrated, 'constitutes a rich ethnographic source, both for attitudes and practices'.[41]

The above discussion could be magnified several times by spreading the net wider in any one country or by drawing in other comparative contexts. No claims for an exhaustive treatment are made but rather pointers are given towards the sources that in one way or another may be considered ethnographic. Considering the literature of confutation, antiquarian accounts, travel literature and statistical enquiry, it is clear that there is a gradual increase in scientific knowledge and methods over time. Condemnation gives way to a more disinterested scientific curiosity in the practices of scholars and travellers as enlightened thought breaks with traditional models of the foundation of truth. Instead of condemning the people it is proposed to know the people and by knowing them it will be possible to govern them better. Travellers sought information in order to better humanity – Arthur Young, for example – or to enrich their lives with experience. Under the influence of pre-Romantic and Romantic ideas aesthetic experiences were increasingly sought. The Romantic's wandering has been seen as the desire of the poet 'to imprint on his soul a variety of vivid and lasting impressions'.[42] This wandering led to sublime landscapes, and to the inhabitants of them. The distinctiveness of folklore was attributed to the fact that it existed in distant regions and was isolated from contemporary social processes. Hence it gave information on the past, and its authenticity was guaranteed 'by the distance which separates [it] from the impositions of present life'. Renato Ortiz argues that 'popular culture implies heterogeneity, spatial discontinuity, and therefore can be integrated by the movement of the journey' which he maintains was the purpose of the Romantics with their interest in picturesque journeys and remote places.[43]

The Brothers Grimm and the Rise of Folklore Scholarship

With the above comments we already approach the foundational notions of folklore. If the word 'folklore' dates from mid-nineteenth-century England, it represents an intellectual development originating in Germany. The Grimm brothers were among the most famous scholars of their day and an essential reference for early nineteenth-century European scholars of what was soon to be called folklore. The pioneering tale collection of the Irishman, Thomas Crofton Croker (see Chapter 3), was translated by them and introduced with a scholarly essay of their own (which in turn appeared in English translation in a subsequent collection of Croker's, dedicated to the brothers). The word 'folklore' was coined in a review of the second English edition of Wilhelm Grimm's *Deutsche Mythologie*. The contributions of Jacob (1785–1863) and Wilhelm (1786–1859) to Germanistics, folklore scholarship, the history of German law, Germanic antiquities and philology were fundamental. Jacob was the foremost folklorist of the first half of the nineteenth century, and the founder of comparative research on the folktale. The influence of the Romantics, but of the Grimm brothers above all, was instrumental in inspiring the collection of folklore on a vast scale and at an international level.

The brothers are best known today for their famous collection of folktales, *Kinder- und Hausmärchen* (1812), the second most widely read book in nineteenth-century Germany. There were no less than seven revised and enlarged editions of the *Kinder- und Hausmärchen* in the brothers' lifetime. The tales were mostly recorded from petit bourgeois or bourgeois individuals and were substantially reworked, the brothers arguing in the preface that they had given the substance of the stories as they had received them, but had provided the form themselves. By removing the traces of the original narration they were highlighting the supposed communal and collective creation of the folktale form. The *Kinder- und Hausmärchen* had an impressive international resonance throughout the century, leading to pioneering national folktale collections such as those of Aleksandr Nikolaevič Afanas'ev in Russia, Peter Christen Asbjörnsen in Norway, Evald Tang Christensen and Svend Hersleb Grundtvig in Denmark, Giuseppe Pitré in Sicily and Emanuel Cosquin in Lorraine.[44]

The brothers began their collection in 1807, on the suggestion of Ludwig Achim von Arnim (1781–1831) and Clemens Brentano (1778–1842), Romantic writers best known for their famous collection of folk songs, *Des Knaben Wunderhorn* (1805–8). The brothers saw the origins of folk poetry in the epic, which was a collective creation of the people itself rather than of individuals. The notion was very influential, as was the idea developed by the brothers of folklore as not just an artistic, but as a historical, source. Jacob's *Deutsche Mythologie* (1835) was a pioneering attempt to scientifically systematize folklore and was of great importance in the development of folklore scholarship. Jacob believed that much of the ancient German mythology had disappeared. Written accounts, however, and especially oral tradition from generation to generation – which he believed to be a faithful source, incapable of distortion – had preserved much evidence. Thus the idea of continuity, which gave equal originality to ancient and contemporary sources. *Deutsche Mythologie* used the evidence of comparative linguistics, old Norse literature, the descriptions of classical writers, the poetry of the Christian Middle Ages as well as contemporary folktales and legends for the reconstruction of ancient German mythology.[45]

The brothers were the first to seriously consider the folktale. Two of the ideas associated with Wilhelm were to be long lasting and widely discussed. His theory that the commonest folktales belonged to the domain of the Indo-European languages and were part of a common Indo-European inheritance derived from contemporary developments in comparative philology. From this it was concluded that the original Indo-European language, from which most European and many West and South Asian languages derive, had been spoken by a unified population group. The place of origin of this group was discussed by using philological evidence, and the most ancient evidence was in the form of the Sanskrit text the *Rig-Veda*. This led to the theory that folktales had their origins in Indo-European myths. The 'Broken-down Myth' theory is eloquently expressed in Wilhelm's own words:

> Fragments of a belief dating back to the most ancient times, in which spiritual things are expressed in a figurative manner, are common to all stories. The mythic element resembles small pieces of a shattered jewel which are lying strewn on the ground all overgrown with grass and flowers, and can only be discovered by the most far-seeing eye. Their significance has long been lost, but it is still felt and imparts value to the story, while satisfying the natural pleasure in the wonderful.[46]

While the Indo-European and 'Broken-down Myth' theories fell out of favour – the latter famously exploded by Andrew Lang and Henri Gaidoz (Gaidoz, in a celebrated essay, showing how Max Müller, the standard-bearer of the Mythological School, was himself a nature myth!) – other ideas about folktales were to have a longer currency.[47] Wilhelm Grimm admitted the possibility of polygenesis in the case of simple tales and of the borrowing – though exceptional – of tales from one people to another, ideas which in time were to be very influential in folktale scholarship. Theodor Benfey (translator of the *Panchatantra*) opposed the idea of a common Indo-European inheritance. He saw folktales (with the exception of Aesop's fables) as originating in India. They spread westwards through oral dissemination, through literary tradition *via* the Islamic world to Byzantium, Italy, Spain and then the rest of Europe, through Buddhist literature *via* China and Tibet to the Mongols and then to Europe, and through the influence of Persian,

Arabic and probably Jewish writings. Benfey offered comprehensive comparative notes to each of the *Panchatantra* tales, a stimulus to intense comparative study of tale collections.[48] Subsequent studies showed that Benfey had exaggerated the importance of India. Emmanuel Cosquin, while by and large subscribing to Benfey's theory, pointed out Egyptian collections of tales which were too early to have been borrowed from India, and this point was further elaborated by Andrew Lang, who also mentioned the tales appearing in the works of Herodotus and Homer, and used parallels from the contemporary world.[49]

Naming 'Folk-lore'

In a letter to the English intellectual magazine *The Atheneum* on 22 August 1846, the antiquary William John Thoms, writing under the pseudonym Ambrose Merton, suggested his own coinage 'Folk-lore' ('a good Saxon compound') in place of 'Popular Antiquities, or Popular Literature (though by-the-bye it is more a Lore than a Literature . . .)'. The letter sought the editor's aid 'in garnering the few ears which are remaining, scattered over that field from which our forefathers might have gathered a goodly crop'. Thoms asserts that two conclusions can be drawn by anyone with an interest in 'the manners, customs, observance, superstitions, ballads, proverbs, etc., of the olden time': that much 'is now entirely lost' and that 'much may yet be rescued by timely exertion'. *The Atheneum* could do much because of its wide readership and preserve folklore in its pages 'until some James [*sic*] Grimm shall arise who shall do for the Mythology of the British islands the good service which the profound antiquary and philologist has accomplished for the Mythology of Germany'. Thoms asserts that the century 'has scarce produced a more remarkable book' than *Deutsche Mythologie*. He argues that the folklore of England and that of Germany are so intimately connected that 'such communications will probably serve to enrich some future edition of Grimm's Mythology'.[50]

The word 'folklore' itself is 'not the happiest of terms, savouring as it does of the mental slumming of a victorian savant . . .' as Caoimhín Ó Danachair puts it.[51] 'Lore' originally had a semantic range which included teaching and education but particularly from the eighteenth century onwards it had become limited to referring to the past, and included the connotation of 'traditional'. Thoms' use of 'folk' instead of 'popular' belongs to the same conscious Anglo-Saxon revivalism that motivated the suggestion in 1830 that 'lore' should be used in place of the Greek scientific endings in '-onomy' and '-ology'. The word 'folk-song' first appears in 1870, and came to be limited to 'the pre-industrial, pre-urban, pre-literate world'. Raymond Williams sees the genesis of the 'folk' term in the context of the new industrial and urban society. It has the effect of 'backdating all elements of popular

culture', in contradistinction to modern forms of popular culture, 'either of a radical and working-class or of a commercial kind'.[52]

The word 'folklore' spread quickly into other languages, to a large extent through the influence of the pioneering Folk-Lore Society, founded in 1878 in London. The society's organ, the *Folk-Lore Record* – later the *Folk-Lore Journal* – looked beyond England's shores, accepted the work of foreign authors and contained regular bibliographical information from foreign countries. It became a model for similar societies in other countries and its success and prestige helped to establish the word 'folklore' as the international name for the field of interest. It was Andrew Lang who first spoke of a 'science of folklore'. The first international congress of folklore was held in Paris in 1889. The pioneering French journal edited by Paul Sébillot from 1882 was called *Revue des Traditions populaires*, and 'traditions populaires' and its equivalents became widespread in the Romance languages. It was with a degree of reticence that Sébillot accepted the use of the term *'folklore'* in France.[53] The word 'popular' itself has its origins as a legal and political term meaning 'belonging to the people'. It took on the additional colouring of 'low' or 'base' from the sixteenth century and the dominant present-day meaning of 'widely favoured' or 'well liked' from the eighteenth century onwards.[54] 'Popular culture' is first evidenced in the 1780s in Herder's *'Kultur des Volkes'*, where it is contrasted with learned culture.[55] In Italy *Storia delle tradizioni popolari* became the accepted denomination of the research field, although *demopsicologia* (from the German *Völkerpsychologie*) was used by the great pioneer Giuseppe Pitré in his courses at the University of Palermo from 1911 to 1915. Early in the twentieth century, particularly in France and Italy, 'folklore' and a word of early nineteenth-century origin, 'ethnography', used much the same perspective and methodology with the difference that the first term applied to the folk culture of Europe and the second to the so-called primitive culture of the colonies.[56] This same distinction was to be found in German *Volkskunde* and *Völkerkunde*.

'Ethnology', one of the terms used today for the discipline that studies folk and popular culture, was coined by Chavannes in 1787 in his book *Essai sur l'éducation intellectuelle avec le projet d'une science nouvelle*, but referred to the history of the successive stages towards civilization.[57] The word has since had a very complicated history, from the early nineteenth-century 'science of the classification of races', it became in the first half of the twentieth century 'the whole of the Social Sciences which study so-called "primitive" societies and fossil man'[58] and which, in the British social anthropological tradition, 'is interested primarily in the past history of peoples without written records, and is therefore closely allied with archaeology'.[59] The word in various central and Northern European countries – where as the term for a discipline it established a close relationship with regional museums – became synonymous with 'folklife research', 'regional ethnology' and later 'European ethnology', proposed as a new name in 1955. The word 'folklife' (*folkliv*) was already used in Sweden in the first half of the nineteenth century and the term 'folklife research' (*folklivsforskning*) was coined early in the twentieth century. The writings of Sigurd Erixon (1888–1968) were instrumental in the spread of the term in Europe. Erixon argued against European ethnology being distinguished as a discipline from general ethnology or anthropology – the *Volkskunde- Völkerkunde* opposition – and called for the general usage of the term ethnology in place of the various national denominations. In that sense European ethnology would be a 'regional ethnology', and this latter term was to be commonly used to refer to the field.[60] In Ireland, where the usage of 'folklore' reigned supreme, Caoimhín Ó Danachair (Kevin Danaher) supported this view. Don Yoder in the United States pointed to the tendency in usage in the English language to 'define *folklife* by default, as material culture only', which goes against Erixon's notion.[61] The Department of European Ethnology and the incorporated Folklore Archive in Lund University today bear witness to both terms in a single institution (*Etnologiska institutionen* but *Folklivsarkivet*). In Sweden, ethnology is seen as the study of folk and popular culture with folklore as a specialization within it.[62]

In France, in the absence of any presence in the universities, the study of folklore was concentrated in the Musée national des Arts et Traditions populaires, founded in 1937 (although there had been a 'Salle de France' in the Musée d'Ethnographie founded in 1878). In the post-Second World War period the concept of *ethnologie de la France* became definitively established. This replaced the notion of '*folklore*', tainted by its old-fashioned connotations and by the enthusiastic support of the Vichy regime.[63]

The word *béaloideas* has been established as the Irish for 'folklore' probably from the early years of the Gaelic League (founded in 1893). The word has been used at least since the late 1620s, when Geoffrey Keating (Seathrún Céitinn) used it in his Irish history, *Forus Feasa ar Éirinn*. But the concept of folklore did not then exist, so we must expect a different meaning to the word: its rebirth with a contemporary meaning was typical of efforts to renew the Irish language. Keating had tried to counter pejorative accounts of Ireland, and complained that the writers of those accounts neglected the description of the Irish nobility and concentrated instead on the ways of the lower orders, to the detriment of Ireland:[64] hardly the evidence of any proto-folkloric interest. Keating's *béaloideas na sean* ('of the ancients') is given as one of the three sources outside of the Bible for ascertaining the truth of history, along with 'old writings' (*seinscríbne*) and what are called in Latin *Monumenta*.[65] A compound, from *béal*, 'mouth', and *oideas*, 'instruction, teaching', *béaloideas* seems to have indicated oral instruction within the learned tradition.[66]

Institutionalizing Folklore

In England, the interest in folklore was first organized around antiquarian clubs, particularly those named after Camden and Percy. Among the important figures in the 1830s and 1840s were two Irishmen. Thomas Crofton Croker (1798–1854) was the author of 'the first intentional field collection' made in the then United Kingdom (see Chapter 4), and Thomas Keightley (1789–1872) published 'the two most mature English studies on comparative folklore in the first half of the century' – *The Fairy Mythology* (1828) and *Tales and Popular Fictions* (1834); he used a broad comparative perspective.[67] The British 'great team' of folklorists who instituted the Folk-Lore Society and brought it to its greatest eminence in the London Folklore Congress of 1891 were private scholars: Andrew Lang, a free-lance writer, George Laurence Gomme, clerk of the London County Council, Edwin Sidney Hartland, a solicitor and later mayor of Gloucester, Edward Clodd, a banker, and Alfred Nutt, a publisher. Mostly London-based professionals, they did not engage in fieldwork. Instead 'they supplied the theoretical frame and the personal encouragement for vicars and country ladies and colonial administrators to collect folklore survivals from "peasants" and "savages"'. In the years after the First World War, with the decline of the private scholar, the position of a scholarly field independent of the university became anomalous. Academics dismissed the Folk-Lore Society as an antiquarian club and the field of folklore studies became marginal to the scholarly community.[68]

The failure of the Académie celtique retarded the development of folklore studies in France, one of the last European countries in which folklore studies developed. The foundation of the journal *Mélusine* (1877–1901) deliberately established a link with the earlier collections and with the project of ordering that material, and it was soon followed by other journals, the *Revue des Traditions populaires* (1888–1919), the *Revue du Traditionalisme français et étranger* (1898–1914) and *La Tradition* (1887–1907).[69] As in England, the failure to establish a discipline of folklore study in the universities marginalized it.

The English and French folklorists by and large were not alienated intellectuals and did not share the sense of national mission that allowed folklore to find a privileged intellectual niche in other countries. With long-established national languages and national cultures, England and France had no ideological need for folklore. They were colonial powers, whose anthropological gaze was directed outwards, towards the colonies, and it was perhaps the usefulness of that to the imperial enterprise which ensured anthropology's position in the academy. Sweden, like England and France, had a long established state, national language and high culture, but unlike them did not have colonies, and it directed the anthropological gaze inwards, to the interior of the state, where folklore/ethnology's prior position as commentator on national cultural diversity ensured that it could maintain a prominent position within the academy.

Evolutionists and Diffusionists

From the middle of the nineteenth century, evolutionism, deriving from the writings of Charles Darwin (1809–1882) and Herbert Spencer (1820–1903), who developed 'social Darwinism', tended to dominate scholarly thinking. This thinking saw unified processes of development in the world in strict accordance with certain laws, and it was strongly positivistic, demanding the accumulation of evidence on which to base conclusions. It influenced the study of folklore, not least through concentration on the scrupulous collection and publication of testimonies from living oral tradition. It also allowed folklore to develop in a more scientific direction and to distance itself from Romantic orientations, which were becoming discredited in a more scientific age. For evolutionists, oral tradition meant 'the end-point of a development leading upwards, towards something wider and more perfect, and not to scattered fragments of ancient entities of a high quality, as the Romanticists had thought'.[70] The latter has been famously termed 'the devolutionary premise' by Alan Dundes and is exemplifed, perhaps best of all, by Hans Naumann's notion of '*gesunkenes Kulturgut*', articulated in the 1920s. This saw a degradation of the cultural heritage as it passed – 'sank' – from the upper to the lower social classes.[71]

The notion of 'survivals' is associated with the evolutionist Edward Tylor (1832–1917). He provided a famous anthropological definition of culture. 'Culture or Civilization, taken in its widest ethnographic sense, is that complex whole which includes knowledge, belief, art, morals, custom, and any other capabilities and habits acquired by man as a member of society'.[72] *Primitive Culture* (1871), the source of the definition, besides being a foundational anthropological text, was immensely influential among folklorists. What most attracted them were the comparisons Tylor made between the primitive and the European peasant. Tylor saw survivals as historical evidence of an earlier cultural state, and for this he used the analogy of geology.

> Just as the forms of life . . . of the Carboniferous formation may be traced on into the Permian, but Permian types and fossils are absent from the Carboniferous strata formed before they came into existence, so here widow-inheritance and couvade, which, if the maternal system had been later than the paternal, would have lasted on into it, prove by their absence the priority of the maternal.

He saw 'the institutions of man . . . as distinctively stratified as the earth on which he lives', succeeding each other everywhere in the same order, 'shaped by similar human nature acting through successively changed conditions in savage, barbaric and civilised life'.[73] He preferred to think of 'survivals' rather than superstitions and thus saw various marginal and residual cultural phenomena in modern society as analogous to primitive mentalities. Witness a reference to

> the appearance in modern Keltic districts of . . . widespread arts of the lower culture – hide-boiling, like that of the Scythians in Herodotus, and stone-boiling, like that of the Assinaboins of North America – [which] seems to fit not so well with degradation from a high as with survival from a low civilization. The Irish and the Hebrideans had been for ages under the influence of comparatively high civilization, which nevertheless may have left unaltered much of the older and ruder habits of the people.[74]

Tylor's influence was decisive in establishing an understanding of folklore – in England, France and elsewhere – as tales, legends and beliefs of those groups less exposed to education and progress and sharing many aspects of the mentality of savages: archaic survivals in the modern age.[75] Two of the founder members of the Folk-Lore Society, Andrew Lang and Edward Clodd, found their vocation through reading Tylor, and its prominent members in general shared this enthusiasm. By the end of the century, comparisons between European folklore and the traditions of exotic peoples became frequent in the search for 'elementary' forms of human belief. Folklorists sought the key to ancient 'survivals' in their own societies in the behaviour of 'primitives'. Journals like the English *Folk-Lore Journal*, the French *Revue du folklore français et colonial* and the Italian *Lares* brought together peasant and primitive. Sir James Frazer (1854–1941), a student of Tylor's and later occupant of the first chair of 'social anthropology' (in 1908 at the University of Liverpool),[76] wrote the most famous example of this approach, *The Golden Bough* (1890), a twelve-volume compendium of belief and ritual from all around the world, indebted to Tylor both in concept and in methodology.

The comparison between the primitive and the peasant had significant implications at a time when the modern state was multiplying its functions greatly. One of the tasks of the state was to integrate the peasant into modern life and many folklorists saw their own work in the same terms, helping to reconcile the peasant with modern civilization. With the intensification of class conflict in the nineteenth century, the bourgeoisie regarded the working class in negative terms. The folklorists, unlike contemporary elites in England and France, were not defenders of the notion of progress and did not identify ignorance with superstition, argues Renato Ortiz. Hence popular culture was not automatically devalued as a form of barbarism, but was seen as survival, a historical source which, additionally, was not without its own aesthetic charm.[77] In this vein, Tylor wrote about 'arrest and decline in civilization'.

> In judging of the relation of the lower to the higher stages of civilization, it is essential to gain some idea how far it may have been affected by such degeneration . . . . In our great cities, the so-called 'dangerous classes' are sunk in hideous misery and depravity. If we have to strike a balance between the Papuans of New Caledonia and the communities of European beggars and thieves, we may sadly acknowledge that we have in our midst something worse than savagery. But it is not savagery: it is broken-down civilization. Negatively, the inmates of a Whitechapel casual ward and of a Hottentot kraal agree in their want of the knowledge and virtue of the higher culture. But positively, their mental and moral characteristics are utterly different. Thus, the savage life is essentially devoted to gaining subsistence from nature, which is just what the proletarian life is not. Their relations to civilized life – the one of independence, the other of dependence – are absolutely opposite. To my mind the popular phrases about 'city savages' and 'street Arabs' seem like comparing a ruined house to a builder's yard.[78]

In this way, primitive culture, 'although considered inferior to that of industrial civilization, when compared by the scale of social evolution, analysed in the time and space which correspond to it, is superior to decadence'.[79]

As George W. Stocking points out, '[f]or Tylor – as for European folklorists generally – folklore was continuous with the culture in which it appeared, but no longer functionally integral to it'.[80] Tylor and Frazer are evidence of the overlap between early folklore study and anthropology. Gomme, a prominent member of the Folk-Lore Society, published *Ethnology in Folklore* in 1892 while Frazer was to publish a three-volume work entitled *Folk-Lore in the Old Testament* in 1918.[81] Alfred Cort Haddon, occupying the chair of zoology in the Royal College of Science in Dublin from 1881, proposed an ethnographic survey of Britain and Ireland to the Anthropological Institute, the Folk-Lore Society and the Society of Antiquaries in 1892. In 1893 he published 'The Ethnography of the Aran Islands' with C. Browne and in 1898 led the famous Torres Straits expedition, an acknowledged landmark in British anthropology.[82] The amalgamation of the Royal Anthropological Institute and the Folk-Lore Society was given serious consideration at this time.[83]

Until the early 1940s in the United States, folklore and anthropology were closely associated, in the American Folklore Society and in the *Journal of American Folklore*. The differences in perspective were attributed to 'literary' and 'anthropological' folklorists, a difference that had existed more or less from the beginning, when the American Folklore Society was founded in 1888.[84] The presence of indigenous populations made their traditions a valid subject of interest for American folklorists from the beginning, while for European scholars, the study of such peoples belonged to the domain of anthropology or ethnology. The American anthropologists tended to limit the term 'folklore' to oral literature since otherwise all of culture would be folklore whereas, for the folklorists, 'folklore was part of the unlettered tradition within literate European and Euro-American societies'.[85] Franz Boas (1858–1942), the father of American anthropology and the founder of ethnography in the modern anthropological sense, had an abiding interest in folklore and was a long-time editor of the *Journal of American Folklore*. He argued for 'the immense importance of folklore in determining the mode of thought', and saw it as revealing the 'genius of a people' and embodying its values. Moreover, it was easily collected on short ethnographic visits. Stocking observes, however, that Boas often equated 'folklore' and 'culture', and reminds us that before 1900 or so 'culture' had not yet generally acquired its modern anthropological connotation.[86]

Evolutionism pushed diffusionism aside in British anthropology from the 1860s, but by the early twentieth century, diffusionism had reasserted itself. Diffusionism is traced to German anti-evolutionism. Adolf Bastian (1826–1905) in his *Elementargedanken* saw similar ideas everywhere due to the 'psychic unity' of the human species, but these took their special ethnic form in the *Völkergedanken*, appearing in '"geographical provinces" of cultural similarities'. Friedrich Ratzel (1844–1904) saw humans as generally lacking in inventiveness and borrowing cultural traits, which were invented by relatively few individuals in relatively few places. His *Anthropogeographie* (1883) was a pioneering diffusionist work.[87] There was a similar development in folktale scholarship with the Indo-European inheritance thesis corrected by the diffusionist arguments of Benfey and Cosquin. Of evolutionist inspiration, this was the first fully scientific method for studying the folktale, but it developed marked diffusionist orientations.

The national epic, *Kalevala* (1835), synthesized by Elias Lönnrot from his extensive collections of oral epic songs, was of central importance in Finnish folklore research. But it could not be used for research into the original poems. To study the evolution of the poetry, it was necessary to undertake large-scale collecting projects in the various regions in which the poetry was found. The Finnish or historical-geographic method was elaborated by Julius Krohn (1835–1888) from his study of the sources of *Kalevala* and by his son Kaarle (1863–1933), and by the latter's student Antti Aarne (1867–1925). It has been called, as Jouko Hautala says, 'Darwinism adapted to folklore', but Julius Krohn from the beginning connected the evolution of the poems to the diffusion of tradition.[88] Kaarle's *Die Folkloristische Arbeitsmethode* (1926) was the accepted methodological guide.

The method, applied to folktales above all, was to dominate folklore scholarship until the mid-twentieth century. Its basic premise was that a folktale known from hundreds of oral 'variants' had been invented in one time and one place and thereafter had spread outwards in ever-widening waves, rather like those caused when a stone is thrown into water. In the same region, the tale could maintain its stability over long periods of time, but migrating, it was transformed, adapting to new cultural environments.

Language and culture were no barrier to the tale's diffusion, which tended to be from more complex to less complex societies, with India and Western Europe as the most important centres of diffusion. The method was based on extensive studies of individual tales, often on the comparison of several hundred variants in many different languages and dialects. Indeed the logistics of such colossal research undertakings on top of the provisional nature of the conclusions helped to undermine the method. The aim of the method was to write a 'life history' of the tale that would best explain its distribution and variation, working backwards and arriving at an approximation to the hypothetical ur-form and its place and time of origin.

From the beginning of the twentieth century a number of scholarly tools towards comparative folktale research appeared which greatly facilitated historic-geographic studies: Aarne's *Verzeichnis der Märchentypen* (1910), a system for classifying international folktales, translated and expanded by Stith Thompson as *The Types of the Folktale* (1928); Johannes Bolte's and Georg Polívka's exhaustive five-volume work of comparative annotations to Grimms' tales, *Anmerkungen zu den Kinder- und Hausmärchen der Brüder Grimm* (1913–32); Stith Thompson's six-volume *Motif-Index of Folk-Literature* (1932–6); and following on Aarne's *Verzeichnis*, a number of national catalogues ('type indices') of folktales (including Seán Ó Súilleabháin's and Reidar Th. Christiansen's *Types of the Irish Folktale* in 1963). With the exception of the *Anmerkungen*, all these volumes appeared as numbers in a publication series of the Finnish-based organization of folklorists, FF (Folklore Fellows) Communications, from 1907.

The main objections to the Finnish method emphasized the fact that it was basically a philological approach, far removed from the cultural context of the tales, and that it underestimated the active role of storytellers in the development and propagation of the tales. The Swedish folklorist Carl Wilhelm von Sydow (1878–1952) emphasized local historical and cultural factors in the development of specific regional subtypes, and the role of the few 'active bearers of tradition', as opposed to the many 'passive'.[89] As we have seen, Finland was among the pioneers of folklore research, its influence due largely to the Finnish method. A chair of folklore, perhaps the first in the world,* was established in the University of Helsinki as early as 1898.[90]

Ethnographic Collections and Museums

The first collections that could be called ethnographic were in the cabinets of curiosities of the sixteenth and seventeenth centuries, selected usually according to 'criteria of originality, curiosity or exoticism'.[91] The Irish antiquary

---

* Kaarle Krohn was appointed Docent in Finnish and Comparative Folklore in 1888, *extraordinarius* of the same in 1898 and occupant of a permanent chair from 1908.

Crofton Croker left a typical example after his death in 1854: 'a curious double bodied Peruvian bottle, the silver seal of the Cork Orange Lodge, Esquimaux tools, an Irish harp, a mummified alligator, and a cap worn by Charles I at his execution'.[92] Ethnographic collections that resulted from the travels of explorers or the expansion of colonial empires were assembled in a single museum for the first time in 1837 with the establishment, at the command of the king of Holland, of the Museum voor Volkenkunde in Leiden. Subsequently, similar museums were established in other countries. Ethnographic objects tended to be exhibited by type, demonstrating 'the linear development of humanity, the progressions realized by the species according to its degree of civilization . . .'[93] The museum of the Academy of Sciences of St Petersburg, devoted to the cultural diversity of the Russian Empire, was opened in 1836. The first museum devoted to the ethnography of its own country was that of Denmark, opened in Copenhagen in 1840. An Ethnological Gallery was opened in the British Museum in 1845 and the Peabody Museum of Archaeology and Ethnology within Harvard University in 1866.[94]

Bjarne Stocklund points out that it was only after the middle of the nineteenth century that the interest in folk culture was extended to its material aspects and he attributes that to the role of international exhibitions. While the first, 'The Great Exhibition of the Works of all Nations', held in London in 1851, did not include an ethnographic dimension, subsequent ones did, in particular that of Paris in 1867. A subtext of competition between national cultures brought folk culture to the fore, with its national specificity resting on its 'supposed timelessness, continuity and independence of international fashions', while the visual requirement of the exhibition format logically pointed to the material aspects of folk culture. The sort of objects displayed were being referred to as 'folk art' by the turn of the century. Paris introduced the pavilion concept and afterwards ethnographic buildings became a constant, with Vienna planning an 'ethnographic village' with houses from all over the world in 1873 (though only seven appeared). Paris invited participating countries to send wax figures in folk costume, and Sweden's attracted most attention at the exhibition.[95]

Artur Hazelius applied this idea to the new kind of museum he founded in Stockholm in 1873, the Nordic Museum (Nordiska Museet), devoted to all the Scandinavian countries (Swedish patriotic sensibility at the time having a pronounced pan-Scandinavian bent). It exhibited objects from rural and urban life along with representations of typical scenes. Nearby in 1891, he established Skansen, the first open-air museum in the world. Its characteristic procedure involved the removal of buildings representative of the various Scandinavian regions and their reconstruction in the museum, furnished and decorated in the appropriate regional style. Craft activities, agricultural practices and archaic techniques were demonstrated in or around the buildings. The intention was 'not so much to reproduce as to simulate a concrete habitat'. The open-air museum represented national unity in diversity, a sort of nation in microcosm.[96] It has since been imitated all over the world.

The ethnographic museum of the Trocadéro, founded in 1878, opened a European room in 1884 with a life-size model of a Breton domestic scene, and from 1889 there was a gallery for the regional cultures of France.[97] The idea of an ethnographic museum had appeared in the folklore journals *Mélusine* and *Revue des Traditions Populaires* and the exhibits at the Universal Exhibition in Paris in 1878 formed the embryo of future French collections. The Musée d'Ethnographie du Trocadéro coincided with the interior industrial development of France and the creation of a French colonial empire, while the strong interest in regional museums at the time was characterized, argues Montserrat Iniesta i Gonzàlez, by 'an idealized and archaizing image of rural life, which counterposed the urban world'.[98] In the United States in the late nineteenth century, heritage was the preserve of the old elites for whom this interest was a form of distinction both from the philistine *nouveaux riches* and an intellectual tendency which saw progress and disdain for the past as quintessential American values. The open-air museum appeared in the 1920s and 1930s, 'in the context of serious labour difficulties on the domestic front', and one of the first, in Greenfield Village, was built ironically by the man for whom famously 'history is bunk' – Henry Ford – as a celebration of the Common Man rather than the 'folk', 'an Americanised Skansen', as Tony Bennett terms it.[99] Other representations of the folk characterized the museological discourses of totalitarian regimes. The National Socialist regime in Germany promoted its *Heimatmuseen* and Fascist Italy its folkloric exhibitions, while the socialist countries saw the task of the museum as three-fold:

> to conserve the cultural inheritance of peoples and to show their recent and contemporary development; . . . to contribute to the scientific and aesthetic education of the masses, as well as to cultivate the idea of fraternity among peoples; and . . . to preserve the identity and to develop in their originality the cultures of the peoples of the USSR, according to the principles of cultural inheritance pronounced by Lenin.[100]

The age of museums is also the age of nation building. The Estonian nation and national culture date from the same period as the Estonian National Museum, which was founded in 1909, and represented an important aspect of national identification to the young state, which was to declare its independence in 1918. To a large extent the museum was devoted to peasant culture and beholden to ethnology in the 1930s. The subsequent loss of national independence meant a downgrading of the museum. Relocated and renamed the Ethnographical Museum, it became an ethnological research institute with little or no access to the public. The years of the 'Singing Revolution' in the late 1980s led to a renewed focus on the museum with a demand for the restoration of its original site, which was occupied by a Soviet air base,* and its original name: an acknowledgement of its role as a central national symbol.[101]

In the post-Second World War United Kingdom, a large number of new museums 'orientated towards the collection, preservation, and display of artefacts relating to the daily lives, customs, rituals and traditions of non-élite social strata' have appeared.[102] These were in the form of folk museums and 'living history farms'. The first open-air museum was the Welsh Folk Museum at St Fagan's, outside Cardiff, which was opened in 1946, and the Ulster Folk Museum can be understood in the same context.

E. Estyn Evans (1905–1989) came to Queen's University, Belfast in the late 1920s and developed an interest in folklife, publishing in the field from 1939. His publications, particularly *Irish Folk Ways* (1957), were read widely and established him as perhaps the best-known scholar in the field. The idea of a folk museum of the Skansen type was his, probably conceived before the Second World War. Although it was 1954 before a committee was established to investigate the matter, eventually the Act establishing the Ulster Folk Museum was passed by the Northern Ireland parliament in 1958 with the brief of 'illustrating the way of life, past and present, and the traditions of the people of Northern Ireland'. A site on 136 acres east of Belfast, Cultra Manor, was purchased in 1961 and the first house, an eighteenth-century cottage from near Limavady, was erected in 1963. Others followed, along with exhibition centres for the display of traditional artefacts. The first director, George B. Thompson, and his successor, Alan Gailey, were both geographers by training.

From 1955, the journal *Ulster Folklife* was published and the recording of folklore was organized through the circulation of questionnaires and the employment of field-collectors. The Ulster Folklife Society was established in 1961 and worked closely with the museum. In 1967, the museum was merged with the Belfast Transport Museum to form the Ulster Folk and Transport Museum. The museum is the major centre for folklife research in the island of Ireland, and has become a major touristic and educational attraction.[103] Recently it was amalgamated with other heritage institutions in the umbrella grouping of the National Museums and Galleries of Northern Ireland.

In the southern Irish state, folklife studies did not achieve the same institutional footing, although they formed part of the brief of the Irish Folklore Commission. The National Museum from the late 1920s set about assembling a folklife collection, later in cooperation with the field staff of the Folklore Commission and with the Irish Countrywomen's Association (who had surveyed traditional craft workers). A.T. Lucas (1911–1986), was put in charge of the Folklife Collection in 1947, the first such full-time appointment.

---

* Ironically, commanded by General Dzhokhar Dudayev, who was to lead the Chechen drive to independence in the 1990s.

Lack of funds for acquisitions meant that a lot of the collection, totalling several thousand items, was donated.[104] It was never given a permanent home. The Irish National Folk Museum is to be opened near Castlebar, Co. Mayo by 2000 or 2001. As a national institution, its distance from the main research and training centres in the field of folklore and folklife may disadvantage it, even if it should benefit tourism in the region.

A Note on the Making of Heritage

Choosing which cultural elements to preserve by definition recontextualizes them and the choice has too often been made according to aesthetic criteria foreign to the culture of origin of the artefact. For example, in Estonia early in the twentieth century, two essential criteria for the selection of the ethnographic heritage were the age of the artefact ('the older, the more national it was') and its artistic merit – it had to be attractive.[105] Singularity has always been taken to distinguish the work of art from the work of craft. The work of art, with its sacred aura, was to be displayed for hushed and reverential contemplation in a museum and removed from everyday life. As Barbara Kirshenblatt-Gimblett points out, the process of collecting creates scarcity, so scarce objects become singular by being removed from their normal context to be displayed as art in ethnographic and anthropological museums despite being multiple objects in the ordinary context of their use.[106] This is one of the dangers of aestheticism, of dissociating objects from their function and from social life.[107]

Cultural heritage is part of identity. Not everything inherited from the past is considered worthy of preservation nor is every part of everyday culture symbolically significant. Stuart Hall argues that in every period the cultural process involves drawing a line, always in a different place, 'as to what is to be incorporated into "the great tradition" and what is not'.[108] Thus, cultural heritage can be a resource for reproducing social differences. It is the dominant groups that determine which elements are superior and worthy to be preserved. The popular classes may create cultural products of great aesthetic value, as García Canclini points out, but they have not the same possibilities to accumulate these products over time and to gain recognition for them as part of the general cultural heritage.[109]

Folk or Peasants?

Empirical research on peasant society contradicts the Romantic autonomy of the folk. This is not to say that folk and peasantry are synonymous. 'Folk' was a projection of an idealized peasant society onto the nation. Peasants in the anthropological literature are rural cultivators, raising crops and livestock, but at the same time are not agricultural entrepreneurs. As Eric Wolf puts it, the peasant 'runs a household, not a business concern'.[110] Research on peasants has constantly emphasized their relationship of dependence on a larger outside world, unlike 'primitives', more or less independent of state organization. A.L. Kroeber emphasized this lack of autonomy and called the peasantry a 'part-society', stressing its relationship to market towns, while Robert Redfield emphasized the 'moral guidance' of the peasantry by the elite. The peasantry then was as a part of a whole society, which included cities and towns, and it was not isolated, nor complete in itself. Among the peasantry lived an intelligentsia consisting of functionaries, teachers, doctors or churchmen, who were mediators between local life and the wider world. In particular they represented the state to the local community.[111]

The opposition of tradition to modernity led to the Romantic idea of the 'folk', contrasted with cosmopolitan groups and with the modern urban proletariat in national society. Folklore research pioneered a type of peasant studies, since through the nineteenth and much of the first half of the twentieth centuries it was the only discipline to concern itself with peasant culture, though without ever clearly defining its subject. Anthropology, as Michael Kearney outlines it, was based on the opposition of the primitive and the civilized, later envisaged, as the 'primitive' disappeared, in terms of the traditional and the modern. From the middle of the twentieth century the polarity came to be expressed in terms of underdeveloped and developed, with the peasant taking up the position vacated by the primitive. Peasant studies became a growth area from the 1960s in the context of the Cold War and the US need to contain Communism.[112]

Robert Redfield (1897–1958) was a key figure in peasant studies, influenced both by the urban sociology of the University of Chicago and Tönnies' *Gemeinschaft* and *Gesellschaft* (see Chapter 1). His concept of a 'great tradition' and a 'little tradition' is well known. The great tradition 'of the reflective few', the philosopher, theologian or literary person, is consciously cultivated in schools or temples and is consciously handed down. The little tradition 'of the largely unreflective many' 'keeps itself going in the lives of the unlettered in their village communities' and is 'for the most part taken for granted and not submitted to much scrutiny or considered refinement or improvement'. But the two traditions are interdependent and co-exist in the same civilization.[113] Redfield's perspective, argues Kearney, fits the old traditional/modern opposition, with modernization gradually leading to the diffusion of ideas from the city to the countryside.[114]

Interrogating the word 'peasant', and its often negative connotations in Ireland, Gearóid Ó Crualaoich finds that the following qualifications have been argued for in the Irish case:

> That the alleged 'peasantry' includes large elements of a depressed aristocracy (thus maintaining everyone's chances of being, in reality,

descended from high kings); that a literate tradition of poetry and learning survives among the people at large, if only in a vestigial way (there is the tradition of Greek and Latin-quoting farm labourers); and that, unlike – so it is alleged – the case of Central European or Central American populations, the memory of past glory and of another order of social organization perpetually fuels a desire to throw off the demeaning yoke of foreign oppression and to resume a very different life style from that prevalent in the countryside in recent centuries.[115]

This notion tended to dominate folklore research, with its emphasis on the oral traditions which seemed to transcend the peasant condition, as opposed to the material culture which underlined it.

Because of the origins of the interest in folklore as implicit critique of the Enlightenment, of modernity, industrialization and urbanization by non-hegemonic, or regional, intellectuals, the discipline of folklore has maintained a certain integrity in its respect for local and small-scale particularities,* even if often coloured by a residual Romanticism. Anthropology is effectively a universalistic discipline, centred in a small number of Western countries and publishing overwhelmingly in English. Folklore and ethnology are multi-centred disciplines in Europe, with strong national research traditions in national languages, close relationships with ethnographic and local museums and local amateur societies, as well as shifting (and nationally significant) relationships with other disciplines: history, archaeology, geography, literary studies (usually in terms of the dominant national or local language), musicology, comparative religion and, since the 1960s, with the social sciences.§ The origins of folklore and ethnology in a sort of inward

---

* A good example of this are the various attempts to map this local diversity. A German linguistic atlas was begun in 1876, Wenker's *Deutscher Sprachatlas*, and from the 1930s atlases of traditional culture were begun, the pioneers being in Germany and Sweden. The *Atlas der deutschen Volkskunde* was planned before 1930 but it came under the influence of National Socialist ideology. A new series was begun after the war, the first volume being published in 1958. The Swedish *Atlas över Svensk Folkkultur*, being prepared from 1937, appeared as a first volume, covering material culture and aspects of social life, in 1957. Heinrich Wagner's *Linguistic Atlas and Survey of Irish Dialects* (Dublin: Dublin Institute for Advanced Studies, 1958–69) is the only comprehensive Irish atlas of this kind; many ethnological maps, of course, have been published but no atlas, although there have been plans to do so. See Alan Gailey (ed.), *Ethnological Mapping in Ireland. A Document for discussion towards an ethnological atlas of Ireland* ([Cultra, Co. Down:] Ulster Folk and Transport Museum, 1974), pp. 1–3, 5–6 and Alan Gailey and Caoimhín Ó Danachair, 'Ethnological Mapping in Ireland', *Ethnologia Europaea* vol. IX, no. 1 (1976), pp. 14–34.

§ According to a survey of the position of 'regional ethnology and folklore' in European universities, published in 1955,

As a free reading course, folklife research exists for example at the Belgian universities of Liège (Walloon folklore) and Louvain (Flemish folklore), under the direction of temporarily appointed teachers. At some Austrian universities (Innsbruck, Salzburg)

anthropological gaze, their past role in nation building and their use of local languages in research has sometimes tended to hinder international understanding, if not cooperation. Isac Chiva points out that there is no 'common and dominant' scientific language in the field but rather a dozen or more languages used 'for extra-scientific reasons'. Research, thus, carried out on a continental scale, is 'deprived of a *lingua franca* and, in consequence, of a common language, definitions and analytical concepts' and even of a common name for the discipline.[116]

'European ethnology' was proposed as a new name for the overlapping fields of folklife research, *Volkskunde* and folklore at the International Folklore Conference in Arnhem in 1955. The idea for the new name represented 'a move from a narcissistic preoccupation with one's "own" to an ethnology which constantly reflects on, and incorporates the "other"', in Klaus Roth's words. The name has been accepted in many Scandinavian and German-speaking institutions since then, and a journal bearing the name (*Ethnologia Europaea*) was founded in 1967.[117] In some countries folklore and ethnology are still close to nationalist or regionalist ideologies; Irish folklore research is occasionally informed by the discourse of the Gaelic revival. But folklore and ethnology are often central disciplines in the academy, often among the oldest university disciplines, and sometimes privileged commentators on the changing nature of national society, rather as historians are in Ireland.

There has been a significant difference between the 'folklife' and the 'folklore' orientation. The former cannot easily escape from the pragmatic function of the phenomenon under investigation, usually a peasant artefact. Folklife research has usually been studied in the context of the museum, where it is displayed, and, like the museum itself, bears some relation to the natural sciences: it deals with what can be observed, quantified and mapped,

---

and some German (Münster, the philosophical–theological Academy of Paderborn and occasionally at some universities) certain aspects of folklife research enter as optional into the training of students of law and divinity (Münster). At several universities, certain aspects of folklife research are dealt with in connection with philology and dialect studies (at several German universities, in Vienna, Uppsala, Helsingfors etc.), in connection with sociology (Hull, Leeds, Leicester and other English universities), general ethnology and physical anthropology (Cambridge, Toulouse, Coïmbra, Lisbon, Genoa, Naples, Ankara etc.), geography (Belfast, Manchester, Vienna, Sofia etc.), architecture and agriculture (Wageningen), and possibly also in other combinations.

Research institutions without any obligation to teach exist for example in France (Laboratoire d'Ethnographie Normande, at Caen), Germany (Abteilung Volkskunde of the Institute for German Philology, at Greifswald), Northern Ireland (Committee of Ulster Folklife and Traditions, at Belfast), Scotland (School of Scottish Studies, at Edinburgh), Ireland (Irish Folklore Commission), Portugal (Centro de Estudos de Etnologia peninsular, at Porto), and Spain (Centro de Estudios de Etnología peninsular, at Barcelona, and Instituto Bernardino de Sahagum [*sic*] in Madrid).

Sigurd Erixon, 'The Position of Regional Ethnology and Folklore at the European Universities: An International Inquiry' in *Laos* no. III (1955), pp. 116, 180.

and the pioneers were usually individuals with a scientific training. In that sense, folklife research is in an enlightened tradition of scientific observation of the outlying parts of the national territory, regionally significant, but not pertaining to a central part of the national heritage. Folklore, on the other hand, is closer to the humanities, dealing with an obviously more 'spiritual' and less quantifiable part of culture and, even if recorded from the mouths of peasants, socially transcending them. Strongly influenced by Romanticism, folklore research was a central national concern, which is why various movements for national emancipation provided an ideal environment for folklore research to thrive. It is also the reason why the Irish Folklore Commission could be established with the support of the government of the Irish Free State in the 1930s and folklife study neglected, while in Northern Ireland it was folklife study that was eventually institutionalized. Gaelic folklore was understood as the channel for the subterranean continuity of a Gaelic aristocratic tradition through centuries of foreign oppression, and hence the historical continuity of the Irish nation (see Chapter 5). Unlike Estonia, where the peasant origins of the modern nation and its ideologues were undeniable, and hence where both folklore and folklife represented the core national heritage, the Irish nation was not envisaged as a nation derived from the peasantry (and the key nationalist and Gaelicist ideologues were not predominantly of peasant origin) so the obviously peasant-based folklife seemed to be at odds with the '*gesunkenes Kulturgut*' which was folklore. These issues are properly the subject of the next chapter, where the question of the relationship between folklore and the nation will be discussed in depth.

3. Folklore and Nation-building

The question of nation building impinges both on folklore as subject matter and as scholarly discourse. The discussion here considers various aspects of the relationship between folklore and nation. It looks at folklorists as nation-builders, who 'map' the nation through the project of intensive folklore-collecting throughout its territory, and who use folklore as a national resource, whether for national history or for the construction of a national high culture. And it looks at folklorists as defenders of regional culture. The wish to use folklore as a national resource when the nation does not have its own state comes from a context in which the putative nation has none of the trappings of nationhood and is little more than a province of a metropolis. In that sense, those who make national claims for folklore belong to a group that rejects its own provincial status, on historic or on ethnic grounds, and argues for folklore as a proof of the historical depth of the nation in the absence of firm documentary evidence or of documented continuity with the past. Hence we see that questions of ethnicity and identity are raised. Indeed such debates are commonest in ethnically stratified societies where one group's lowly status is the result of conquest at the hands of the group whose status is the highest. The former's rejection of its status is based on its knowledge of or belief in an anterior situation, recorded by history or tradition, in which it occupied its rightful place. An appeal to a better past comes from the rejection of an ignominious present. There are, however, a number of variables involved, and it is necessary to consider these in order to appreciate the different national trajectories of folklore scholarship.

Among them are the ethnic composition of the country in question (e.g. Ireland with its colonial elite and largely native lower classes); the country's political situation (e.g. Finland passing from Sweden to Russia in 1809); its relationship with a metropolis (e.g. that of the eighteenth- and early nine-teenth-century German states with France); the existence of deep social and regional, and sometimes national, differences between different parts of the state (e.g. the Italian North and South, the Brazilian South and North-East, Catalonia, the Basque Country and Galicia within the Spanish state, Ireland within the United Kingdom); the development of industrialization and urbanization (correlated with one or more of the other factors); and so forth. These variables determined crucially whether the popular could be reconfigured as the national and whether there was a social group or a fraction thereof in whose interests the identification could be made. From Herder to the present day, those who idealized indigenous cultural experience (through Scottish 'Highlandism', the Catalan *Renaixença*, Finnish *Karelianismi*, Russian *narodnichevo*, the Gaelic Revival, Latin American *indigenismo*, Francophone West-Indian and West-African *négritude* and a host of other such intellectual movements and tendencies) attempted to reject ill-fitting foreign models by discovering the raw material of high culture in that section of their own population most removed from metropolitan culture and its local imitations. Of necessity, then, there was an unavoidably 'provincial' aspect to all these movements.

Alienated Intellectuals

The model of intellectual alienation was the German bourgeoisie of the second half of the eighteenthth century, politically and socially excluded by a French-speaking aristocracy (see Chapter 1). Their development of the notion of *Kultur* in opposition to 'civilization' reflected this situation. Early nineteenth-century Anglo-Irish writers wrote their fiction not for their compatriots but for a metropolitan readership and tried to establish 'its discreteness, its regionalism *vis-à-vis* an exoteric readership by means of local colour'.[1] Thomas Davis and Young Ireland consciously opposed this; their project, in the words of Davis's celebrated song, that 'Ireland long a province be/ A nation once again'. More recently Roberto Schwarz has written that '[w]e Brazilians and other Latin Americans constantly experience the artificial, inauthentic and imitative nature of our cultural life'.[2] In Latin America, 'the traditional structure of culture – where side by side exist extensive illiteracy and the social but provincial refinement of the cultivated elites – drives the latter not to modernity, but to a kind of inevitable alienation'. Socially distanced from the peasant and indigenous masses, writers and thinkers could not write for a local public but had to redirect themselves to a European audience, as did the Brazilian symbolists, who wrote directly in French.[3] The Brazilian modernists tried to redress this problem in the 1920s by actively engaging with national traditions, listening to 'the profound voices of our race', in parallel with a renewed scholarly dedication to folklore.[4]

The eighteenth-century German intellectuals did not have a 'social hinterland' and were dispersed throughout the small capitals of the various

German states, unlike their French equivalents, united in the metropolis and 'held together within a more or less unified and central "good society" . . .'[5] The nineteenth- and early twentieth-century folklorists in England, France, post-unification Italy and other countries that did not have significant cultural nationalist movements tended to remain provincial intellectuals. It is significant that before the foundation of the Gaelic League in 1893, which 'nationalized' Ireland's provincialism, Irish folklorists were by and large part of a wider United Kingdom interest, and the most famous two – Croker and Keightley – had metropolitan careers.

From Herder's time folklore has been commonly understood as an authentic and uncorrupted national inheritance. Interest in it has been called 'a particularist discourse about identity'.[6] 'Nationalistic inferiority complexes' then have been understood as the reason for what Alan Dundes calls the 'fabrication' of folklore, giving Macpherson's *Ossian*, Elias Lönnrot's *Kalevala* and the work of the Grimm brothers as examples.[7] Renato Ortiz argues that popular culture was a symbolic element that allowed intellectuals to express the peripheral situation of their country.[8] In the case of regional elites who resented their marginalization as power became more and more centralized, 'the revalorization of the regional' was a means for them to maintain their cultural capital.[9] Similarly, if regional intellectuals did not identify with the state or with the dominant culture of the state, if they had a memory of previous autonomy, a consciousness of a separate nationhood or the desire to create one, then their provincial status could be opposed. They could posit the regional as representing in fact national difference. Alienated by political or social change, they could then revalorize their cultural capital in national terms: folklore offered them the means to 'de-provincialize' themselves by giving them the basis for a national culture. Folklore then became a national resource and scholarly interest in it led to the establishment of a 'national science'. It was in this way that folklore studies were usually institutionalized and found their place in the academy.

(Internal) Colonialism and Social Mobility

If elite culture could be construed as the national culture (or at least, on the eve of the construction of a modern society, was a national culture in waiting) and if state elites were also national elites (were hegemonic), then folklore had little national significance. The provinces are always peripheral and, despite carping at the capital's concentration of power and resources, they may well accept the situation as the natural order of things. But the inequality of the relationship between the provinces and the capital may also be interpreted as having nothing inevitable about it. It may represent a historic wrong that is capable of being redressed. It may be the obvious result of conquest and colonization. Colonialism, after all, unlike provincialism, always entails unequal rights:[10] The characteristic colonial situation is outlined by Michael Hechter as follows:

> it must involve the interaction of at least two cultures – that of the conquering metropolitan élite (cosmopolitan culture) and of the indigenes (native culture) – and that the former is promulgated by the colonial authorities as being vastly superior for the realization of universal ends: salvation in one age; industrialization in another. One of the consequences of this denigration of indigenous culture is to undermine the native's will to resist the colonial régime. If he is defined as barbarian, perhaps he should try to reform himself by becoming more cosmopolitan. Failure to win high position within the colonial structure tends to be blamed on personal inadequacy, rather than any particular shortcomings of the system itself. The native's internalization of the colonist's view of him makes the realization of social control less problematic. Conversely, the renaissance of indigenous culture implies a serious threat to continued colonial domination.[11]

Racist doctrines, bureaucratic authoritarianism and an obvious economic exploitation were the lot of African and Asian colonies. But territorially based ethnic groups within European states also experienced various degrees of economic and cultural discrimination (not to speak of non-territorially based groups such as Jews and Gypsies), and sometimes racist ideas of hereditary inferiority helped to justify their subaltern status. The notion of 'internal colonialism' has sometimes been applied in this context.

Sir William Wilde gives a vivid account of his visit to a remote village in Ireland in the first half of the nineteenth century:

> . . .the children gathered around to have a look at the stranger, and one of them, a little boy about eight years of age, addressed a short sentence in Irish to his sister, but meeting the father's eye, he immediately cowered back, having to all appearance, committed some heinous fault. The man called the child to him, said nothing, but drawing forth from its dress a little stick . . . which was suspended by a string around the neck, put an additional notch in it with his penknife. [We] were told that it was done to prevent the child speaking Irish; for every time he attempted to do so a new nick was put in his tally, and when these amounted to a certain number, summary punishment was inflicted upon him by the schoolmaster.

When questioned, the father, who spoke little English, enthusiastically expressed his affection for the Irish language but explained that the children needed education and, since no Irish was taught in the schools, they had to be encouraged to speak English. The school was more than three miles distant, across river fords and over mountain passes, and an adult escorted the children there and back each day, occasionally carrying the weak.[12]

The Kenyan writer Ngũgĩ wa Thiong'o describes a similar method in the colonial school system he experienced in the 1950s. A child overheard speaking Gikuyu was given a button which was then passed on to the next culprit until at the end of the day the child left holding the button began a chain of denunciation 'and the ensuing process would bring out all the culprits of the day'. The punishment was physical or psychological – being forced to wear a placard with a humiliating inscription.[13] The complicity of the students in the degradation of their own language is obvious. That is how the system worked, and it worked because it was also seen as bringing rewards. Ngũgĩ points out that achievement in English was highly rewarded in school: it was the passport to social mobility, 'the magic formula to colonial elitedom'.[14]

In Estonia in 1911, in a report of the Estonian National Museum, founded only two years before, Oskar Kallas (1868–1946), the first professionally trained Estonian folklorist, found it necessary to justify the interest of ethnic Estonians in their heritage. 'We have been told: we are nothing, we possess nothing. And it has been explained to us so thoroughly that even we ourselves believe it, and we are not able to feel and exist in our own way. We have to fight against this opinion.' At the time there was little public support for the notion of preserving peasant culture. The ethnic Estonian Students' Society in Tartu (Dorpat) University did not consider the collecting of folklore and peasant artefacts to carry any prestige. The university, Russian-speaking at the time, had been German-speaking until some years before (since the elite, high culture and political and economic power were German). The folklorist Oskar Loorits (1900–1961) summed up the dilemma of the young Estonian: 'outwardly an Estonian, but a gent by nature [*väliselt küll eestlane, sisemiselt aga paratamatult saks*]'.[15] The paradox in this statement lies in the very words *eestlane*, 'an Estonian' (itself a nineteenth-century neologism), and *saks*. The latter word is glossed as 'gentleman', 'toff', 'master', but crucially its archaic meaning and etymology reveal the historical power on which the connotation of the word rested: 'German'.[16] An educated Estonian found identification with German culture unavoidable. Only with independence (declared in 1918), could the power of the new state allow a national culture to be consolidated.

The implications of minority, or general subaltern, status for an ethnic group within a wider society have been explored by Fredrik Barth in a classic study.

> In the total social system, all sectors of activity are organized by statuses open to members of the majority group, while the status system of the minority has only relevance to relations within the minority and only to some sectors of activity, and does not provide a basis for action in other sectors, equally valued in the minority culture. There is thus a disparity between values and organizational facilities: prized goals are outside the field organized by the minority's culture and categories.[17]

Social mobility then, unless a racial bar existed, meant moving outside of the bounds of one's own ethnic group and assimilating to the dominant ethnic group. In eighteenth- and early nineteenth-century Ireland, the assimilation of aristocrats and social climbers of Gaelic and Old English descent to the Anglo-Irish (through 'conforming' to the Anglican established church) was an obvious strategy to further individual (or family) interests at a time when the subaltern ethnic group controlled a very circumscribed domain. Finnish-speaking officials and ministers tended to be assimilated to the dominant Finland – Swedish ethnic group in eighteenth-century Finland, and, until the early nineteenth century, educated Estonians to the Baltic Germans.[18]

Ethnicity and Identity

Ethnicity and nationality have to do with feelings of belonging within large groups of people, supported by a relatively well-established consciousness of a common history and a common culture. Both concepts can be used to reconcile differences and oppositions within a group or a territory, such as those based on gender, class, religion, language, and so on. Unlike ethnicity, nationality is tied to a state, or to the desire to create a state.[19] Ethnicity as a concept is only significant when groups of different ethnic origin are in contact with each other in some common context. Barth defines an ethnic group as being to a large extent biologically self-perpetuating, sharing basic cultural values, forming a field of interaction and having a membership identified as distinct, both by itself and by others. But he argues that this definition assumes that the cultural boundaries of an ethnic group are unproblematic, and his study shows that that is not necessarily the case. He argues that circumstances exist in which the value standards of an ethnic group can be satisfactorily realized, but also that there may be limits beyond which they cannot. He maintains that if individuals need to go beyond those limits, then ethnic identities cannot be retained.[20]

Beyond those limits the culture of the subaltern ethnic group is not valid, but the question of assimilation is not always relevant. If one does not permanently venture beyond the limits but has occasion to do so frequently or from time to time, one nevertheless has to master a new way of behaving which often includes a new language. The characteristic feature of groups whose culture is subaltern within the modern state can be compared to the bilingualism of the dialect ('low', informal)/national language ('high', formal) type, a sort of 'biculturalism', where the individual is enculturated into his or her native community, and acculturated through having to participate in the dominant culture.[21] This form of bilingualism is called diglossia, a term which carries clear connotations of social difference. 'High' forms and situations, in Ferguson's schema, include a sermon in church or mosque, a personal letter, a speech in parliament or a political speech in general, a news broadcast, a newspaper editorial, a news story, a caption on a picture, a university lecture and poetry. Instructions to servants, waiters, workmen and clerks, a conversation with family, friends or colleagues, a radio soap opera, a caption on a political cartoon and folk literature are, on the other hand, 'low'.[22] Diglossia may be a transitional phenomenon, or it may be stable. The varieties involved may be considered as dialects of the same language, such as with Arabic, German or Italian, or separate languages (bilingual diglossia), as with Spanish and Guaraní in Paraguay, or Irish in Ireland (with the situation becoming more complicated in the twentieth century with state recognition and support for Irish). In some cases the informal variety may have strong associations with national identity, as with Guaraní or Swiss German.

The modern notion of German culture derives from Luther's translation of the Bible. Remaining faithful to the existing sacred or classical models, he expanded the register of the national, as Kristeva puts it. Beginning with language, he set in motion a process that would culminate in Romanticism. 'The national is founded then on an extended translatability . . .'[23] The linguistic dimension of nineteenth- and early twentieth-century nation building also involved the raising of the status of a demotic language so that it could encompass the whole of high culture. This was characteristic of European cultural nationalism in the nineteenth and early twentieth centuries.

Diglossia is not necessarily relevant to national questions. If the informal variety can be construed as a dialect of the formal variety (let us here remember the ironic definition of a language as 'a dialect with an army and a navy', attributed to Max Weinreich), whether linguistically the two varieties are close to or distant from one another, then its ideological weight in national terms is slight. The abbé Grégoire's enquiry, begun in 1790, which led to the report *Sur la nécessité et les moyens d'anéantir les patois et d'universaliser l'usage de la langue française*, investigated linguistic difference in order to lay the ground for its destruction.[24] The implications of the report were only likely to cause disquiet if the existence of the informal variety could be explained as the survival of a *distinct* language, in which case the language and the cultural forms specific to it (folklore, literature) could be taken as evidence of a distinct identity. This distinct identity is based not on social status or geographical location but on national distinctiveness – this indeed was the claim of Breton nationalism.

If worldview is universally conceived in terms of spatial relationships, as has been argued by Jurij Lotman, in the form of oppositions such as top/bottom, right/left, concentric/eccentric, then a fundamental question is how the world structured by the worldview is organized. It can be envisaged in terms of two spaces, an internal space that is surrounded by, hence bounded by, an external space. The external space itself then is unbounded, since it is limitless. Because the internal space is closed and the external open, the opposition internal/external can be understood as bounded/unbounded, organized/disorganized, or having structure/not having structure. Thus organization is an entrance to a closed world.[25] This model can be exemplified by the Greek notion of the non-Greek, the 'barbarian', *bárbaros*, one who stammered (according to the etymology of the word) and was, in other words, incapable of organized speech; or by a host of ethnocentric traditions which characterize foreigners by their stupidity (lack of organization in thought), drunkenness, sensuality and dirtiness (lack of bodily control).[26]

The selection of elements for an identity system takes place as part of a polemic with other groups, and this is where the spatial interpretation of worldview allows an easy reckoning of what is 'ours' and what is not. It is through such a debate that a position is formulated. The meaningful elements tend to come from areas of culture which are under pressure from outside, as Lauri Honko points out.[27] The identification of what is proper to the group is a systematization whereby cultural elements are placed on either side of the boundary, fitted into the system or excluded from it. But,   .

> the description of the systematic (the 'existing') is at the same time an indication of the nature of the extrasystematic (the 'non-existing'). One could speak, then, of a specific hierarchy of extrasystematic elements and their relationships, and of the system of the extrasystematic. From this standpoint the world of the extrasystematic could be seen as the system inverted, its symmetrical transformation.[28]

Logically, then, that which is outside the system is a resource for reforming or overthrowing it. The Enlightenment used the notion of reason – organization *par excellence* – to reject much of the accumulated human cultural heritage while the Romantics, in their turn, exalted that which was outside and beyond reason, which transcended it. Regions which had been denigrated as a result of their geographical and political peripherality became spiritually central (for example the Irish-speaking regions). The countryside, rather than the city, traditional source of civility and politeness (Latin *civitas*, Greek *polis*) was asserted as the wellspring of national culture and human values. Peasant languages were elevated in place of cosmopolitan *Kultursprache*.

Tradition, culture and identity have usually been central concepts in the study of folklore. Honko has attempted to create a 'division of labour' between the three terms. Tradition, according to his perspective, refers only to materials. It is 'an unsystematic array of cultural elements and features that have been made available to a particular social group during a longer period of time and in different contexts'. It has been inherited from previous generations or offered to the group from outside. Some of it has been accepted by the group, and adapted, and some of it has been rejected. It is generally believed to be 'old', 'to have been in the transmission process for a long time'. Tradition 'would span the past and present cultures within reach of the group we are studying'. It could be compared to a store, 'only some

parts of which are in use at any given time, the other parts simply waiting
be activated (memory culture) or gradually vanishing'. The store is no
system, but a haphazard array of cultural elements, which changes as in
viduals enter or depart from the group. Tradition, then, 'would denote the
cultural potential or resource, not the actual culture of the group'. Three
forms of tradition can be defined:

> Dead traditions (stored in archives, libraries, etc., waiting for possible
> recirculation and revival), living but passive traditions (stored in the
> memory, inactive) and living, active traditions (performed and/or commu-
> nicated, sometimes difficult to single out and define, e.g. to delimit against
> popular culture, media lore, semi-literary phenomena, etc.).

Tradition may be seen as synonymous with 'cultural elements', but not
with culture, which implies the ordering of elements into a system. The
haphazard accumulation of cultural materials is 'made relevant to the
community, integrated into a life-style' through acquiring a 'systemic character', by becoming culture, which is not so much in the materials
themselves as in how the materials are thought with. Selection is central to
the ordering process: 'Without alternatives, without the potential for adop-
tion and rejection, without the adaptation of available elements into
contemporary systems of interests and values, without social control and
interpretation, no tradition can pass into culture'. In that sense, 'selective
tradition', 'tradition system', 'collective tradition' could be seen as broadly
synonymous with culture. Culture organizes tradition.

The elements form a system of symbols, and represent the group's sense
of cohesiveness. There is a strong rhetorical element to their use, and both
emotional and spiritual connotations. Identity functions in a similar way, 'but
as an ordering principle of the second degree'. What this means is that some
of the traditions of the group are set apart and come to stand for more than
themselves. They take on a symbolic meaning and represent the group in its
dealings with other groups. These symbols are particularly evocative and
take on a sacred air. They may refer to language or music or costume or
place, or they may be names or colours or flags or whatever. But they stand
for more than themselves, expressing the identity of the group.[29]

Nations, National Movements and Nationalism

Most definitions of the nation include among their criteria territoriality (the
claim to a historic territory), a named human population, a common historical memory and a density of socio-cultural communications. Features such
as a common economy, common legal rights and duties, an impersonal
power structure, the monopoly of the use of violence and a claim to legitimacy belong to the nation already constituted as a state.[30] The two distinct

modern ideas of the nation tend to reflect respectively the German experience, with an ethno-cultural definition going back to Herder, and the French, with Ernest Renan's famous 'Qu'est-ce qu' une nation?' (1882) consciously opposing the former. Renan's concept of the elective nation, the result of the 'daily plebiscite' which is the underlying solidarity and fellow feeling of its members, was a reaction to the recent loss of Alsace and Lorraine, and helped to move him away from earlier, more 'German' orientations. 'I like ethnography very much, and find it a peculiarly interesting science', he said. 'But as I wish it to be free, I do not wish it to be applied to politics'.[31]

The European national state is usually seen as a response to the transition to modernity. By politically activating the people through the democratic legitimation of the state, a national identity was able to compensate for the destruction of the social integration which pre-modern identities provided.[32] Nation-states that replaced dynastic-religious ones from the late eighteenth century onwards took two different routes in the move to a capitalist economy and civil society, and in this the theorists of nationalism, the historian Miroslav Hroch and the anthropologist Ernest Gellner, seem to be in broad agreement. One route is when the early modern state developed under a pre-existing ethnic high culture. Here England, France, the Netherlands or Sweden are typical examples. The second situation involved a ruling class of foreign origin dominating ethnic groups that occupied a compact territory, but lacked their own aristocracy and a continuous high culture. Typical examples here would be Estonians, Latvians, Ukrainians or Slovenians (all achieving statehood – even if only nominally within a multi-national entity – after the First World War). In the latter case it was necessary to create a high culture from existing folk traditions, which presupposed ethnographic investigation. On the other hand, the folk tradition of the first kind of state had to be obliterated. So the different options for the two kinds of states are, in Gellner's words, either 'created memory or induced oblivion'.[33] There is also a transitional type, the ethnic community with its own ruling class and literary traditions, but lacking a common statehood – typically Italy and Germany (unified respectively in 1861 and 1871), but also Poland after partition (in 1795).[34] The first type of state will concern us somewhat less in the discussion that follows since folklore was less relevant to that kind of nation-building.

It is the monopoly of legitimate education, rather than of violence, that is at the base of the modern social order, according to Gellner. The industrial era is the age of a universal high culture.

> In the old days it made no sense to ask whether the peasants loved their own culture: they took it for granted ... But when labour migration and bureaucratic employment became prominent features within their social horizon, they soon learned the difference between dealing with a co-national, one understanding and sympathizing with their culture, and

> someone hostile to it ... In stable self-contained communities culture is
> often quite invisible, but when mobility and context-free communication
> come to be the essence of social life, the culture in which one has been
> *taught* to communicate becomes the core of one's identity.

Nationalism is a response to this transformation from agrarian to industrial
society, argues Gellner.[35] Here Hroch disagrees and argues that most European national movements long predated industrial society. There are
antecedents for modern nation-building in late medieval and early modern
times, often in aborted earlier efforts, he argues. These leave certain
resources for a later period, in the form of relics of an earlier political autonomy, in the memory of former independence or statehood and in the survival
of the medieval written language.[36]

The classic national movement (again following Hroch, who looks particularly at small nations in Central and Eastern Europe) had goals covering
three main demands. Firstly, the development of a national culture based on
the local language, and its normal use in education, administration and
economic life. Secondly, the achievement of civil rights and political self-
administration, initially in the form of autonomy and ultimately of
independence. Thirdly, the creation of a complete social structure from out
of the ethnic group, including educated elites, an officialdom and an entre-
preneurial class, but also free peasants and organized workers. This took
place in three structural phases. The first is that of intellectuals who took
an academic interest in the language, culture and history of the common
people, without making any specific national demands. The second phase is
the so-called national awakening, whereby programmes of action were
drawn up and contacts between the intellectuals and the people established. The third phase is a mass movement, involving broad cross-sections
of the people.

In the move from phase two to phase three, the mass movement, Hroch
considers that three factors were decisive: a social and/or political crisis of
the old order, the emergence of discontent among significant elements of the
population, and loss of faith in traditional moral systems, above all a decline
in religious legitimacy, even if this only affected small numbers of intellectuals. The national movement that succeeded seems to have included at least
four elements: a crisis of legitimacy in the dominant social order; a certain
amount of social mobility (some educated people came from the non-dominant ethnic group); a fairly high level of communication within society,
including literacy, schooling and market relations; and nationally relevant
conflicts of interest.[37] Ernesto Laclau argues that 'the emergence of populism
is historically linked to a crisis of the dominant ideological discourse which is
in turn part of a more general social crisis'. The problem is the result either
of 'a fracture in the power bloc, in which a class or class fraction needs, in
order to assert its hegemony, to appeal to "the people" against established

ideology as a whole' or of 'a crisis in the ability of the system to neutralise the dominated sectors'.[38] This, as we can see, provides similarly propitious circumstances for the cultivation of an interest in popular culture, though the classic Latin American populist examples differ insofar as the element of 'ethnic' liberation is usually lacking.

Hroch's three structural stages in the life of a national movement are well known and have been applied to various countries. The first phase included the ethnographic exploration to which Gellner refers, a period of pioneering interest in language and folklore. With the succeeding two phases the importance of 'ethnographic exploration' lessened, but remained an intrinsic and to some extent defining part of both until it was finally institutionalized with the triumph of the national movement. In Ireland, as in Estonia, the interest of exogenous elites in folklore was part of the first phase. Anglo-Irish Protestants such as Brooke and Bunting in Ireland, 'Estophile' Baltic Germans such as Johann Heinrich Rosenplänter in Estonia (indeed Herder, one time resident of Riga, included eight Estonian songs in his collection of folk songs) may serve as examples. The first phase has been placed in the first half of the nineteenth century to about 1860 in Estonia and Latvia, the second phase from 1860 to 1885 and the third phase from 1885.[39]

To Hroch, a national movement involved a disadvantaged non-dominant ethnic group reaching a level of self-awareness sufficient to see itself as a real or potential nation, and to set about achieving all the attributes of a nation.[40] This seems to coincide with Peter Alter's category of Risorgimento nationalism. This he defines as 'an emancipatory political force that accompanies the liberation both of new social strata within an existing, formerly absolutist western European state, and of a people that has grown conscious of itself in opposition to a transnational ruling power in east-central Europe'. This kind of nationalism 'serves as a medium for the political fusion of large social groups, the formation of nations and their self-identification in the national state'. The model here is nineteenth-century Italian nationalism, and its aim is liberation from political and social oppression. Herder and Mazzini were perhaps the most influential 'prophets' of this kind of nationalism. Anti-colonial nationalism can be considered as a form of it, but because of greater linguistic and cultural diversity in European colonies, ethnicity, history and culture could only rarely form the bases of the nation[41].

Partha Chatterjee argues that anti-colonial nationalism divided the world into two domains, the material and the spiritual. The material is the domain of the outside, 'of the economy and of statecraft, of science and technology . . .' The spiritual is the inner domain, 'bearing the "essential" marks of cultural identity'. This he considers to be a fundamental feature of Asian and African colonial nationalism. 'The greater one's success in imitating Western skills in the material domain, therefore, the greater the need to preserve the distinctness of one's spiritual culture'.[42] This was the dilemma of subaltern European ethnic groups in the transition to modernity. To preserve their culture and language was to be traditional and to be modern was to lose them. The paradox was overcome by 'nationalizing' modernity – and the model here was German – by giving that which was supposedly universal a particularist form.

Hroch's model applies to small nations in Central and Eastern Europe. While 'ethnographic exploration' already took place in the closing decades of the eighteenth century in Ireland, the national movements of the first half of the nineteenth century did not primarily rest on a cultural definition of the nation. In that sense there was an 'ethnographic' hiatus between the pioneers of the first phase and the triumphal mass movement of the last, not because an interest in folklore was not cultivated, but because it remained an apolitical endeavour. The extensive collection of folklore falls into Hroch's third phase of the development of a national movement. 'Folklore scholarship has created a "national text" that is considered to have been authored by the "folk" speaking in the "voice" of the nation', is how Pertti Anttonen puts it, articulating the unmistakably nation building aspects of the folklorist's work.[43] The process of cataloguing, storing and archiving of folklore and folklife helped to map the national territory, to 'nationalize' the land, and to present it in microcosm in the folklore archive or in the ethnographic museum. The ethnographic museum, by bringing together large numbers of artefacts in the capital, 'announces that here the intercultural synthesis is produced', the national culture (which leads to García Canclini's question whether national identity can be affirmed 'without reducing ethnic and regional peculiarities to a constructed common denominator').[44]

The most celebrated debunkers of the national aspirations of some of the European small nations were none other than Marx and Engels. They argued that the growth of the nation should lead to the formation of national states in which the bourgeoisie could secure its hegemonic position, essential for the subsequent revolt of the proletariat. Nations that had not developed their own bourgeoisie thus were reactionary relics, anachronisms which must 'perish culturally and politically in order to make way for the progressive unifying role of the bourgeoisie'. They used the notorious term, *geschichtslosen Völker*, 'peoples without history', to refer to these peoples who had been and who would remain incapable of creating a state: 'ethnographic monuments', in Engels's unfortunate phrase.[45] Giuseppe Mazzini had different criteria for nationhood, but only recognized the claims of a few European countries. He believed that nationhood should have a democratic foundation, but that there should be a moral purpose behind it. A nation had a distinct mission to serve humanity – for example, England's was industrial and colonial, Russia's to civilize Asia – and on those grounds, Ireland, despite his sympathy, did not have a valid claim.[46]

Folklore and Nation Building

There was an unavoidable idealization of the people in national movements of subaltern ethnic groups or peripheral countries. Distinguished by a predominantly agrarian culture (the Estonians, for example, called themselves *maarahvas*, 'people of the land') and a weak bourgeoisie, they were not in control of the socio-economic processes transforming their world. Folklore scholarship thrived above all in countries whose histories had been characterized by rupture rather than continuity and where a new hegemony was being created. There was a liberating and validating dimension to the discovery of folklore, legitimizing the traditions of a population that had usually been denigrated, giving them the status of culture, and allowing ordinary people to participate in the building of a nation. Folklore archives were ideologically informed, but represented the cultural production of the common people and formed a unique body of documentary evidence, which by their very existence offered an alternative to a view of history and culture as the work of 'great men'.

Let us return to Gellner's explanation of the growth of nation states from the eighteenth century. Developing either from 'pre-existing states and or/high cultures', or rolling their culture 'out of existing folk traditions', the folk tradition of the first kind of nation state had to be destroyed and the second cherished. The resort by middle-class intellectuals to the culture of a subaltern group, folk culture, as the basis for the building of a national culture of necessity involved idealization. Romanticism was the ideological support for the construction of the second kind of state, and it involved the 'ethnicization' of folk culture. For the first, folk culture was of less interest, though it could provide a model of national community in a period of social or political stress (characteristically in the era of industrialization and urbanization). Otherwise in the first kind of state, folklore study was carried out in order to accumulate scientific data, as a scientific (and hence patriotic) endeavour, without an obvious cultural nationalist or regionalist sub-text. It belonged to an Enlightenment tradition. Folk culture was not ethnicized, but was seen as a valuable strand in the national heritage, which had to be documented because of its scientific value. This to a large extent was the context for the interest in Gaelic culture in late eighteenth-century Belfast; the revolutionary United Irish movement, even if many of its members shared this interest, worked with the notion of a non-cultural foundation for Irish nationhood. Being of scientific value (even if scientific endeavour could be seen as something generally patriotic), folk culture was primarily of interest to scholars, but understood as being of essentially national value, its importance could be appreciated by large populations mobilized by a national movement: indeed the collection of folklore itself was an activity that allowed ordinary people to participate in nation-building. A number of countries provided official support for folklore collection projects in the twentieth century. The Irish Folklore Commission was perhaps unique in the democracies of Western Europe, but in Central and Eastern Europe state support for such projects was widespread, for the same reasons.

Mythical Landscapes and Nationalist Heartlands

Hroch has shown how the regions with the best networks of communications, particularly literacy, schooling and market relations were the strongholds of national movements. But these regions were not the regions in which folklorists concentrated their efforts. The latter regions tended to have the lowest levels of literacy, schooling and market relations; they were the least modern, and hence the most different from the dominant culture. There was a salient difference between the physical, as it were, and the spiritual national core. The discovery of spiritual values in the countryside reacted against the modern industrial way of viewing the landscape, as a resource to be utilized. Industrial production, as Orvar Löfgren points out, created a new distance between raw materials and nature on the one hand and finished product and consumer of that product on the other.

> These new ways of using and experiencing nature contain some striking paradoxes. Science and technology clear the landscape of all peasant mystiques and superstitions, but in its place a new mysticism colonizes the landscape. A new division of labour creates two types of landscape, which rarely overlap. The landscape of industrial production is ruled by rationality, calculation, profit, and effectiveness, while another new landscape of recreation, contemplation, and romance emerges – a landscape of consumption.

The Romantics' view of nature and nineteenth-century bourgeois society shared the values of 'the novel ideas about individuality, the nostalgic search for a utopian past and an unspoilt natural state'. Nature came to be opposed to the artificial industrial and materialist world of the city. It represented purity, authenticity, simplicity and lack of affectation.[47] Associated with authentic national values, the countryside took on a deep symbolic importance.

It is possible to identify a number of 'mythical landscapes' in nineteenth- and twentieth-century history, 'mythical' in the sense of foundational, sacred and ideal since these landscapes were not objectively delineated historically, geographically or socially. Indeed like the Romantic notion of the folk, the inhabitants of these territories, mythical landscapes, were experienced more as revelation than as observation, as vision rather than sightseeing. They represented a sort of national *dénouement* to an otherwise incoherent and dispersed narrative. Such landscapes, with a greater or lesser degree of sacralization, included the West of Ireland (especially the Irish-speaking parts), and of the United States (the frontier), the East of Finland (namely Karelia), the land in a more generalized way (compare the ruralist movements of Catalonia or Israel), the mountains (as in Austria, particularly the Tyrol), the plain (the *puszta* of Hungary), and so forth. Those who idealized rural landscapes tended to be members of the urban middle classes. The inhabitants of the countryside, the peasants, conversely saw the landscape in practical rather than aesthetic or 'national' terms.

The following passages will briefly discuss some of the above issues in the context of a few countries (excluding Ireland, which will be discussed in greater detail in Chapters 4 and 5). Not all the information is broadly comparable, for various reasons, including limitations of source material, but it should point out some obvious similarities in the uses of folklore and popular culture.

Estonia

In Estonia, the elite played an insignificant role in providing intellectual leadership for the national movement, though from among them came the pioneering figures who first showed a scholarly interest in Estonian culture. The elite was Baltic German, ruling the three Baltic provinces where the majority was Estonian and Latvian. The fact that the same aristocratic families were split between the Estonian north (the province of Estland), the Latvian south (Courland) and the ethnically mixed Livland, arguably prevented the development of a 'privileged' relationship between the elite and one or other ethnic group. The land and its inhabitants had been owned by the Baltic Germans since the Middle Ages and only after the abolition of serfdom (between 1816 and 1819) and the reforms of 1849 and 1856 could the peasants buy land. The agriculturally rich region of Viljandimaa, which had the highest rate of economic growth and the highest incidence of peasant purchase of farms, was the leading region in the national movement.[48]

From the 1870s, agricultural associations, aiming to encourage rational farm management and new agricultural methods, became an important part of the national movement. Since they had the aim of improving the lot of the peasants in general and since the peasants were ethnic Estonians, these associations had implications for the construction of an Estonian nation.[49] The development of an Estonian civil society and public sphere were of great significance since an Estonian political party could be formed only after the Revolution of 1905. At the beginning of the twentieth century, nevertheless, the economic and political base of the native middle class was so weak that most Social Democrats dismissed an Estonian high culture as the creation of a small elite for its own consumption.[50] The stronger peasants tended to be the strongest supporters of the national ideal, along with the middle class, developing in the towns. There was a significant industrial working class, since the Baltic provinces were the most industrialized part of the empire, while 60 per cent of the rural population was landless at the end of the nineteenth century: indeed in the 1917 elections, the Bolshevik wing of the Social Democrats won 40 per cent of the vote.[51]

In the 1930s Oskar Loorits identified five periods in the development of Estonian folklore research (compare Hroch's three phases in the development of a national movement).[52] First was that of the interest of the German Estophiles. The second was that of 'the great dreamers and idealists of the national awakening who desired to give a history and an epic to the people ...' The third was the 'glory days' of pastors Jakob Hurt (1839–1907) and Mattias Johann Eisen (1857–1934) whose work culminated in the great folklore collection of the 1880s and the 1890s. Appeals for the collection of folklore had been launched through newspapers by Hurt from 1871, and they were continued by Eisen. The appeals were answered by contributions from all levels of society, from country tradesmen, farmers, teachers, factory workers and school children, and amounted to more than 200,000 pages.[53] The fourth of Loorits' periods was the beginning of a scholarly systematization of Estonian folklore, exemplifed by Oskar Kallas (1868–1946), the first Estonian to gain a doctorate in folklore (in Helsinki University in 1901). And lastly the institutionalization of folklore research in the independence period which the existence of an Estonian state (declared in 1918) made possible. A department of folklore was established in Tartu University in 1919 in which Eisen and the noted Baltic German scholar Walter Anderson (1885–1962) worked as professors, and the Eesti Rahvaluule Arhiiv (Estonian Folklore Archive) was founded in 1927.[54] In 1934 a system of awards, to be bestowed by the president of Estonia, was established to recognize the efforts of the best folklore collectors.[55] In 1938/9 the Folklore Archive, collaborating with the Ministry of Education, organized a folklore competition through the schools, which can be compared to the Irish project of the previous year (see Chapter 4). Over 1,000 pupils entered, from 269 schools, and contributed more than 16,000 pages.[56]

Finland

Finland ceased to be a Swedish province when it was conquered by Russia in 1809. In many ways it took on the trappings of an independent state long before independence. It was established as a Grand Duchy in 1809 with considerable autonomy (eventually even having its own currency and army), Russia seeing the building of a Finnish national culture as a means of winning Finnish assent and stymieing any possible Swedish revanchism.

Obvious cultural differences, rooted in part in the divide between Western and Eastern Christianity, and culturally based notions of nationhood spread through the so-called Turku (Åbo) Romantics, strengthening a Finnish sense of distinctiveness. Henrik Gabriel Porthan (1739–1804), professor in Turku University, had already been instrumental in instilling a sense of pride in Finland's past in his students. A man of the Enlightenment, he was aware of the works of Percy, Macpherson and Herder. His *De Poësi Fennica* (1766–78) does not treat of folk poetry alone, but he discusses it in such detail that he has been considered the first Finnish folklorist.

Adolf Ivar Arwidsson (1791–1858) collected folk poetry and called for it to be the foundations of a developed Finnish language and literature. His clarion call, 'We are not Swedes; we can never become Russians; let us therefore be Finns', was answered in various ways. Johan Vilhelm Snellman (1806–1881) has been called the 'father' of Finnish nationalism. He converted much of the elite to the idea of a Finnish-speaking Finland through becoming Finnish-speaking themselves. The ideas of Porthan along with Romanticism informed the 'Fennomans', who came to dominate nineteenth-century intellectual discussion. The wish to reconstruct the original epic, strengthened by the influence of Macpherson's *Ossian*, was manifest in the work of Elias Lönnrot (1802–1884), creator of the national epic, *Kalevala* (1835), from oral epic songs. *Kalevala* was seen as either history or myth and it was greeted with great enthusiasm on its publication: Finland could now say 'I too have a history'.[57] Its importance to Finnish national culture aside, it was also to be of fundamental importance for comparative folklore research since, in the first half of the twentieth century, this was principally carried out according to the Finnish historical-geographic method, developed from research into the oral sources of *Kalevala* (see Chapter 2).

The national movement in its beginnings consisted almost exclusively of members of the Swedish-speaking upper and middle classes. Only from the middle of the nineteenth century did the Finnish-speaking lower classes become involved. The cultural-nationalist Fennoman vision of a rural society excluded both the rural and the urban proletariat.[58] Landless peasants, tenant farmers and urban workers made up 60 per cent of the population at the beginning of the twentieth century, reflected in the overall majority won by the Social Democrats in the parliamentary elections of 1916.[59] Pietism was the point of departure for the economic basis of Finnish nationalism. It 'recruited its followers above all from the richest and most innovative part of the peasantry' and in Ostrobothnia (Pohjanmaa), which was later to be to the fore in the national movement, and the home region of its leading personalities.[60] But the economically marginal region of Karelia was the spiritual core of Finnish nationalism.

'Karelianism' has its origins in the collecting work of Lönnrot, creator of *Kalevala*, the most important part of which was based on epic poetry collected among the inhabitants of Karelia. The region was a medieval borderland between the Catholic West (Sweden) and the Orthodox East (Russia). Its remoteness and the dominant Russian Orthodox faith of its inhabitants allowed it to retain cultural elements such as epic poetry which had more or less long disappeared from Finland (i.e. the formerly Swedish part of the Finnish-speaking language area). After the publication of *Kalevala* in 1835, Karelia came to be seen as a reservoir of ancient Finnish traditions, writers, artists, folklorists and linguists travelling there as pilgrims to a national shrine – Jean Sibelius, the most illustrious of the many artistic visitors, went there on his honeymoon. This movement intensified in the more disturbed political climate of the 1890s, rather as the fall of Parnell encouraged an engagement with cultural questions in contemporary Ireland. Karelia had a profound influence on Finnish national culture and on intellectual life.[61]

Karelia meant different things to different ideological tendencies. It gave living testimony to Finnishness or to Finland's ancient civilization and suggested the future of a greater Finland, uniting the country with its ethnic kin across the Russian border. In the words of K.A. Grönqvist's rhapsodical account from 1884, in Karelia 'anyone can see hundreds of years both forward and back'. The Karelians were understood as the people of *Kalevala*. They were idealized as 'an icon of of Finnishness: as an origin, as an ideal', contends Lotte Tarkka. Karelia 'was archaized, archived and turned into a museum piece: raised from the periphery onto a pedestal'. She points to two intellectual tendencies in fact relating to Karelia: the Romantic and the acculturating. The latter saw Karelia's political significance as well as its economic and social backwardness. The aims of improving the cultural level of the Karelians and strengthening them against russification came together in Lutheran proselytizing efforts.[62]

The collection of folklore in Finland was mostly carried out by academics until about 1870, but after that the general public participated. The level of participation was an index of growing national sentiment.

> The public schools, the folk schools, and the public press all encouraged their patrons to collect the lore of their home regions and to submit it to the Finnish Literature Society. The collecting instructions distributed by the Society made clear that participants would be performing a 'patriotic work' for their country. As a result, men and women from all ranks of society, determined to preserve the spiritual heritage of their forefathers, swelled the archives of the Finnish Literature Society to 43,000 items in 1887 and to over 200,000 by 1900.

The collectors were rewarded with 'a handsome certificate from the Finnish Literature Society thanking them for the work they had performed in preserving for the benefit of posterity the spiritual inheritance of their forefathers'.[63]

In Finland, a democratic republic after 1917, folklore had been an essential part of the building of a national identity, and it was embraced by the irredentism of the Right in the years between the two world wars. The country suffered grievous human and territorial losses to the Soviet invasion in 1939, but in 1941 seized the opportunity to reclaim the annexed territory. The Finnish army had strategic reasons for moving into East Karelia, never part of the Finnish state. But this was a region that had helped to provide the spiritual basis for a Finnish nation, 'where Elias Lönnrot and his disciples had once collected the *Kalevala* poems and where great artists like [Akseli] Gallén-Kallela [the painter] and Sibelius had gained the inspiration for their masterpieces'. Folklore collectors soon followed the soldiers, 'to save the last remnants of the old folk traditions and to stress the cultural and therefore political unity of Finland and Karelia'.[64]

Italy

In pre-unification Italy, folklore was understood as a specifically national inheritance, its interpretation following the Romantic perspective.

> *Il popolo* were more or less defined as people immune to any form of cosmopolitan culture, as speakers of one of the dialects of the peninsular language, and as creators of a communal and traditional culture. In this perception, *il popolo* embodied the essence of what it was to be Italian, the essence of that spirit of nationality that survived and prospered apart from the cultural internationalism of many Italians and in spite of the presence of foreign rulers in the peninsula for so many centuries . . . The nationalist impulse drove them [the folklorists] to the cause of unification, and in the folklore of the peninsula they found one of the important repositories of whatever national sentiment did exist.[65]

As Lombardi Satriani and Meligrana express it, interest in folklore sought 'a cultural matrix capable of sustaining the aesthetic concept of creativity and the political [concept] of the people-nation'.[66]

Folklore interest developed conservative tendencies as the idealization of the people outlived its usefulness in the post-unification period. The Romantic notion of the creativity of the people became problematic in the light of the difficulties that seemed to threaten Italy's unity, especially the Southern question, which attained a central importance. A governing alliance had been formed between northern capitalists and the southern land-owning aristocracy, leading to the political isolation of an impoverished and discontented southern peasantry, their malaise substantiated in rebellion and brigandage (which were tying down over 100,000 regular troops in 1862[67]). Besides the repressive use of the military and police, scientific methods were developed to investigate the problem, and criminal anthropology developed an interest in folklore. The earlier interest in popular poetry began to wane as the contemporary 'people' became an object of dread: 'the "people" is identified with the nascent bourgeoisie and there is a refusal to recognize it in the modern peasants'.[68]

After unification, ethnography grew with the need of the state to know the inhabitants of the new national territories. Between 1870 and 1873, the parliament carried out various enquiries following the precedent of the agrarian enquiry of 1869. De Sanctis, the minister of education, insisted 'on the necessity of overcoming particularisms in order to establish the national idea and to forestall the dangers of anarchy'. The problem was to channel the centrifugal tensions of the masses into the life of the state. D'Azeglio's famous statement of 1867, 's'è fatta l'Italia, ma non si fanno gli Italiani' (Italy is made but the Italians are not being made), memorably presented the problem.

The contradictions between the new state legal system based on the Napoleonic code and customary notions of right and wrong were the reason why an interest in 'juridical folklore' became a notable tendency in folklore research in the South, and why a link between popular culture and delinquency came to be implied. The aim was to understand the 'anomalous' nature of southern society, but also to eventually harmonize custom and current legislation. The contemporary conception of 'survival', derived from Tylor, helped to make sense of southern folklore and explained the South's backwardness while at the same time isolating folklore as something specifically southern. There was a 'folklorization' of the South, as Lombardi Satriani and Meligrana term it, and it became one of the privileged fields for folklorists after unification, as for journalists, dialectologists, criminal anthropologists, psychiatrists, political theorists and travel writers.[69] With Italian colonial expansion, a link was established between colonial ethnography and folklore research, both providing information of administrative use. This was pointed out by Lamberto Loria, editor of the folklore journal Lares, in 1912 in an article entitled 'L'etnografia strumento di politica interna e coloniale' (ethnography as an instrument of internal and colonial politics).[70]

The paradox of Italian folklore was that it supposedly reflected the spiritual unity of Italy – the Romantic and Risorgimento perspective – while at the same time in its obviously local and regional character it reflected the historical disunity of Italy – the post-unification concern. The state, of course, was interested only in the former and its efforts inspired Mussolini to claim that d'Azeglio's project of 'making Italians' had been finally accomplished under his regime. The fascist regime actively supported folklore, but this interest was informed by the concern that it should help to consolidate national unity. A national congress held in Florence in 1929 was attended by King Victor Emmanuel III and led in the following year to the re-establishment of the folklore journal, Lares, originally published from 1912 to 1915. Il Folklore Italiano had been already founded in 1925 by Raffaele Corso, an enthusiastic supporter of the regime. Both journals became openly propagandistic during the war years. Corso had, after some consideration, opted for 'folklore' in the title of his journal, but with *tradizioni popolari* as the subtitle. The word *'folklore'* itself, well established in Italian, was banned in 1933 as a foreign word and the word *popolaresca* ordered in its place.

The Comitato Nazionale Italiano per le Tradizioni Popolari sought, in the words of its chairman, 'to frame the traditional arts and folklore of the various provinces of Italy into a unified vision'. He added that the regime wished 'to cancel all forms and all vestiges of the ancient regional divisions from the context of national life'.[71] Mussolini himself inaugurated provincial exhibits of traditional arts. The Comitato Nazionale was instructed to establish provincial committees and to provide them with whatever assistance they required, but any publications by them had to be authorized by its chairman. The Museo Nazionale delle Arti e Tradizioni Popolari was established by the regime in Rome in 1941. An official interest in 'juridical folklore' – long established in the South – was in part a reflection of the concern of the Minister of Justice that customary law was often stronger than that of the state. In 1930, a royal commission was established under the ministry to collect juridical customs and uses. At its inauguration the minister made clear that this was not meant to call the state legal system into question. An initial project to collect legal customs from Tuscan farmers was begun.[72] Reminiscent of officially sponsored Greek folklore research, the Italian folklorists also sought to prove continuity with the admired culture of the past. 'Rome', according to Corso, 'which took its power and civilization to so many countries, imposes on our folklorists the noblest duty to trace the vestiges of the great mother . . .' It was not only at home that such evidence was sought. Folklorists too supported the Italian claims to Corsica, Malta and Dalamatia (with its Italian minority) on cultural grounds.[73]

Spain

In the Spanish state, as in the contemporary United Kingdom, ethnographic research in the closing decades of the nineteenth century could be divided into two main orientations.[74] One can be explained respectively in terms of the Enlightenment, positivism and evolutionism, leading to an anthropological discourse, and the other in terms of Romanticism and regionalist and nationalist movements, leading to a folkloric discourse. Physical anthropologists and naturalists – 'naturalist anthropologists' – were mostly scholars influenced by the Institución Libre de Enseñanza (Free Institution of Education) or doctors educated in France and under the influence of evolutionism. They were centred in Seville above all, their influence radiating outwards to Madrid, the Canary Islands and beyond. Politically, this line of thinking was particularly associated with liberalism, and had an anti-clerical and agnostic tint, leading to conflict with the church. In the North and the East, particularly Galicia, the Basque Country, Catalonia and Valencia, where a distinct language and history were the focus of cultural identity, writers were the ethnographic pioneers. There it was an interest motivated by nationalism, emphasizing the national specificity of landscape and, in Galicia and the Basque Country, of ethnicity as well. In the Basque Country, the idea that the authentically Basque was no longer found in the regions influenced by industrialization and urbanization was shared by political nationalists and folklorists.

Antonio Machado y Álvarez was the pioneer of scientific folklore research in the peninsula, founding the society of El Folk-Lore Español in 1881, modelled on the London society. The aims of the society included the collecting, copying and publication of scientific information as 'materials indispensable for the knowledge and the scientific reconstruction of Spanish history and culture'. Among the different branches of science specified in the constitution of the society were medicine, hygiene, botany, politics, morals and agriculture. Machado y Álvarez considered folklore to be a scientific discipline, 'a powerful auxiliary to anthropology', rigorous in its use of empirical and positivistic methods, and he hoped to see folklore societies covering the length and breadth of the Spanish state. He saw the society as being of national interest, and hence 'should be favoured and supported by all good Spaniards, without distinction of sex, class or opinions'. Other 'naturalist' societies had a similar approach, that of Castille circulating in 1883 a *Cuestionario para Sacerdotes, Maestros y Médicos* (for priests, schoolmasters and doctors) on popular culture. From 1880, the Institución Libre de Enseñanza and later the Ateneo of Madrid promoted questionnaires on popular custom. In 1901, the Ateneo circulated a questionnaire on rites of passage to schoolmasters, priests, doctors, lawyers and other professionals throughout Spain and received in reply tens of thousands of items of information on birth, marriage and death customs, more than half of which disappeared under suspicious circumstances during the Civil War.

The nineteenth-century Catalan cultural movement, the *Renaixença*, brought folklorists together with writers and jurists. Together they fashioned one of the central symbols of the movement, 'ancestral ruralism'. The symbolic representation of the rural world involved 'a mythical description' of the countryside and of traditional culture and a normative codification of the values pertaining to it, argues Llorenç Prats. Thus the rural world was opposed to the urban world and traditional culture to that of foreign derivation. The intellectuals of the *Renaixença* wrote for a predominantly urban audience who, separated from everyday rural life, but themselves of recent rural origin, were open to a sacralized representation of the countryside and to rural values. They thus could see the vices of the city as deviations from an original essence.[75] A central part of this cultural renaissance was *excursionisme*. It was not just organized tourism, as Robert Hughes explains, which did not exist in Spain at the time.

> Rather, excursionism meant purposeful, educated travel with the aim of discovering one's own country and learning to value it. It brought poets together with intellectuals, botanists with architects, antiquarians with geologists. It was Ruskinian adventure – active, inquisitive, melding scientific curiosity about plants with aesthetic appreciation of old buildings, folk art, frescoes, and crafts. One did not set out to reach a few climactic sights. One noted everything along the way, and the reward for one's efforts was not only knowledge but a kind of historicist rapture, an ecstatic dreaming about the lost cultural past.[76]

The first excursionist societies were founded in 1876 and 1878, with the aim of physical recreation allied to 'a declared scientific and Catalanist vocation', and the intention of gaining a thorough knowledge of the Catalan countryside. The first society, the Associació Catalana d'Excursions Científiques, while emphasizing its scientific, literary and artistic interests, took little interest in popular culture. The Associació d'Excursions Catalana, founded two years later, explicitly mentioned the study of traditional culture among its objectives and was a pioneer in the field, creating the first group, Folklore Català, and the first series of books specifically dedicated to the theme. Francesc de S. Maspons i Labrós, president from 1883 until its dissolution, emphasized the patriotic aspect of its mission which was 'to tear from the bowels of the earth that native spirit, that nature characteristic of it, in which to establish, uniting it with the advances of the century, the beautiful future of splendour and glory which it merits'. The two societies united in 1891 and in the first issue of the new Centre Excursionista de Catalunya's bulletin reiterated their aims.

> We come to take part in the present Catalan crusade on the peaceful terrain of folklore and of the natural, historical and geographical sciences, removed from the field of the outstanding political questions but not thus indifferent insofar as referring to the betterment in all senses and conditions of this country which we esteem so much.[77]

The reference to the apolitical nature of folklore is reminiscent of the contemporary interest in Irish culture in Ireland, where nationalist and unionist could meet.

The principality of Catalonia was an economically advanced region with its traditional elite in place, though incorporated into an economically backward state. In that sense its situation was different to that of Ireland or the small nations of Central and Eastern Europe. Nineteenth-century Catalan folklorists ostensibly were trying to renew those forms of life that were declining as a result of modernization, according to Prats' analysis. In reality, as peasants left the land and the traditional social order and moved *en masse* to the industrial cities, the folklorists sought folklore elements to express conservative cultural values and on which to base a Catalan identity, emphasizing traditional values of work, private property and patriarchal authority. The hegemony of the traditionally dominant sectors of Catalan society was undermined by modernization. These sectors needed to establish a new hegemony, through the creation of a modern Catalan national identity different both from the subaltern identity developing among migrants to the industrial city through radical politics, and from a Spanish national identity being promulgated by the state.[78]

Catalan *'Noucentisme'* ('Nineteen-hundredism') was modernist and nationalist, going beyond the *Renaixença*. Folklore research in this period became professionalized, not just carried on by writers and philosophers any more, but by jurists interested in the system of inheritance, by architects interested in popular architecture, and by others. From 1915, the Arxiu d'Etnografia i Folklore de Catalunya (Catalan Archive of Ethnography and Folklore), closely associated with the University of Barcelona, had the aims of creating a data base of Catalan folklore and traditional culture, a bibliography on the subject and a specialized library. It used questionnaires, publishing a guide for collectors in 1922 (*Manual per a recerques d'Etnografia de Catalunya*, with twenty-two sections, from worldview to economic techniques). It also collaborated with the linguistic atlas of Catalonia. Much data was accumulated (and disappeared almost completely during, or immediately after, the Civil War).[79] Josep M. Batista i Roca, ideologue and co-founder of the Arxiu d'Etnografia i Folklore, shared the interest of many Catalan intellectuals in Ireland. He visited Ireland between 1919 and 1922 and made contacts with Irish intellectuals.[80]

The Basque and Galician folklorists sought to recover the original ethnic culture through archaeology, pre-history and rural traditional culture. From early in the twentieth century, these efforts were intensified in order to record traditional culture as industrialization proceeded apace. In the Basque Country, the Sociedad de Estudios Vascos (Eusko-Ikaskuntza), founded in 1918, and in Galicia, the Seminario de Estudos Galegos (1923) were as rigorous as the Arxiu in observation and accumulation of data, which was the proclaimed positivistic objective, in the absence of any avowed theoretical speculation. Joan Prat contends that the unstated theoretical premises were really political: the project of the folklorists was to scientifically endorse nationalist theory. Hence the Arxiu validated the theory articulated by the most important Catalanist party, the Lliga Regionalista; the leading Basque folklorist, Fr J. M. de Barandiarán, that of the Partido Nacionalista Vasco; Vicente Risco, the pre-eminent Galician folklorist was also the inspiration behind the nationalist ideology of *galleguismo* ('Galicianism').

The folklorists rejected 'paradigmatic concepts such as evolution and progress, which . . . constituted the theoretical axes of the anthropological and general discourse on man'. Instead, they wished 'to discover and recuperate the "essences" of very particularized human groups', and, as part of the *Volksgeist*, these were, 'by definition, eternal and immutable and do not change with the passing of time'. But the 'supposed immutability and permanence of societies guaranteed by tradition' can be threatened by social change and progress. Hence the 'phobia', as Prat calls it, of Catalan, Basque and Galician folklorists towards industrialization. The anthropological discourse saw survivals as means to reconstruct the process of evolution and the progress of human groups, but the folkloric discourse saw them as ends in themselves, storing the treasures of the past: a prehistoric past in the Basque Country, an idealized Celtic and medieval past in Galicia, a medieval past in Catalonia. The leading folklorists in Catalonia, the Basque Country and Galicia were politically conservative, close to Catholic social and political thought. These Northern and Eastern regions opposed themselves to Castile and to Andalucia, military invasion coming from the former as a later invasion of migrants would come from the latter, as Aguirre Baztán puts it. Franco's triumph in the Civil War led to the repression of many of the Basque, Galician and Catalan institutions, and the exile of many of the key personnel.[81]

Sweden

In Sweden, a long-consolidated nation state, the role of folklore was less central than in countries such as Finland or Estonia. For a start, the notion of *folkliv* (folklife) was long established and was to take a more holistic view of folk culture than the folklore orientations in many other countries – Sigurd Erixon (see Chapter 2) was to insist in the early 1950s that folk culture was not to be opposed to urban culture (disagreeing in person with Robert Redfield in this) or to be associated with 'a particular socio-psychological category' of the countryside.[82] A once great power, Sweden nevertheless had no colonies in the modern period to which to direct the anthropological gaze. An anthropological gaze directed inwards – but without the overwhelming neuroses of national identity felt by culturally alienated intelligentsias of peripheral countries – characterized Swedish interest in folk culture.

At the same time there was an especial folkloric interest in the province, and local museums were established from the middle of the nineteenth century. Since the universities were organized around provincially recruited student 'nations', much information on regional culture was accumulated through the efforts of their members: for example, the largest nineteenth-century collections of folk music. Folklore played an important role in the nineteenth century as an assertion of national identity at a time when Finland had been lost to the Russians (in 1809) and a French king had been forced onto the Swedish throne. Folklore for some also represented a retreat from a despised urban industrial world.

Jakob Fredrik Neikter, the pioneering figure to whom we have already referred, was the teacher of Erik Gustaf Geijer (1783–1847), co-editor, along with Arvid August Afzelius (1785–1871), of the classic collection of Swedish folk songs, *Svenska Folk-Wisor*, published between 1814 and 1816. Geijer was a historian and a philosopher and had been familiarized with Herder's ideas through Neikter. He showed a perceptive recognition of different attitudes to folklore in different countries: 'those among Europe's nations who speak subjugated languages or are ruled by a nationality who are of a different language to them generally compose and possess more folk poetry'. The Geijer-Afzelius collection was published in association with the Götiska förbundet (Gothic Association), a patriotic grouping of young academics and officials keen to investigate Sweden's great past as an inspiration for the present at a time of national humiliation. This was a time of intense interest in the Nordic past. Geijer was among the first historians to place the people in the title of the history of his country (*Svenska Folkets Historie* [1832]).[83]

Another figure of importance was Richard Dybecks (1811–1877), a lawyer whose ill-health caused him to devote himself to recording folklore and folksong throughout Sweden. He was a propagandist for folk music, an inveterate opponent of the 'repulsive spirit of the times' who despised the contemporary high and popular music that spread from the cities. Like Afzelius, he wrote songs to folk tunes, and he was the author of the Swedish national anthem.[84] The later idealization of the countryside and of a harmonious peasant life was, as in many other countries, an attempt to project a national ideal that would transcend the heightened class conflict of an industrial society which was destroying the peasant way of life. Both liberals and socialists used the same ideal of an egalitarian peasant society as a model for the future.[85]

The industrialization of society meant that folklore collectors, in Löfgren's words, 'saw themselves as a rescue team picking their way through a landscape of cultural ruins, where scraps and survivals of traditional life-styles could still be found'. The province of Dalecarlia (Dalarna), somewhat like Karelia or the Irish Gaeltacht, came to represent the quintessential national traditional culture for two reasons that made it atypical, as Löfgren outlines. Firstly, a picturesque peasant life was still observable there in the early twentieth century and, secondly, the social differences were smaller there than elsewhere, with 'no large rural proletariat to disturb the image of a happy village *Gemeinschaft*'. The Dalecarlians were understood as a virtuous peasantry, 'freedom-loving, individualistic, and principled', and attached to national traditions: 'the kind of ancestors the middle class wanted to have in their cultural charter'. The discipline of ethnology, fashionable in the 1890s, was based on this 'cult of nature and the peasant heritage'. The first generation of scholars concentrated on Dalecarlia, 'thus helping to give this idiosyncratic region a central position in the construction of "traditional peasant life"'.[86]

Brazil

Interest in folklore and popular culture in Brazil was concerned with establishing the essential qualities of identity in a country whose colonial history and peripheral situation had made the European metropolis a constant and overbearing reference for intellectual and cultural life. The North East in the works of the pioneering folklorist Sílvio Romero (1851–1914) and of the noted sociologist Gilberto Freyre (1900–1987) was the essential Brazil. It was contrasted in the former's collection of traditional songs, *Cantos populares do Brasil* (1883), with the culture of the imperial court in Rio de Janeiro (Brazil only became a republic in 1889), and with the industrializing South – particularly São Paulo – in the latter's sociological work.[87]

In the period between 1947 and 1964 folklore studies reached their apogee. Luís Rodolfo Vilhena refers to a 'folklore movement' in this period, whose object, he argues, was to bring intellectuals together from all the regions of the country in order to define the national identity. The creation of the Comissão Nacional de Folclore (National Folklore Commission) affiliated to UNESCO, mobilized most intellectuals interested in folklore. It galvanized interest in the various Brazilian states through a series of conferences that appealed for state support to protect and research Brazilian folklore and to establish a co-ordinating agency. Previous to this – since the 1930s – popular music had been the dominant interest of Brazilian folklorists, owing much to the prestige of Mário de Andrade (1893–1945), and to the fact, as Vilhena points out, that music rather than oral literature in Portuguese, the language of the colonizer, could be posited as quintessentially Brazilian. The Comissão was the first initiative that united all those interested in folklore throughout the country. It established a number of constituent commissions on state level, usually around a prominent local intellectual. The commission's two periodicals, circulated to folklorists, libraries and other appropriate institutions, circulated articles and bibliographical information widely. The first Brazilian Folklore Congress in 1951 approved the Brazilian Folklore Charter (*Carta do Folclore Brasileiro*). This document defined the 'folkloric fact' by its collective nature, its anonymity and its popular, though – significantly – not necessarily traditional, quality. It called for the study of folklore to be included among 'the anthropological and cultural sciences'. The populist president of Brazil, Getúlio Vargas, was guest of honour at the congress, and an appeal was made for his support to defend the 'folkloric heritage' and protect 'the popular arts'.

The setting-up of the Campanha de Defesa do Folclore Brasileiro (Campaign for the Defence of Brazilian Folklore) in 1958 was a response to the appeals of folklorists for more focused state support. It established a specialist library, the Biblioteca Amadeu Amaral, made agreements with the universities of Ceará and Bahia in the North East to carry out folklore surveys in their respective states and founded the *Revista Brasileira de Folclore*. Nevertheless, the folklorists' long-term aims to have their discipline recognized in the universities were unsuccessful. The coup d'état of 1964 that overthrew João Goulart's government did not end the Campanha's activities, but greatly reduced them and eventually led to the virtual eclipse of folklore studies as an important part of intellectual discourse. The military were particularly hard on the Left and on nationalists: the director of the Campanha, Édison Carneiro, of known Marxist views, was dismissed.[88] An earlier Sociedade Brasileira de Folclore had been founded in 1941 in the North-Eastern state of Rio Grande do Norte by Luís da Câmara Cascudo (1898–1986), the folklorist who was best known both at home and abroad, but a fully harmonious working relationship was never established between this and the initiatives in the South, based in the capital, Rio de Janeiro. Câmara Cascudo's 'limbo', as a recent article calls it, was due to three factors: he spent his life in a poor state, distant from the power centres of the South, Marxism was not a point of scholarly reference for him, and indeed he was a fervent Catholic all his life with conservative political views.[89]

The Instituto Superior de Estudos Brasileiros, created by the Ministry of Education in 1955, was the focus of what E. Bradford Burns calls the developmental nationalist movement.[90] According to Renato Ortiz, the ISEB was the matrix for an intellectual approach which set the agenda for the debate on culture in Brazil since then, influencing the Left as well as Catholic social thought in addition to the arts: for example the theatre of Augusto Boal and *Cinema Nova*.[91] It was preoccupied with the question of overcoming Brazil's status as a periphery of the metropolitan developed world through industrial development and national integration. According to Roland Corbisier, one of the key figures of the ISEB,

> [i]f an authentic culture is that which is elaborated from and as a result of the country's own reality, of its being, the colony cannot produce an authentic culture by itself . . . Its culture can only be a reflex, a by-product of the metropolitan culture, and the inauthenticity that characterizes it is an inevitable consequence of its alienation.[92]

One result, reflected in the other cultural nationalist currents, including folklore studies, was an engagement with the 'reality' of Brazil, an interest in the people and popular culture, a concern with cultural alienation and a wish to overcome underdevelopment through creating a new consciousness among the people.

This led to various populist initiatives, such as the Centros de Cultura Popular in Rio de Janeiro which tried to bring a politically activist theatre to the streets, the Movimento de Educação de Base, organized by the Catholic Church, and Paulo Freire's method of teaching literacy.[93] The first of these movements was the Movimento Cultura Popular de Recife set up in 1959 or 1960 by Miguel Arraes, who was running for governor of the poverty-stricken state of Pernambuco, of which Recife was capital. The immediate aim, according to Roberto Schwarz, was electoral, 'to educate the masses who would surely vote for him if they could . . .' (since illiterates had no right to vote).

> He also tried to encourage the setting up of all kinds of community groups for people to take an interest in real matters such as their city, district and even their local folklore, which would compensate for the misery and marginality of the masses . . . Inspired by the tenets of Christianity and reformism, the central idea behind the programme was 'the improvement of mankind'.[94]

Paulo Freire argued that a dependent society is 'by definition a silent society' since its voice 'is not an authentic voice, but merely an echo of the voice of the metropolis . . .' Hence, within the dependent society, the elites, 'silent in the face of the metropolis, silence their own people in turn'. It is only when the people 'break out of the culture of silence and win their right to speak', as a result of the structural transformation of society, that the relationship of dependency can be broken.[95]

These initiatives came to an end with the military coup of 1964. The Movimento Cultura Popular de Recife was abolished and replaced by a social security office,[96] while Freire was arrested and went into exile.

The reasons for an interest in folklore varied substantially from country to country. Scientific enquiry; self-affirmation within a movement for national liberation; the assertion of regional identity within the nation; nostalgia for a harmonious rural society at a time of urban proletarian radicalism and, as was more common, some combination of various of these. The countries we have chosen to discuss in brief do give characteristic instances of the uses of folklore and popular culture, though the experiences of no two countries were alike. The well-known case of Germany, to an extent, is paradigmatic insofar as the linkage of folklore and nationalism is concerned, though in many ways it is similar to Italy, with folklore interpreted as evidence for national unity before this was politically achieved, and associated with reactionary politics under fascism to the extent that there were calls for the abolition of *Volkskunde* after the Second World War.[97] This chapter has focused on the use of folklore as part of a nationalist discourse rather than on discussing the question of political discourses within folklore and popular culture, within a subaltern public sphere. Nevertheless, in order to emphasize the fact that the latter may be amenable to the former, a few pointers will be made in the lines that follow.

The public sphere is defined by Habermas as 'a domain of our public life in which such a thing as public opinion can be formed'. Both terms, the public sphere and public opinion, were formed in the eighteenth century. They derived from a distinction made between opinions, defined as 'things taken for granted as part of a culture, normative convictions, collective prejudices and judgments', and public opinion, which 'can be formed only if a public that engages in rational discussion exists'.[98] In this sense opinions belonged to folklore, but one could also speak of a popular, a subaltern, public sphere, separate from the bourgeois public sphere originally formed by the print media. In other words, oral tradition and popular literature could also spread information, inform opinion, motivate action and disseminate interpretations of events, relating them to earlier precedents and helping to create feelings of wider solidarity.[99] In Ireland, political songs formed an important part of a subaltern public sphere, from the Jacobite *aisling*, which circulated orally and in manuscript, to the United Irishmen's and Young Irelanders' use of ballads, which depended on print, and were circulated by pedlars and ballad singers at fairs.[100] The seditious nature of much popular literature was noted in the 1820s by Crofton Croker, who was very concerned by the popular songs in circulation. The point that can be made about these songs is that in their origin they were not popular songs. But they became popular, and in a society where literacy and illiteracy coexisted, they circulated both through writing and through oral transmission. How did they become popular? Serge Ouaknine makes a perceptive observation:

> folklores are not the production of peoples but of individuals, artefacts or legends afterwards assimilated and recuperated by the collective. Great songs are first of all emotional extensions of poets and it is when the intimate model has succeeded that it can give elements of identification to a community.[101]

With these observations on folklore and popular culture as part of a public sphere, we have touched briefly on a matter which is properly the subject of another book. But we have also glanced in brief at the complex question of orality and literacy, and of the transition from an agrarian to an industrial popular culture which will be discussed in greater detail in the final chapter. We have also brought the discussion to Ireland, which is the exclusive subject of the next two chapters. In them we will plot the development of the interest in Irish folklore from its beginnings in the late eighteenth century to its blossoming in the institutionalization of folklore studies in the first half of the twentieth century.

- folk song
- Gaelic poetry

4. Irish Pioneers

A historical overview of Irish folklore must take cognisance of the varied understandings of what folklore is. Understood as purely oral, traditional and rural, folklore was easily isolated from modern social processes. To consider it ancient made it a historical source, of scholarly interest in the same way that historical documents or archaeological artefacts were, all unified in the notion of antiquities. With emphasis on the native Irish aspect of folklore, it shared a common subaltern status with the language, so that folk song and eighteenth- and nineteenth-century poetry composed within the Gaelic literary tradition could be combined in the same category. The pioneers of the interest in Irish folklore (in the various senses outlined above) include General Charles Vallancey (1721–1812), 'the first practitioner of ethnology in Ireland';[1] Charlotte Brooke (1740?–1793), 'the first mediator of importance between the Irish-Gaelic and the Anglo-Irish literary traditions',[2] who published Irish texts and translations from oral and literary traditions; Edward Bunting (1773–1843), the first collector of Irish music, from both the popular and the learned traditions; Thomas Crofton Croker (1798–1854), correspondent of the Grimm brothers and Sir Walter Scott and author of the first collection of oral tales published in Ireland or Britain; and Robert Mac Adam (1808–1895) who made the first collection of Gaeltacht folklore.[3]

The nineteenth-century antiquaries brought the history and culture of Gaelic Ireland to the attention of the Anglo-Irish Protestant elite and indirectly prepared the symbols that cultural nationalists could later draw on. Unlike eighteenth-century Patriotism, nineteenth-century nationalism rested on the knowledge of Ireland's cultural distinctiveness, and increasingly on its Gaelic inheritance, which the colonial elite gradually identified with. From the Act of Union (1800), historical awareness became intrinsic to political thought. Leerssen points out that the prerequisite for that, the collection, systematization and dissemination of the remaining evidence of Gaelic history, had been accomplished roughly between 1620 and 1770, and 'as relations worsened between the Anglo-Irish elite and the British government, this Gaelic history was slowly absorbed into the national narrative'. In the second half of the eighteenth century, enlightened Anglo-Irish scholarly societies were able to devote themselves to the study of Irish antiquity and came to rely on the assistance of native Gaelic scholars. Thus Vallancey benefited from the assistance of Charles O'Conor of Belanagar as Joseph Cooper Walker and Charlotte Brooke did from that of Theophilus O'Flanagan.[4] After the rising of 1798 and the Act of Union, the Anglo-Irish elite distanced themselves from this field of interest.

Vallancey was considered the leading antiquary of his time, was behind many scholarly initiatives, and was a founder member of the Royal Irish Academy. Born in England in 1721 to a Huguenot family, he came to Ireland as a military engineer in 1762. The fancifulness of his ideas today has to be understood in the context of the contemporary scholarly world, whose conceptual framework was based to a large extent on the authority of the Old Testament.[5] He was the first 'to turn an attentive eye and ear to the doings and sayings of the common people', devoting part of volume 12 (1783) of his great work on Irish culture, *Collectanea de rebus Hibernicis* (1770–1804), to the festivals of Lúnasa and Samhain (respectively the harvest festival and Hallowe'en).[6]

Northern Pioneers

Charlotte Brooke played an important role in bringing the Gaelic tradition to her own Anglo-Irish Ascendency class. She recorded poetry from local Irish speakers. Her inspiration was hearing a labourer on the family estate reading heroic poems of the Fianna aloud from a Gaelic manuscript, reminding her of Macpherson's *Ossian*. She was encouraged by her father to study Irish antiquities. The poet and scribe Muiris Ó Gormáin, who had taught Irish to Vallancey and also collaborated with Charles O'Conor, helped her in her work of compiling and translating. It took some encouragement, notably by Bishop Percy, who was a friend and mentor to her, to persuade her to publish her efforts. The title of her book, *Reliques of Irish Poetry* (1789), reflected the influence of Percy. It included heroic lays of the Fianna as well as folk songs, translated into an ornate English style, with introductory comments and notes on each section, an introduction in which she asserts the greater antiquity of Irish literature over the English, as well as the original texts at the end (mindful as she was of the Macpherson controversy). The book too seems to be a subtle assertion of the Irishness of the material that Macpherson used. *Reliques* won immediate popularity, and in it Brooke expressed the hope that her work would further cordial relations between the two islands.[7] *Reliques* intended to present Gaelic literature to an Irish audience unacquainted with it and was not primarily intended for a British audience: the

discourse was 'primarily intra-Irish' as Leerssen puts it, unlike the early nineteenth century Anglo-Irish writers, who wished to explain Ireland to the
English, and whose perspective was from outside.[8]

In 1795, a magazine appeared in Belfast, published from the offices of the
Northern Star, the newspaper of the political society, the United Irishmen.
The advance publicity had described it as follows:

> ...the first edition of Bolg an Tsolair* or the Gaelic Magazine containing
> Laoi na Sealga or the Famous Fenian Poem called The Chase With a collec-
> tion of choice Irish Songs Translated by Miss Brooke To which is prefixed
> an abridgement of Irish Grammar A vocabulary, and Familiar Dialogues ...

The magazine offered itself to the public 'with a view to prevent in some
measure the total neglect, and to diffuse the beauties of this ancient and
once admired language ...; hoping to afford a pleasing retrospect to every
Irishman, who respects the traditions, or considers the language and composition of our early ancestors, as a matter of curiosity or importance'. It was to
be the first and only issue. The printing presses of the *Northern Star* were
destroyed in a raid by the Monaghan Militia in 1797, part of General Lake's
repressive measures against the United Irishmen.[9]

The magazine was evidence of the thriving interest in Irish culture in
Belfast at the time, largely among the mostly Presbyterian middle class, the
main local support for the United Irishmen. Belfast then was a small town,
only beginning to be seen as the regional focus of North East Ulster.
Neither an administrative nor a legal centre and supporting no cathedral, it
offered no attractions to the aristocracy, leaving the middle class to run it.[10]
Unlike the Romantic urban intellectuals of the Gaelic revival of a hundred
years later, who valued popular agrarian culture as a spiritual alternative to
industrial modernity, these individuals were part of the enlightened bourgeoisie of a rapidly industrializing town. For them the investigation of
native culture was an undertaking of rational enquiry and an endeavour
which could interest all those who took the interests of their country to
heart. Mostly bourgeois Dissenters in a society ruled by aristocratic Angli-
cans whose minority church was the official state church, they were
enthused by the American and French revolutions, familiar with Enlightenment thought through the Scottish universities in which they were
educated, and avid readers of Locke, Rousseau and Tom Paine. They
sympathized with the oppressed native Catholic majority – a small minority
in Belfast at the time.

Breandán Ó Buachalla gives a compelling account of this rich intellectual
milieu. The house of Mary Ann McCracken was the centre of this activity
(and outside it her brother Henry, the United Irish leader, was to be hanged

---

* Usually written *bolg an tsoláthair* today, this is the name for the Irish equivalent of the
horn of plenty.

in 1798). It was there that the pioneering student of native Irish music Edward Bunting lived and where Wolfe Tone (1763–1798), Thomas Russell, Samuel Neilson (editor of the *Northern Star*) and other United Irish figures met. Bunting was born in Armagh, the son of an English colliery engineer and an Irish mother. Staying with the McCrackens he claimed to have first discovered 'the structure of Irish Music', and it was through another McCracken connection that he set about the pioneering work on which his fame rests.

Henry Joy, a leading Belfast businessman and relative of the McCrackens, circulated a notice in 1791.

> Some inhabitants of Belfast, feeling themselves interested in everything which relates to the Honor, as well as the Prosperity of their country, propose to open a subscription which they intend to apply in attempting to revive and perpetuate THE ANCIENT MUSIC AND POETRY OF IRELAND. They are solicitous to preserve from oblivion the few fragments, which have been *permitted* to remain as Monuments of the refined Taste and Genius of their Ancestors.
>
> In order to carry this project into execution, it must appear obvious to those acquainted with the situation of this country, that it will be necessary to assemble the Harpers, almost exclusively possessed of all the remains of the MUSIC, POETRY and ORAL TRADITIONS of Ireland.

The appeal resulted in the Belfast Harpers' festival, held in July 1792 in the Assembly Rooms. It brought together ten harpers, six of them blind, mostly from Ulster and mostly middle-aged or elderly.[11]

The harp itself – chosen as the symbol of the United Irishmen – formerly held an esteemed place in Gaelic elite culture. But it had long been in decline. By the time the festival had been held, its dwindling number of practitioners were wandering musicians playing a repertoire mostly composed of folk music, along with some of the compositions of the famous Carolan (Toirdhealbhach Ó Cearbhalláin 1670–1738), who had benefited from Anglo-Irish patrons and was often regarded as the last representative of an ancient tradition. In 1808, the Irish Harp Society was founded in order to promote the harp. The founders were Bunting and Dr James McDonnell, a Protestant doctor from an old Gaelic family and a leading patron of Gaelic culture, of science and of medicine. Their intention was both to teach the harp to blind boys and girls so that they could make a living and 'to promote the study of the Irish language, history and antiquities'. Nevertheless, the old harp tradition died out within a few years. In 1819 the only surviving harpers were those who had been trained by the Harp Society.[12]

The festival was a remarkable affair, 'the last of the Irish harpers gathered in Belfast, the most recent town founded in Ireland', the nineteen-year old Bunting transcribing the tunes and 'the ladies and gentlemen of the first fashion in Belfast and its vicinity looking on and listening attentively'.[13]

Among those who went to hear the harpers was Tone, though his diary entry on the thirteenth showed his opinion: 'The harpers again. Strum. Strum and be hanged . . .'. The last day of the festival was on the fourteenth of July, and was begun after the march of the Volunteers through the streets of the town, commemorating the fall of the Bastille. Bunting had been asked by Dr McDonnell to transcribe the music and immediately after the festival he set off, enthusiastically, collecting music in Derry, Tyrone and Connacht. He published a first collection in 1796, *A General Collection of the Ancient Music of Ireland*, in which were sixty-three tunes. Bunting continued his collection after the publication of his book, going as far afield as Tipperary.

The words of the songs had not been transcribed at the harpers' festival, and neither did they appear in Bunting's volume. Hence it was decided, at the McCrackens' expense, to send Patrick Lynch (Pádruic Ó Luingsigh) to collect the words of the songs. Lynch was well qualified for the task. He was a member of a Co. Down family versed in Gaelic learning which had run a school in Loughinisland and it was he who had published *Bolg an Tsolair*. The collecting work was co-ordinated from the McCrackens' house, and Lynch's letters to Mary Ann give a vivid account of the fieldwork. The following is from 29 May 1800:

> I made good progress in Castlebar. I got forty seven songs in it, having stayed ten days, it cost me just two guineas . . . I walked about the town not knowing whom to apply to and passing by a brogue-maker's shop, I heard him singing a good Irish song. I stepped in and asked him if he would take a pot of beer. He came with me to the house of John McAvilly, a jolly publican, who sang well, and was acquainted with all good singers in town. Under Tuesday I found out a hairdresser, a shoemaker, a mason and a fiddler – all good singers . . . I send you here a list of 150 songs with the names of the persons and places where I got them for Mr Bunting's use . . . I heard of a blind piper, a Billy O'Maily, who had the greatest variety of Irish songs . . . Paid my bill 2s. 2d., and went to the house where I had seen Blind Billy yesterday, sent for him, gave him a shilling and grog, took down six good songs, cost me 2s. 8½d.

Lynch had stayed with McDonnell and had taught Irish to Thomas Russell, librarian of the Linen Hall Library in Belfast (on McDonnell's recommendation). Russell went on the run after his part in Robert Emmett's unsuccessful rising in 1803. McDonnell, to his later regret (being ostracized by Mary Ann McCracken and other friends), contributed to the reward for information leading to Russell's apprehension while Lynch, apparently under the pressure of a charge of high treason, identified Russell, who was hanged on a similar charge.[14]

Robert S. Mac Adam, born in Belfast in 1808 to a Presbyterian family with an ironmonger's and saddler's business, was a central figure in the cultivation of Irish studies in the nineteenth century. He was a member of the Harp

Society and with a small group of its members – including McDonnell – established an informal Irish society in 1828. This was formally established as the Ulster Gaelic Society in 1830, with the Marquis of Downshire – whose father had already been patron of the Harp Society – as president. Mac Adam travelled Ulster selling the family's wares, taking advantage of his travels to collect Irish manuscripts and record oral traditions. His collections were entered in Irish in a book, often indicating the person from whom he recorded and the year of the recording. The book consists of tales, proverbs, verses and songs – 'the first collection of folklore from the Gaeltacht'.[15]

Mac Adam amassed a substantial number of manuscripts. When the Gaelic Society received a manuscript on loan in order to copy it, Mac Adam in his capacity as secretary wrote a grateful letter in Irish to its owner in Inishowen, Co. Donegal, promising to 'do my best as much as I can to help to save the songs, old stories and old poems that are not yet put down on paper and that will die in a few years'. He complained that young people were not learning them. In another letter – in English – in 1833, Mac Adam expressed a willingness to travel to Inishown to collect the 'old poems and Fenian tales' that his correspondent has told him were known by some of the local old people, and he explained that in the previous week he had spent 'several days engaged in that manner in the Glens of the County Antrim and succeeded in writing a good number from the old people there'. In a letter in Irish to a friend in Scotland (c.1833), he showed his great interest in what would soon be called folklore.

> If the Scottish Gaels are like their brothers in Ireland they cannot but get solace from listening to old stories and traditional lore (*seanchas*). We have great mountains and beautiful green valleys as you have and often the people who live there far from the towns are accustomed to sit with each other by the big turf fire every winter's night to hear tales of the old times and sing sweet Irish songs. Oh! Is this old practice not better than sitting in an alehouse drowning reason in rough fiery whiskey?[16]

Mac Adam made the largest single collection of proverbs in Ireland. He saw them as 'the fragmentary relics of days gone by', revealing of 'the national mode of thought and tone of morality'. He considered it 'as worth-while to record the obsolete words or phrases in our old national language, as to preserve descriptions or representations of material objects of antiquity still existing among us'. 'Six Hundred Gaelic Proverbs Collected in Ulster' was published in the journal which he had founded and of which he was the first editor, *The Ulster Journal of Archaeology*, between 1853 and 1862. As Fionnuala Williams shows, the collection was scrupulous and scholarly and showed a wide comparative knowledge. The expansion of the family business, with the establishment of the Soho Foundry in 1835, limited Mac Adam's endeavours in the cultural field. Nevertheless he recruited others to help him in this, and some of them became his employees in the foundry.

The foundry was a great commercial success, exporting its produce as far afield as Egypt. Mac Adam frequently travelled to the continent on business and became fluent in thirteen languages.[17]

In the first quarter of the nineteenth century, antiquarian interest no longer benefited from the patronage of the Anglo-Irish elite and was concentrated among Catholic intellectuals, but benefited from the general scientific prestige of native scholars such as Charles O'Conor.[18] *Irish Melodies* (1808–), by Thomas Moore (1779–1852), helped to make an interest in the Irish past respectable to the elite once again, as Douglas Hyde pointed out, and had its influence on nationalist rhetoric.[19] *Irish Melodies* consisted of 124 songs and of them 'some 85 are primarily anecdotal or sentimental in nature' while the rest have political connotations, including a number dealing with themes of Irish and Gaelic antiquity and patriotic events, with the historical information derived from various past and contemporary antiquaries.[20] Moore used tunes from Bunting's published Irish music collections for many of his poetic compositions.

Croker

Irish Melodies link us to another figure of importance, who had offered his own collected texts to Moore. Thomas Crofton Croker was born in Cork in 1798, the son of an army officer. His family was of English origin, established in Ireland for some two hundred years. In 1818 he obtained a position as an admiralty clerk in London, where he remained for the rest of his life. But he continued to visit Ireland during his holidays. His abiding interest was in the Irish popular tradition. He persuaded friends to help him by recording tales, which he was to edit, polish, refine, colour, and publish. He was prominent in English antiquarian circles, a member of the Society of Antiquaries, the Camden Society and the Percy Society. With Croker and his contemporaries, '[t]he Irish peasantry, until then seen as the pauperized, brutish and sullen dregs of a dead old culture, full of disaffection and hatred for their new rulers, gain cultural interest'.[21]

In 1824, Croker published in London *Researches in the South of Ireland, Illustrative of the Scenery, Architectural Remains and the Manners and Superstitions of the Peasantry with an Appendix containing a Private Narrative of the Rebellion of 1798*. It is a major source for contemporary Irish popular culture, with specific chapters devoted to 'History and National Character', 'Fairies and Supernatural Agency', 'Keens and Death Customs' and 'Manners and Customs'. The first chapter is of great interest with its discussion of Irish character and its reference to 'the secluded Irish mountaineer' in whom 'the nobleness of savage nature has merged into the dawn of civilization, that without conferring one ray to cheer or ameliorate his condition, affords him imperfect glimpses of the superior happiness enjoyed by the inhabitants of other countries'. The Irish character 'is a compound of strange and apparent inconsistencies, where vices and virtues are so unhappily blended that it is difficult to distinguish or separate them'.

> An Irishman is the sport of his feelings; with passions the most violent and sensitive, he is alternately the child of despondency or of levity; his joy or his grief has no medium; he loves or he hates, and hurried away by the ardent stream of a heated fancy, naturally enthusiastic, he is guilty of a thousand absurdities.

Croker concludes the first chapter with an assertion that 'the present stage of Irish superstition closely resembles that of England during the age of Elizabeth', and he sees this state as 'a strong proof of those who have stated a space of two centuries to exist between the relative degree of popular knowledge and civilisation attained by the sister kingdom'.[22]

In terms of the history of folklore research, Croker's second book is of especial importance. Published anonymously in London in 1825, *Fairy Legends and Traditions of the South of Ireland* was the first collection of oral tales to appear in the then United Kingdom. It was an immediate success and won the praise of such figures as Sir Walter Scott and the Brothers Grimm, who translated it into German as *Irische Elfenmärchen* within a year. A second and a third volume of tales appeared under Croker's name in 1828, the first dedicated to Scott, the second to the Brothers Grimm, the latter including a translation of an essay on Irish and Scottish fairy traditions which the brothers had written for *Elfenmärchen*. The two later volumes included British and continental European material and excited some controversy. It appears that Croker used stories collected by others, particularly by the author of *The Fairy Mythology* (1828), his compatriot Thomas Keightley, who claimed to be the source of most of the comparative notes as well. Croker's tales are legends, short believable narratives of the supernatural, rather than long elaborate folktales (*Märchen*). Or rather they are based on legends since he expands them with colourful 'stage Irish' dialogue into full stories.[23] A book dealing with the lament tradition, *The Keen of the South of Ireland*, appeared under his name in 1844.

Various criticisms have been made of Croker, as an exploiter of Irish material, 'spiced' for an English audience as Douglas Hyde put it, and as reflecting a typical perspective on the Irish peasantry from the standpoint of the Protestant Ascendency. C. Hultin and U. Ober, explaining these Irish peasant images in *Researches*, maintain that Croker's 'fastidiousness as a member of the Ascendency, his desire to be one of the London literati, and his instincts as a popular writer lead him to employ these stereotypes in his own writing'. They contend that the inappropriate inclusion of a Protestant woman's memoir of the horrors of 1798 in *Researches* is a reminder to the English of 'the inevitable consequence following upon continued application of unjust laws . . .' and of the contemporary volatility of the situation in Ireland. Croker seems to have been obsessed with the rebellion and a feared recurrence, and the capacity and willingness of the peasantry to participate in insurrection. His disapproval of the circulation of seditious songs derives from the same fear. In *The Keen*, however, he openly took the side of O'Connell and the repeal of the Act of Union, and Hultin and Ober wonder if this position did not cost him his job at the Admiralty.[24]

W.B. Yeats writes of Croker and Samuel Lover (1797–1868), author of *Legends and Stories of Ireland* (1831, 1834) and of other works, that

> full of the ideas of harum-scarum Irish gentility, [they] saw everything humorised. The impulse of the Irish literature of their time came from a class that did not – mainly for political reasons – take the populace seriously, and imagined the country as a humorist's Arcadia; its passion, its gloom, its tragedy, they knew nothing of. What they did was not wholly false; they merely magnified an irresponsible type, found oftenest among boatmen, carmen, and gentlemen's servants, into the type of a whole nation, and created the stage Irishman. The writers of 'forty-eight [Young Ireland], and the famine combined, burst their bubble. Their work had the dash as well as the shallowness of an ascendant and idle class, and in Croker is touched everywhere with beauty – a gentle Arcadian beauty.[25]

Cultural nationalism was largely introduced to Ireland *via* the Young Irelanders, the difference between them and Daniel O'Connell's earlier movements deriving in large part from the influence of Romanticism. Until the 1870s cultural matters had little political significance, it being generally accepted that nationalists and unionists could meet on the neutral ground of an interest in Irish antiquity. This was the accepted ground rule of various scholarly bodies, including the Society for the Preservation of the Irish Language, founded in 1877, and from which a group constituting itself as the Gaelic Union – reiterating the ground rule – seceded in 1880. Douglas Hyde was a member of the group and in time the Gaelic Union became the Gaelic League (see Chapter 5). The popular tradition itself came to be seen as a cultural asset in this period, both the proof of continuity from the ancient Gaelic past, and a resource for artistic inspiration to the elite.

The vibrant traditional world that drew many writers like Croker to it in the course of the century was dealt a devastating blow by the Great Famine of 1845–48. Evidence enough of its impact is the decline in the housing of the poorest category of the population, one-roomed cabins and hovels, by some 330,000 or three-quarters between the census of 1841 and that of 1851.[26] The most authoritative estimates indicate well over a million deaths in the Famine years.[27] The speed with which the country changed certainly helped to give folklore studies – the term itself, as we have pointed out, dates only from 1846 – 'a sense of combined urgency and nostalgia'.[28] It is clear too that change had been hastened by the Famine, and it is important to note that the antiquary Sir William Wilde (1815–1876) attributed the decline of popular tradition as much to modernity as to the catastrophic years of 1845–48. His book, *Irish Popular Superstitions*, was one of the most insightful and sympathetic of the nineteenth-century antiquary-folklorists'. In a striking passage in the book, he portrays the 'civilizing process' which came to dominate the popular culture of post-Famine Ireland.

> We are now in the transition state, passing through the fiery ordeal from which it is hoped we are to arise purified from laziness and inactivity, an honest, truth-telling, hard-working, industrious, murder-hating, business-minding, rent-paying, self relying, well-clad, sober, cooking, healthy, thriving, peaceable, loyal, independent, Saxon-loving people; engaged all day long, and every day except Sundays . . ., in sowing and mowing, tilling and reaping, raising flax, fattening bullocks, and salting pork, or fishing and mending our nets and lobster pots; instead of being a poor, dependent, untruthful, idle, ignorant, dirty, slinging, *sleeveen*, cringing, begging set; governed by the bayonet or the bribe; generally misunderstood; always *sould* by the agitator at home, and the mimber [Member of Parliament] abroad; ground down by the pauper absentee or his tyrannical agent; bullied by the petty sessions magistrates; alternately insulted and cajoled by the minister of the day, misrepresented and scandalized as Whig and Tory prevailed; bullied by the Browns and Beresfords to-day, worshipping O'Connell to-morrow; vilified by the London press, and demoralized by charity jobbing.[29]

Wilde made substantial collections of folklore, and these were to form the basis for the anthologies published by his wife, Lady Jane Wilde (1826–1896), under the pen name 'Speranza' (the name under which she made her famous contributions to the Young Ireland newspaper, *The Nation*). Yeats preferred those above any of the works of her predecessors. Many collections of tales derived from the popular tradition appeared in the course of the nineteenth century, but few of these – until the beginning of the language-revival movement – are of major interest to folklore studies. The Irish-speaking peasant background of William Carleton (1794–1769) gave him much insight into that life as evidenced by *Traits and Stories of the Irish Peasantry* (1830) and his novels. Patrick Kennedy (1801–1873), a bookseller of peasant background from Wexford, emphasized the importance of recording the disappearing traditions of Ireland and was familiar with contemporary folklore studies. He published a number of collections of tales,* divided into a great variety of different narrative genres, with the

---

* *Legends of Mount Leinster* (1855), *The Banks of the Boro* (1867), *Evenings in the Duffrey* (1869), *Legendary Fictions of the Irish Celts* (1866), *The Fireside Stories of Ireland* (1870) and *The Bardic Stories of Ireland* (1871).

Hero Tales
Fairy tales
The Ghost World

stories linked by running commentary and characterized by often ponderous moralizing. Jeremiah Curtin (1838–1906), an American linguist and ethnologist, made pioneering and scrupulous collections in the West of Ireland, particularly Kerry, with the assistance of interpreters: *Myths and Folklore of Ireland* (1890), *Tales of the Fairies and of the Ghost World* (1893) and *Hero Tales of Ireland* (1894).He had also published collections of myths and folktales of Russians and Hungarians and joined the U.S. Bureau of Ethnology in 1883, working with various native American peoples, learning their languages and recording their myths.[30]

Yeats

The literary movement of which W.B. Yeats (1865–1939) was to be the leading light is dated from around the time of the fall of Parnell (*c.*1890). It was rooted in earlier antiquarian study, the popular nationalist literature of Young Ireland and, above all, in folklore. As a young man Yeats was strongly influenced by the poetry of Young Ireland, to which John O'Leary (1830–1907) had introduced him. O'Leary, whose association with revolutionary nationalism – Young Ireland and the Fenians – led to many years of imprisonment and exile, was an important influence on the literary revival. In 1885, Yeats met him, and O'Leary brought translations of Irish literature to his attention. Yeats' reading of Standish James O'Grady's historical fictions and the translations of Samuel Ferguson and James Clarence Mangan thus combined with the tales and supernatural beliefs he had heard in his native Sligo and his interest in theosophy and esoteric religion.[31]

He insisted that the folklorist should not be alone in interpreting peasant supernatural beliefs, but that the occultist was as well qualified to do so; after all, the occult was 'an enlargement of the folklore of the villages'.[32] Yeats was central to the role of folklore in the literary revival: 'poet, playwright, fictionist, field-collector, anthologist, theorist of folklore, and student of matters spiritual'. He was 'the first major talent of the Irish revival to contemplate fiction's respectful emulation and appropriation of folklore . . .'[33] In 1893 he wrote:

> Folk-lore is at once the Bible, the Thirty-nine Articles, and the Book of Common Prayer, and well-nigh all the great poets have lived by its light. Homer, Aeschylus, Sophocles, Shakespeare, and even Dante, Goethe, and Keats, were little more than folk-lorists with musical tongues.

He was well read in contemporary folklore scholarship, and enthusiastic about mythological interpretations of Irish folklore, despite scholarly scepticism at such explanations.[34]

Mary Helen Thuente sees his folkloric interest evolving through successive themes – 'fairies, contemporary peasants, eighteenth-century rogues and rapparees, and ancient heroes' – and genres – 'folk belief legends, Anglo-Irish fiction, folk hero legends, and ancient myth'.[35] His early dissatisfaction with the urban, materialistic, modern world led him to English Romanticism, but he soon felt that its models were sterile, cut off from a living popular tradition. An engagement with Irish folklore filled the void. By the late 1880s, having praised ballads and folk songs and written an article on them, he was writing poems in imitation of or based on them. Later in his life he wrote songs to popular tunes, hoping that they might become a part of oral tradition.[36] He considered folklore to be a continuation of the same imagination that created medieval Irish heroic literature. Realizing that nineteenth-century ballad writers such as the Young Irelanders or William Allingham, whom he had tried to emulate, were distant from the folk tradition, he set out to know the peasantry and read exhaustively in Irish folklore collections. He published *Fairy and Folk Tales of the Irish Peasantry* in 1888 and *Irish Fairy Tales* in 1892, both of them anthologies.* In them he made clear the distinction between the genres of folktale, legend and myth.

Yeats rejected stories which were obviously moralistic, and which were tinted by anti-Catholicism (such as some of Carleton's). He also rejected those which were 'concerned with earthly matters only', which took place in countries other than Ireland, and in which Irish country people were characterized in derogatory or patronizing terms. He thought the folk tales 'full of simplicity and musical occurrences',

> for they are the literature of a class for whom every incident in the old rut of birth, love, pain, and death has cropped up unchanged for centuries: who have steeped everything in the heart: to whom everything is a symbol. They have the spade over which man has leant from the beginning. The people of the cities have the machine, which is prose and a *parvenu.*

The introduction to the first volume reviews the work of his predecessors whose great merit, Yeats argues, was 'to have made their work literature rather than science . . .' Thus 'they have caught the very voice of the people, the very pulse of life, each giving what was most noticed in his day'. The greatest since Croker, he argues, is Lady Wilde's *Ancient Legends*:

> We have here the innermost heart of the Celt in the moments he has grown to love through years of persecution, when, cushioning himself about with dreams, and hearing fairy-songs in the twilight, he ponders on the soul and on the dead. Here is the Celt, only it is the Celt dreaming.

---

* The first included sections on 'The Trooping Fairies', 'The Solitary Fairies', 'Ghosts', 'Witches, Fairy Doctors', 'Tir-na n-og', 'Saints, Priests', 'The Devil', 'Giants' and 'Kings, Queens, Princesses, Earls, Robbers'; the second 'Land and Water Fairies', 'Evil Spirits', 'Cats' and 'Kings and Warriors'.

Of Hyde, who had yet to publish a collection in book form, he comments that he is, 'perhaps, most to be trusted of all'. Hyde 'knows the people thoroughly' and understood all the elements of Irish life. In 1892 Yeats published *Irish Fairy Tales*. It contains a revealing introduction.

> I am often doubted when I say that the Irish peasantry still believe in fairies. People think I am merely trying to bring back a little of the old dead beautiful world of romance into this century of great engines and spinning-jinnies. Surely the hum of wheels and clatter of printing presses, to let alone the lecturers with their black coats and tumblers of water, have driven away the goblin kingdom and made silent the feet of the little dancers.

At the end of the introduction he asks:

> Do you think the Irish peasant would be so full of poetry if he had not his fairies? Do you think the peasant girls of Donegal; when they are going to service inland, would kneel down as they do and kiss the sea with their lips if both sea and land were not made loveable to them by beautiful legends and wild sad stories? Do you think the old men would take life so cheerily and mutter their proverb, "The lake is not burdened by its swan, the steed by its bridle, or a man by the soul that is in him," if the multitude of spirits were not near them?[37]

The Celtic Twilight (1893), a mixture of oral testimony and tradition, his own spiritual experiences and his commentary and speculation, was very influential, on the revival and much later on Lady Gregory's important collection *Visions and Beliefs in the West of Ireland* (1920). Unlike the anthologies, most of this material was elicited at first hand, and included his own visionary experiences as well as those of his informants. It is less concerned with peasants and with the fairies. By 1902 and the second edition of *The Celtic Twilight*, he was much more preoccupied with heroic themes, seeing ancient Gaelic heroes and modern peasants sharing 'the vast and vague extravagance that lies at the bottom of the Celtic heart'. Peasants were in touch with and inherited a heroic ancient Ireland. Elsewhere he wrote: 'In Ireland today the old world that sang and listened is, it may be for the last time in Europe, face to face with the world that reads and writes, and their antagonism is always present under some name or other in Irish imagination and intellect'. He noted that the specificity of Irish peasant life and its usefulness to writers as a source of inspiration was declining, the writers now 'sail the sea of common English fiction'. The mid-nineteenth century was the time of 'the great famine, the sinking down of popular imagination, the dying out of traditional fantasy, the ebbing out of the energy of race'.[38]

Hyde

Douglas Hyde (1860–1949) was introduced to the Irish language and story-telling tradition by the local keeper of the bogs where Hyde's father had hunting rights, and who had been charged with keeping the young Douglas from falling into bogholes. A cook to his family knew a Fenian lay, while he heard and recorded other stories from the father of one of the family's servants. Studying in Trinity College Dublin, he joined the Society for the Preservation of the Irish Language, the Young Ireland Society and the Contemporary Club, a debating society, meeting individuals involved in the leading contemporary cultural and political movements: Yeats, O'Leary, Michael Davitt, founder of the Land League, and others. Yeats has left an account of his first impressions of Hyde:

> . . .there was something about his vague serious eyes, as in his high cheek-bones, that suggested a different civilization, a different race. I had set him down as a peasant, and wondered what brought him to college, and to a Protestant college, but somebody explained that he belonged to some branch of the Hydes of Castle Hyde, and that he had a Protestant Rector for father. He had much frequented the company of old country-men, and had so acquired the Irish language, and his taste for snuff, and for moderate quantities of a detestable species of illegal whiskey distilled from the potato by certain of his neighbours.[39]

Already he had begun to publish poems in Irish, under the pseudonym An Craoibhín Aoibhinn, and to record stories, songs and phrases from the oral tradition of his native Co. Roscommon. From 1890, he began publishing songs with translations and commentary, at first in *The Nation*; these were to be collected as *Love Songs of Connacht* in 1893. The tales he had collected were published as *Leabhar Sgéaluigheachta* in 1889, followed by a bilingual collection, *Beside the Fire*, published in London in 1890. A small collection of tales in a French translation published in Rennes in 1893 was expanded to appear in a bilingual (Irish-French) collection in 1901 as *An Sgeuluidhe Gaedhealach*.[40]

In the preface to *Beside the Fire*, Hyde tells his reader that Irish and Scottish Gaelic folktales are 'by this time pretty nearly a thing of the past . . . trampled in the common ruin under the feet of the Zeitgeist, happily not before a large harvest has been reaped in Scotland, but, unfortunately, before anything worth mentioning has been done in Ireland . . .' He draws attention to the mysteries of the origin of the folktale, 'part of the flotsam and jetsam of the ages, still beating feebly against the shore of the nineteenth century'. The folktale has been 'swallowed up at last in England by the waves of materialism and civilization combined', but is 'still surviving unengulfed on the western coasts of Ireland . . .'

The preface gives a pioneering overview of the collecting of Irish folklore with Hyde's judgement on the merits of the various writers. Crofton Croker 'led the way', but, despite 'his light style, his pleasant parallels from classic and foreign literature, and his delightful annotations', his stories, with their 'ground-work in his conversations with the Southern peasantry', were 'elaborated . . . over the midnight oil with great skill and dexterity of touch, in order to give a saleable book, thus spiced, to the English public'. Glossing over the 'incidental and largely-manipulated Irish stories' of William Carleton and Samuel Lover he passes on to Patrick Kennedy who, like Croker, neglected to give his sources so that 'we cannot be sure how much belongs to Kennedy the bookseller, and how much to the Wexford peasant'. Lady Wilde's volumes share the same flaw, and the disadvantage of her ignorance of Irish, but are, 'nevertheless, a wonderful and copious record of folk-lore and folk customs, which must lay Irishmen under one more debt of gratitude to the gifted composer'. Jeremiah Curtin is singled out for praise having 'approached the fountain-head more nearly than any other' and his tales told 'with much less cooking and flavouring than his predecessors employed'. But he is dependent on the assistance of interpreters and unfortunately gives no information on the tellers of the tales, or of their provenance.

Hyde complains of no Irish folklorist comparable to the great Scottish collector John Francis Campbell of Islay (1822–1885)* 'in investigative powers, thoroughness of treatment, and acquaintance with the people, combined with a powerful national sentiment, and, above all, a knowledge of Gaelic'. In this respect he laments Irish collectors' ignorance of Irish, so that treatment of the skeletons of the Gaelic stories is second in interest to 'the various garbs in which the sophisticated minds of the ladies and gentlemen who trifled in such matters, clothed the dry bones'. The indifference to the language is the reason why Irish folklore scandalously 'has remained practically uncollected'. In contrast, his own methods were much more scientific, giving 'the *exact language* of my informants, together with their names and various localities – information which must always be the very first requisite of any work upon which a future scientist may rely . . .' There is scholarly commentary in the preface on differences and similarities between the Irish and Scottish Gaelic traditions and on the orality/literacy question ('old Aryan traditions' and 'bardic inventions'). There are also explanations of certain tales in the light of the phenomena of nature – typical of the contemporary Mythological School.

He also gives portraits of storytellers. For example, Shawn Cunningham had been taught in a hedge school and wore the *bata scóir*.§ This leads to a further discussion of the travails of the Irish language:

> the men who for the last sixty years have had the ear of the Irish race have
> persistently shown the cold shoulder to everything that was Irish and

---

* Campbell is known for *Popular Tales of the West Highlands*, 4 volumes (1860-62), *Leabhar na Féinne* (1872) and the posthumous *More West Highland Tales*, 2 volumes (1940,1960).
§ A stick on which a notch was cut whenever the child was heard to speak Irish, his or her punishment afterwards dependent on the number of notches (cf. Chapter 3).

racial, and while protesting, or pretending to protest, against West Briton-ism, have helped, more than anyone else, by their example, to assimilate us to England and the English, thus running counter to the entire voice of modern Europe, which is in favour of extracting the best from the various races of men who inhabit it, by helping them to develop themselves on national and racial lines.

These observations, and others, prefigure the concerns he was later to famously voice in 'The Necessity of de-Anglicizing Ireland' (see Chapter 5). Interesting comments enlighten us on Hyde's methods. The informant is usually a very elderly man who, when finally discovered, may have work to do. At harvest time, the collector's task is next to impossible. To get the informant to tell his stories 'some management' is needed: '[h]alf a glass of *ishka-baha* [whiskey], a pipe of tobacco, and a story of one's own are the best things to begin with'. Writing down the story *verbatim* may cause prob-lems: 'What you must generally do is to sit quietly smoking your pipe, without the slightest interruption, not even when he comes to words and phrases which you do not understand'. Only then can one broach the subject of writing it down. Hyde indicates that 'I have not always translated the Irish idioms quite literally, though I have used much unidiomatic English, but only of the kind used all over Ireland, the kind the people themselves use' – a pioneering use of Hiberno-English. Pioneering too was the collection in terms of scholarly standards of editing, translating and contextualizing. Hyde also included a list of motifs.

Beside the Fire 'brought Irish folktale study to maturity', according to Richard Dorson. Wilson Foster argues that this work is an important part of the fiction of the literary revival and influenced other revival fiction.[41] In that sense *Love Songs of Connacht* was even more important. It was 'the source of what has come to be regarded as the most notable and distinctive characteristic of modern Irish drama – the quality of the writing which gave dialect and English as it is spoken in Ireland a new status in world drama'. It provided the example for Lady Gregory, Padraic Colum, George Fitzmau-rice and most notably J.M. Synge.[42] In the preface, Hyde laments that 'scarcely an effort' has been made to preserve Irish folk songs, noting that the bulk of the songs in his anthology have been noted down from Irish-speaking peasants, 'a class which is disappearing with most alarming rapidity'. *Love Songs* was very influential with its bilingual text and Hyde's own Hiberno-English translations, wherein, indeed, as Declan Kiberd points out, lay the appeal of the book to Yeats and his contemporaries: '[t]he very success of the book caused the defeat of its initial purpose, for, along with popularizing Irish literature, it made the creation of a national literature in English all the more feasible'.[43]

Lady Gregory

Lady Augusta Gregory (1852–1932) was a native of Co. Galway and a member of an Anglo-Irish Ascendancy family. Her husband had been a Member of Parliament and governor of Ceylon. Her experiences of the revolution in Egypt in 1882 had made a great impact on her life, helping to set her on the road as a writer and as a supporter of Irish Home Rule.[44] Through Hyde, she was to experience popular culture as a revelation.

> This discovery, this disclosure of the folk learning, the folk poetry, the ancient tradition was the small beginning of a weighty change. It was an upsetting of the table of values, an astonishing excitement. The imagination of Ireland had found a new homing place.
>
> My own imagination was aroused. I was becoming conscious of a world close to me and that I had been ignorant of. It was not now in the corners of newspapers I looked for poetic emotion, nor even to the singers in the streets. It was among farmers and potato diggers and old men in workhouses and beggars at my own door . . .[45]

Her contributions to Irish life were immense. To a large extent the inspiration behind the literary revival and the Irish National Theatre, she was also a creative writer, an interpreter of the mythological and heroic Gaelic literature and an important student of folklore.

She met Yeats in 1897 and their friendship was to be mutually rewarding. They went on folklore-collecting expeditions together. Her *Poets and Dreamers: Studies and Translations from the Irish* appeared in 1903 and consisted of essays on themes such as 'Raftery' [the blind poet well known in the oral tradition of Connacht], 'West Irish Ballads', 'Jacobite Ballads', 'An Craoibhin's [*sic* – Hyde's] Poems', 'Boer legends in Ireland', and so forth. It also included folktales, legends, verses and beliefs as well as four of Hyde's plays on folk themes. There were many tributes to Hyde in the book. With *Love Songs of Connacht*, she wrote,

> I realized that, while I had thought poetry was all but dead in Ireland, the people about me had been keeping up the lyrical tradition that existed in Ireland before Chaucer died. While I had been looking in the columns of nationalist newspapers for some word of poetic promise, they had been singing songs of love and sorrow in the language that had been pushed nearer and nearer to the western seaboard – the edge of the world. 'Eyes have we, but we see not; ears have we, but we do not understand'. It does not comfort me to think how many, besides myself, must make this confession.

The ballads to be collected are all that remain of 'the great mass of traditional poetry' which was lost 'in the merciless sweeping away of the Irish tongue, and of all that was bound up with it, by England's will, by Ireland's need, by official pedantry'.[46]

Poets and Dreamers does not give the names of her informants, nor does *The Kiltartan History Book* (1909), which consists of a groundbreaking collection of oral historical accounts on a huge variety of themes. The plates of the book and the remaining copies were destroyed in the 1916 Rising, but she added new information for the second edition (1926) as well as some broadside ballads. In the notes to the latter, she comments on the popularity of the book: 'I have always claimed the right to praise it because there is not in it one word of my own: all come from the lips of the people' – 'I do but record what is already in "the Book of the People"'.[47] *Visions and Beliefs in the West of Ireland* (1920),[48] her most scholarly work, 'represented the fruits of more than twenty years of shared study, fieldwork, and thought with W.B. Yeats', and included two essays by him.[49]

Synge

John Millington Synge (1871–1909) visited the Great Blasket Island in 1905, taking perhaps the first photographs there, writing notes on words and idioms of the local Irish and leaving an account of his visit. His earlier visit to the Aran Islands was at the instigation of Yeats, whom he had met in Paris in 1896. According to Terence Brown, before the 1920s most literary treatments of the west and of the Irish-speaking districts in particular were in the form of a journey 'from the bourgeois world of self to an almost pre-lapsarian innocence and community which the writer can enter or, as in John Synge's work, employ to highlight his own Romantic, melancholic alienation'.[50] Synge had studied the Irish language and was particularly taken with *Love Songs of Connacht*, which he reputedly carried with him everywhere he went.[51] He believed strongly in Irish economic self-reliance, defended the preservation of the Irish language in the Gaeltacht, supported the cultivation of a pride in their culture among Irish-speakers, but could not accept the Gaelic League's aim of making Irish the language of all Ireland. He studied comparative mythology and folklore intensively, reading Frazer's *The Golden Bough*, Hartland's *The Science of Folklore*, Miss Cox's *Cinderella*, Le Braz's *La legende de la mort en Basse Bretagne* and Sébillot's *Contes populaires*, among other scholarly works. He brought Hyde's *Beside the Fire* with him to Aran in order to guide him and also made use of Campbell of Islay's methods in *Popular Tales of the Western Highlands*.

Much folklore appears in various of his writings, tales as well as comparative scholarly notes on various aspects of folklore. Kiberd finds comparative folklore notes even in Synge's diary and points out that he deliberately downplayed his scholarship on comparative folklore and mythology in his classic, *The Aran Islands* (1907) out of deference to the general reader. He was familiar with the fundamental distinction made by the Grimm brothers between folktale (*Märchen*) and legend (*Sage*) and his creative work was based on both genres. He accepted that folktales should be collected in Irish, and one of his reasons for going to Aran was to collect them. *The Aran Islands* includes much ethnographic observation and a couple of folktales.

Synge saw great artistic potential in folklore and it had a major impact on his literary career. In an unpublished essay he wrote that with the development of folklore scholarship

> men began to realize that the song and story of primitive men were full of human and artistic suggestion, that the official arts were losing themselves in mere technical experiments while the peasant music and poetry were full of exquisitely delicate emotions.

His creative writings, notably *Riders to the Sea* (1904), *The Well of the Saints* (1905) and *The Playboy of the Western World* (1907), made brilliant use of folk themes. Controversy over Synge's unromantic portrayal of the peasantry led to a falling-out with the Gaelic League and culminated in the notorious riots at the Abbey Theatre on the opening night of *The Playboy*. The Blasket Islanders also took offence to Synge, or at least to some of Synge's account of them, sympathetic and all as it was. Muiris Mac Conghail suggests that the islanders may have read his published account or heard of it after the furore about *The Playboy* and the attack on it by the Gaelic League. He points out that the Irish-American attitude to Synge was also a factor since 'there was constant correspondence between the islanders at home and in America'.[52]

According to Leerssen, Anglo-Irish interest in the popular in general took three forms: song and verse, folklore, and the Irish language. With regard to folklore, he contends that the peasantry was de-politicized and 'translated into the realm of timeless superstition, the folktale, the otherworld and the living past'. He finds that this concentration on fairies and leprechauns had no place in the pages of *The Nation*, but was characteristic of Protestant, conservative and unionist writers and appeared in the pages of publications such as the *Dublin University Magazine* and in the writings of figures such as Croker, William Carleton, Samuel Lover, William Allingham and the early Yeats. This literary mode, common elsewhere in Europe, has been interpreted as an elite reaction to an urban, industrial, rational and modern world. The Anglo-Irish writers were interested in folklore as an artistic resource. The fascination with fairies – something which Catholic intellectuals shied away from as an embarrassing part of their recent peasant culture – was part of a Romantic embrace of the irrational and the mysterious as a source of creative inspiration.[53]

If, as Kiberd suggests, the Anglo-Irish writers' emphasis on place was both to identify with the Gaelic place-lore tradition and to avoid history which was too easily used as a stick with which to beat them, it was also because the supernatural world to which they were drawn was located in the local sites of fairy forts, holy wells, dolmens and standing stones. If later folklore scholarship saw folklore as a literary–historical source, rather than as artistic resource or indeed as art, it was to re-establish continuity with the much-admired art of the ancient aristocratic Gaelic world annihilated in the seventeenth century. But it would be wrong to generalize too much about an Anglo-Irish Protestant versus an Irish Catholic perspective on folklore. After all, the most significant difference between Yeats and Lady Gregory, say, on the one hand and the twentieth-century folklorists Ó Duilearga and Ó Súilleabháin (see Chapter 5), on the other, was that the former were primarily artists and the latter primarily scholars. Hyde is the key link between the literary revival in English and the Gaelic revival, between writing in English and writing in Irish, between the artistic use of folklore and the scholarly study of it. These were not two separate movements, but two sides of the same coin. Nevertheless, it is useful to treat them separately since folklore was used for different purposes by them, and the stress on the importance of the Irish language and its role in a new Ireland also differed. Additionally, the one was predominantly Protestant, the other predominantly Catholic.

5. The Gaelicization of Folklore

Hyde's address to the National Literary Society on 25 November 1892 was a seminal statement on 'The Necessity for de-Anglicising Ireland' (as he entitled his lecture).[1] With it he set the agenda for cultural nationalism in Ireland. Of course he argued that the issue transcended political divisions between nationalists and unionists – as scholarly interest in Gaelic Ireland did – but he admitted that it was 'a question which most Irishmen will naturally look at from a National point of view'. The creation of a movement for the revival of the Irish language and the call for the placing of the language in a central place in Irish life gave new importance to folklore, as a means of knowing those parts of Ireland that were still Gaelic and as the inspiration for a literature which, unlike that of the Anglo-Irish revival, would be 'true' to the original source.

De-Anglicizing Ireland

In his address, Hyde compared the Ireland of his day to the medieval country, 'one of the most classically learned and cultured nations in Europe', and found it wanting in a number of ways, which he explained in terms of 'the race diverging during this century from the right path, and ceasing to be Irish without becoming English'. He instances the paradox of people who gave up Irish for English, translated their names into 'English monosyllables', read English books and were ignorant of Gaelic literature 'nevertheless protesting as a matter of sentiment that they hate the country which at every hand's turn they rush to imitate'.

> I wish to show you that in Anglicising ourselves wholesale we have thrown away with a light heart the best claim which we have upon the world's recognition of us as a separate nationality. What did Mazzini say? What is Goldwin Smith never tired of declaiming? What do the *Spectator* and *Saturday Review* harp on? That we ought to be an integral part of the

United Kingdom because we have lost the notes of nationality, our language and customs.

He saw no prospects of this anomalous position being rectified by the Irish 'becoming good Englishmen in sentiment also'. The contradictoriness of the situation was detrimental to Ireland's production of 'anything good in literature, art, or institutions'. The key to the puzzle was Ireland's Gaelic past which, 'though the Irish race does not recognise it just at present', restrained the Irish from being fully assimilated. This was revealing of the difference between the English and the Irish, that the latter would refuse material prosperity at the price of assimilation. But still the process of Anglicization continued apace and the great Celtic race 'is now – almost extirpated and absorbed elsewhere – making its last stand for independence in this island of Ireland'. Hyde emphasized the Irish contribution to medieval civilization, its singularity in the fact that 'we alone developed ourselves naturally upon our own lines outside of and free from all Roman influence'. The Ireland of today is the descendant of that Ireland, 'then the school of Europe and the torch of learning', and neither incoming Norsemen, Normans or Cromwellian English broke the chain. But 'the continuity of the Irishism of Ireland' was damaged by the Ulster Planters, 'whom our dear mother Erin, assimilative as she is, has hitherto found it difficult to absorb' and by the landlords, 'many of whom always lived, or live, abroad, and not half of whom Ireland can be said to have assimilated'. Ordinary people, 'the mass of the people whom Dean Swift considered might be entirely neglected, and looked upon as hewers of wood and drawers of water', sustained Irish life until today. But now the Irish

have at last broken the continuity of Irish life, and just at the moment when the Celtic race is presumably about to largely recover possession of its own country, it finds itself deprived and stript of its Celtic characteristics, cut off from its past, yet scarcely in touch with its present . . . Just when we should be starting to build up anew the Irish race and the Gaelic nation – as within our own recollection Greece has been built up anew – we find ourselves despoiled of the bricks of nationality. The old bricks that lasted eighteen hundred years are destroyed; we must now set to, to bake new ones, if we can, on other ground and of other clay. Imagine for a moment the restoration of a German-speaking Greece.

He argued that Gaelic civilization died with O'Connell, 'largely, I am afraid, owing to his example and his neglect of inculcating the necessity of keeping alive racial customs, language and traditions'. While Young Ireland brilliantly tried to give the country a new literature in English, 'the old bark had been too recently stripped off the Irish tree, and the trunk could not take it as it might have done to a fresh one'. He chronicled the recent decline of the language and referred to the interest of great continental philologists as proof of the language's importance. Its loss 'is our greatest blow, and the sorest stroke that the rapid Anglicisation of Ireland has inflicted upon us'. He called for 'every Irish-feeling Irishman, who hates the reproach of West-Britonism' to encourage efforts to preserve the language. He argued for the encouragement of a patriotism towards it among the peasantry 'and put an end to the shameful state of feeling – a thousand-tongued reproach to our leaders and statesmen – which makes young men and women blush and hang their heads when overheard speaking their own language'. He insisted that Home Rule, if passed, should ensure the placing of the language at least on a par with Latin, Greek and modern languages in government examinations, the provision of Irish speakers as schoolteachers and officials in Irish-speaking districts and the bringing-about of 'a tone of thought that would make it disgraceful for an educated Irishman . . . to be ignorant of his own language – would make it at least as disgraceful as for an educated Jew to be quite ignorant of Hebrew'.

Hyde enumerated other elements of Irish culture which were, concomitant with the decline of the language, in serious decay. In respect of surnames, he asserted that 'hundreds of thousands of Irishmen prefer to drop their honourable Milesian names, and call themselves Groggins or Duggan, or Higgins or Guthry, or any other beastly name, in preference to the surnames of warriors, saints, and poets . . .' Likewise with regard to Irish given names: 'I *do* think that the time has now come to make a vigorous protest against this continued West-Britonising of ourselves . . .' Place-names, too, had been 'shamefully corrupted to suit English ears'. They 'have been treated with about the same respect as if they were the names of a savage tribe which had never before been reduced to writing, and with about the same intelligence and contempt as vulgar English squatters treat the topographical nomenclature of the Red Indians'. Irish music was similarly threatened. The harp was extinct and the pipes moribund, and in place of the fiddlers and the pipers 'we are now in many places menaced by the German band and the barrel organ', and English music-hall ballads and Scottish songs had taken pride of place in the repertoire of the declining wandering minstrels: 'I must be content with hoping that the revival of our Irish music may go hand in hand with the revival of Irish ideas and Celtic modes of thought which our Society is seeking to bring about . . .'

The position of native games, however, had improved due to the work of the members of the Gaelic Athletic Association. This gave him 'more hope for the future of Ireland than everything else put together', and he considered that the work of the association had 'done more for Ireland than all the speeches of politicians for the last five years'. Expressing his pride in the green jerseys of the GAA, he urged the wearing of Irish dress in place of 'the shoddy second-hand suits of Manchester and London shop-boys'.

> Let us, as far as we have any influence, set our faces against this aping of English dress, and encourage our women to spin and our men to wear

comfortable frieze suits of their own wool, free from shoddy and humbug. So shall we de-Anglicise Ireland to some purpose, foster a native spirit and a growth of native custom which will form the strongest barrier against English influence and be in the end the surest guarantee of Irish autonomy.

Similarly he urged the reading of 'Anglo-Irish literature' instead of English books: 'We must set our face sternly against penny dreadfuls, shilling shockers, and still more, the garbage of vulgar English weeklies like *Bow Bells* and the *Police Intelligence*'.

He finished with an appeal 'to cultivate everything that is most racial, most smacking of the soil, most Gaelic, most Irish' because Ireland '*is* and will *ever* remain Celtic to the core'. The country had to develop along such lines, 'following the bent of our own natures', renounce its 'West-Britonism', cease to be 'a nation of imitators, the Japanese of Western Europe, lost to the power of native initiative and alive only to second-hand assimilation'.

> . . . I would earnestly appeal to every one, whether Unionist or Nationalist, who wishes to see the Irish nation produce its best . . . to set his face against this constant running to England for our books, literature, music, games, fashions, and ideas. I appeal to every one whatever his politics – for this is no political matter – to do his best to help the Irish race to develop in future upon Irish lines, even at the risk of encouraging national aspirations, because upon Irish lines alone can the Irish race once more become what it was of yore: one of the most original, artistic, literary, and charming peoples of Europe.

It is clear that Hyde's ideas reflected much contemporary European thought. Ideas of what elements 'make up a proper nation' had been gradually evolved. Orvar Löfgren points out that 'cultural matrices were freely borrowed across national frontiers', and writes of what he calls '*an international cultural grammar* of nationhood, with a thesaurus of general ideas about the cultural ingredients needed to form a nation'. This was mainly a product of the nineteenth century and included, for example, 'a symbolic estate (flag, anthem, sacred texts, etc.), ideas about a national heritage (a common history and folk culture, a pantheon of national heroes and villains, etc.), and notions of national character, values, and tastes'. He sees this international 'grammar' transformed into 'a specific national *lexicon*, local forms of cultural expression, which tend to vary from nation to nation'.[2] Hyde's organicist vision of community, the specificity of national culture and the linking of language and nation – already made by Thomas Davis – can be traced back to Herder and beyond. The reference to Mazzini makes clear that Hyde was aware of the international context of ideas of nationality. Mazzini thought that Ireland 'did not plead for any distinct principle of life or system of legislation, derived from native peculiarities, and contrasting radically with English wants and wishes' nor claimed 'any "high special function" to discharge in the interest of humanity'. Its need basically was for better government.[3] John Hutchinson stresses that Hyde's resort to the Irish-speaking peasantry should not be read as 'a flight to the archaic', but by a wish 'to scientifically recover from its last remains the history of a once-great nation . . ., and thereby enable the reconstruction of a new high culture based on authentic native values'.[4] The fact that the present cannot be justified does not necessarily mean a retreat to the past but simply that the future must be built on values other than those of the present.

Hyde also reflects a conservative strain of European thought which idealized an imaginary harmonious countryside where a benevolent social order had recently been in place. This opposed the vulgar materialistic world of the cities where traditional hierarchies dissolved and the lower orders did not know their place (see Chapter 7). There was little industry in most of Ireland that was not dependent on agricultural commodities. Despite industrial stagnation and the relative stability into the twentieth century of the urban population outside of the North,* the organization of labour and mass literacy threatened the complacency of the middle and upper classes with the subversion of the status quo. There were working-class protest movements appearing from around 1880 and a wave of strikes among unskilled workers took place between 1889 and 1891.[5] Mass literacy helped to create a market in Ireland for English popular literature and popular culture generally, in Dublin above all, and this was seen as a moral threat in much Catholic and nationalist thought. English popular culture was seen as a corrupting and de-nationalizing influence on the lower classes. The *Catholic Bulletin* in 1911 outlined the problem.

> In the workrooms of mills and warehouses, the books are concealed, to be taken out at the dinner hour and devoured with even greater interest than the scanty meal of the worker. The little maid who pushes your baby's perambulator has her novelette concealed beneath the rug to be easily perused in the park or along the country road, while baby is left to his own devices. The errand boy sitting upon his basket's handle, forgets his errands and grows careless of his master's interests while he burns to emulate Dick Daring, the Gentleman Burglar, or Sappy Sam, the Champion Rider of the Plains.

There were attempts at censorship of offending material – for example, the occasional destruction of imported papers and books after 1910.[6]

---

* The urban population outside of the North actually declined between 1841 and 1911. In this period Belfast's population multiplied by more than five, Derry's by more than two and a half, Dublin's increased by about a third, Waterford's by a small fraction, while that of Cork, Limerick and Galway declined. See Chris Curtin, Hastings Donnan and Thomas M. Wilson (eds), *Irish Urban Cultures* (Belfast: Institute of Irish Studies, The Queen's University of Belfast, 1993), pp. 2–3.

Hyde's view, then, can be seen as representing both an intellectual current fearful of the transformation of (Irish) peasants into the masses of (British) industrial society and the position of a member of a declining social elite. It is true that to a significant extent he equated modernization with anglicization, or confused them, as Joseph Lee argues, since in ways other than language 'Ireland was no more anglicised in 1892 than in 1848'. Lee instances the efforts by British governments and colonists over many centuries 'to impose English ideas of property and God . . . on the [Irish] natives' but it was 'in Hyde's excoriated nineteenth century that England conceded defeat in these two crucial areas' – with the transformation of the land-owning system and the disestablishment of the Anglican church of Ireland.[7]

The Gaelic League

As we have seen, Hyde had already shown a deep interest in folklore and it was to be expected that this would be an important part of the agenda of the Gaelic League. The League was founded in 1893 at a meeting chaired by Hyde, who was duly elected president. Its aim was to maintain Irish as a spoken language in Ireland by preserving it in Irish-speaking districts, by strengthening it in the residually or partly Irish-speaking districts (later to be called the Gaeltacht), by extending its use as a spoken language into the English-speaking parts of the country and by creating a modern literature in Irish. Under the auspices of the Oireachtas, the annual festival (modelled on the Welsh Eisteddfod) founded in 1897, literary competitions were established to encourage original literary composition in Irish. The journal and newspapers founded by, or taken over by, the League (*Irisleabhar na Gaedhilge*, *Fáinne an Lae* and *An Claidheamh Soluis*), as well as its publishing house, provided the means for the publication of such work and for the spread of its message.[8]

The League grew slowly; only forty-three branches had been formed by 1897. After 1901, it grew much more rapidly: 227 branches by 1902 and almost 600, with a membership approaching fifty thousand by 1904. Full-time organizers (*timirí*) travelled the country founding new branches which, in turn, were served by travelling teachers, mostly native speakers of Irish. They taught the Irish language as well as Irish dancing, history, folklore and music, and they organized various competitions and entertainments (*feiseanna, céilithe, aeraíochtaí*). Breandán S. Mac Aodha points out its importance both for adult education and for entertainment, which it shared with similar movements on the European continent, and contends that its success 'may have stemmed in part from a reaction to the superficial standards of the Victorian era'.[9]

Patrick Pearse (1879–1916) was to write that 'when the Gaelic League was founded in 1893 the Irish revolution began'.[10] It has been calculated that half of government ministers and senior civil servants of the first fifty years of Irish independence had been members of the League in their youth: 'In effect, the League educated an entire political class'.[11] If the Land League successfully 'taught the tenants the simple but symbolic gesture of not doffing their caps to landlords',[12] the Gaelic League undermined the automatic deference to English culture and helped to give a sense of self-respect and self-confidence in Irish culture to the Catholic young. Its main appeal was to 'clerks, a minority of the doctors, solicitors, and teachers in country towns', and to relatively few of the middle class, its constituency, according to Tom Garvin, 'in many cases those who were kept out of the charmed circle of Masonic and [Ancient Order of] Hibernian circles and did not have powerful friends or relatives at court'. He argues for a motivation to join in part 'because of career frustration and discrimination against people of their creed and class'.[13] But its ability to mobilize Members of Parliament and local government bodies in support of the language in education, and the fact that half of the country's secondary-school students were taking Irish as an examination subject in 1908[14] cautions against underestimating the League's social base. As the League expanded, the influence of its Dublin membership lessened and Munster came increasingly to the fore. In 1908, 41 per cent of the League's teachers were active in Munster, which sent 42 per cent of the delegates to the 1912 convention.[15]

Garvin contends that the League's politicization of culture 'was to create an official cultural ideology which was arguably hostile to much of the real culture of the community'. He does not answer the question as to whether the ideology it replaced was any more congruent with Irish culture, and neither does he identify 'the real culture' or 'the community'.[16] Oliver MacDonagh's case is that that the original reason for the decline of Irish 'was the popular – or more precisely the Catholic popular – will'. On the other hand, the fact that the majority in the democratic, newly independent, Irish state 'would acquiesce, up to a point . . . in the efforts of the [Irish language] enthusiasts to transform the speech and practices of their country', he attributes to '[a] generation of Gaelic League and similar crusading'. In other words, a disenfranchized majority gave up Irish of their own free will while their emancipated descendants were brainwashed into supporting the revival movement![17]

An Gaodhal, founded by Michael Logan (Mícheál Ó Lócháin) for the Brooklyn Philo-Celtic Society in 1881 with the aim '*teanga na hÉireann a chosnughadh, a haithbheodhughadh agus a chleachdughadh a measg Clann na nGaodhal*' ['the defence, revival and practice of the language of Ireland among the Gaels'] initiated a modern literature in Irish, argues Máirtín Ó Cadhain. It published Irish lessons, sermons, original literary compositions, learned texts, translations and folklore. It was to be the model for the various national and regional journals published by the Gaelic League, all of which published a considerable amount of folklore until the foundation of the folk-lore journal *Béaloideas* in 1927.[18] Indeed *Irisleabhar na Gaedhilge* published an Irish translation of one of the Grimm brothers' stories in 1883 and announced 'that it would ill become it to neglect that department of antiqui-ties and archaeology still existing to a certain extent among the mass of our people, and well denominated folklore'.[19] The League had an important role in the cultivation of an interest in folklore.

Understandably, this attention to traditional culture was an important source of recognition and legitimation to those whose culture it was. Towards the close of the nineteenth century the Irish language had no legal status, was not taught in school, was not used in church, was not a medium of publication of newspapers or books and was spoken by no one of social prominence. What was more, Irish speakers were as often as not compelled to emigrate.[20] Members of the Gaelic League, mostly from the towns, became frequent visitors to Irish-speaking districts in order to learn the language and they befriended local people. The storyteller Mící na gCloch, on hearing that the noted League organizer Tomás Bán Ua Concheanainn was to visit Dingle, 'was like one possessed on that day, standing on the steps in front of the great door of the church, his powerful voice ringing out in triumph at the resurgence of the Gaedheal'.[21] Members of the League published stories and songs that were known to the locals, some of whom were encouraged to write and whose work was published by the League: For many, it was the first time they heard their own speech being read from books. Successful campaigns by the League in support of the language in education allowed Irish-speakers to learn to read and write their own language.[22]

Feiseanna in Ireland and in London awarded prizes for the collection and performance of folk culture. The first Oireachtas, in 1897, awarded prizes for collecting folklore. Hyde announced that the contributions sent to the folk-tale and folk-song competitions of the 1900 Oireachtas amounted to over seven hundred pages. In the same year the League's publication committee announced its intention to include in its annual folklore volumes all other unpublished folklore material that it acquired.[23] The number of the contribu-tions made the goal impossible to reach. The competitions brought storytellers to the attention of scholars. Amhlaoibh Ó Luínse, whose tales were published in two major collections in 1971 and 1980,* won £2 at the 1901 Oireachtas for his collection of unpublished folktales and another £2 in

---

* Seán Ó Cróinín and Donncha Ó Cróinín, *Scéalaíocht Amhlaoibh Í Luínse* (Dublin: An Cumann le Béaloideas Éireann, 1971); Seán Ó Cróinín and Donncha Ó Cróinín, *Sean-chas Amhlaoibh Í Luínse* (Dublin: Comhairle Bhéaloideas Éireann, 1980). He was also the principal informant for Mícheál Ó Briain's collection of words from Co. Cork, edited by Brian Ó Cuív, *Cnósach Focal ó Bhaile Bhúirne i gCunndae Chorcaí* (Dublin: Institiúid Árd-Léighinn Bhaile Átha Cliath, 1947) and for Brian Ó Cuív, *The Irish of West Muskerry, Co. Cork. A Phonetic Study* (Dublin: The Dublin Institute for Advanced Studies, 1968).

1910 for unpublished information about Diarmuid and Gráinne, protagonists of one of the best-known tales of the Fianna. The question of authenticity was raised almost from the beginning when submitted material was identified as being of literary origin: for example, a number of poems by the eighteenth-century poet, Eoghan Rua Ó Súilleabháin. The League published thirty volumes of folklore, as opposed to sixteen books for learning Irish, in its first thirty years. They were usually edited with the necessary information on contributor and provenance, standards encouraged by periodicals such as *Fáinne an Lae*, though there was a tendency to replace Anglicisms by Irish alternatives. Many contributors made clear that the value of the material was primarily linguistic.

Storytelling competitions were held from 1901, with the following instructions given to the competitors: 'The contestant will sit comfortably in a chair and will tell a story in his own Irish as he would tell it by the fireside at home; his own speech and voice and gestures'. At the first there were ten competitors, of whom only two were from Irish-speaking districts; Amhlaoibh Ó Luínse won first prize. There were fifteen competitors in 1902 while in 1903 there were four different competitions, for female and male adults and for females and males under twenty years old. In 1905, 1906 and 1907 there was a competition for storytellers who were not native speakers of Irish. There were two competitions in 1913 and 1914 and a hundred or so competitors at each, all from Irish-speaking parts of Co. Galway the first year and from Munster the second.[24]

Dance was absent from the first Oireachtas. There was an Irish Reel and Jig competition at the second in 1898 and henceforth dance competitions were held. During much of 1901 a debate was carried on in the pages of *An Claidheamh Soluis* about the vexed question of the authenticity of particular dances. Music had a part in the first Oireachtas, harp and pipes being played. There were competitions for instrumental music from 1901. There were also a few occasions when brass and reed bands performed or competed. While individual singers and choirs performed at the first Oireachtas, no competition was organized. The following year, however, there were competitions for male and female singers, all songs to be sung 'in recognized Gaelic metres'. In 1910 a conference on traditional singing was held in Dublin, which led to a special Feis Cheoil in Tuam devoted to traditional singing in Irish.

Choirs were particularly troublesome, since the question of what was traditional was more likely to arise, and they were sometimes disqualified from the Oireachtas on those grounds. Much controversy pursued this question in the pages of *An Claidheamh Soluis*, to which both Pearse and his fellow signatory of the 1916 proclamation of the republic, Éamonn Ceannt (1881–1916), contributed. Pearse's article, 'Traditionalism', in 1906, made some perceptive observations, arguing that 'traditionalism' was not essentially Irish, but that there was a traditional mode of singing and story-telling 'in every land in which there is an unspoiled peasantry . . ..' The traditional style was simply the peasant style; 'it is not, and never has been, the possession of the nation at large, but only of a class in the nation . . . .' This peasant style was different in every country.

> Thus it comes that the only arts which have survived to us from Ireland's past are peasant arts; just as the only Irish speech which is living today is a peasant speech. And those who would build up a great national art . . . must do even as we propose to do with the language: they must take what the peasants have to give them and develop it. And this, indeed, is simply doing over again what was done thousands of years ago by the earliest of the professional musicians and seanchaithe [storytellers].

But he argued that these traditional art forms had their proper place: 'by cottage fires in the winter evenings' and that to 'transplant them were to kill them'. An art culture would hopefully arise in Ireland and the artists 'must imbibe their Irishism from the peasants, since the peasants alone possess Irishism; but they need not, and must not, adopt any of the peasant conventions'. In tune 'with the soul of Ireland, they need not be afraid of modern culture . . .'

From the beginning the League wished to encourage Irish manufacting and particularly that from the Irish speaking districts. Exhibitions at the Oireachtas included arts and crafts, at which artists such as Jack B. Yeats, Sarah Purser, Nathaniel Hone, Walter Osborne and William Orpen exhibited. The first Industrial Exhibition, part of the 1904 Oireachtas, included pampooties from Inishmaan and woollen clothing from Donegal. An account from the *Manchester Guardian* of the 1905 exhibition, reprinted in *An Claidheamh Soluis*, gives a good picture of the event.

> The imperfect embroideries and rough home-spuns of the Congested Districts faced the tapestries, types, and bindings of the Dun Emir looms and presses. Miss Purser's stained-glass windows and panels, with their reminiscences of Botticelli, Angelio [*sic*], and mediaeval tapestry, were faced by Belfast pocket-handkerchiefs and flanked by pillars of soap and pyramids of plate polish. But the unifying idea was there – the idea of Irish self-help.[25]

Folklore was important to the Gaelic League because the spoken Irish language was important. The League wished to restore the language, but Irish had more or less ceased to be a vehicle for literature and had been a predominantly peasant language for two centuries. How was the literary tradition to be renewed? The language had an illustrious literary tradition in the medieval and early modern period, but could the writings of seventeenth-century figures such as Geoffrey Keating serve as a model for prose at the beginning of the twentieth century? The proponents of the spoken language (*caint na ndaoine*) won the often acrimonious debate in which the weight of the eminent scholar priest Peadar Ó Laoghaire (1839–1920), author of original works and modern versions of medieval tales, was crucial.[26] Of necessity modern spoken Irish had a strong dialectal colouring.

There were supposedly only five books in print in Irish when the Gaelic League was founded. Clearly the provision of reading material was an immediate necessity. Folklore texts helped to fill the gap and the 'folk form' was to dominate the prose literature of the revival for a long time despite the objections and alternative models provided notably by Patrick Pearse, who wondered how a relevant modern literature 'could evolve from the folk-tales of a rural peasantry'. Indeed, as O'Leary puts it, 'the role of folk-lore in the development of Gaelic creative prose was to become one of the major battlegrounds in the war between nativism and progressivism'. Folk-lore to the former was able to offer 'safely indigenous models to link the increasingly Anglicized present with the pristine Gaelic past'.[27] Liam P. Ó Riain wrote in 1911:

> Irish writers and Irish students seemed to consider it a sacred duty to be what they regarded as 'traditional': to tell stories and look out on life in the way of their fathers before them. Their philosophy was simple and partial, appealing in some ways but not convincing to more eager spirits of the new generation. So we have our bracing battles over the 'Gaelic Spirit', and over sundry 'modern issues' – in some wise very ancient – that must challenge Irish humanity as well as a great deal of the rest of humanity.[28]

Part of the problem was the nature of the audience to be addressed. Father Ó Laoghaire unequivocally saw native Irish speakers as the imagined audience: 'If someone reads our Irish prose for that public, and if our language goes home with full force and directness to the hearts and minds of that public, then we may feel certain that our work is a success', a passage which suggests that he was writing for illiterates. Pádraig Ó Siochfhradha ('An Seabhac') 'felt that the pseudo-traditionalism of many writers in this regard had led them to patronize Gaeltacht folk by failing to challenge either their intellect or their imagination'. Ó Laoghaire's *Séadna* (1904, though appearing serialized in periodicals from 1894), the first major literary work of the revival, was based on a folktale and intended as reading material for learners of Irish and is 'a virtual handbook of Irish folklore and folklife'.

One clear difference between oral tales and the literary tales based on the 'folk form' was in their treatment of the supernatural. O'Leary shows how the traditional Otherworld is rationalized or discredited in the latter and he cogently contrasts this attitude with that of Protestant writers: 'we are offered, in opposition to this vestigial paganism that so fascinated the Anglo-Irish, a public repudiation of superstition and a communal affirmation of wit, good sense, and rationally orthodox spirituality'. O'Leary is sympathetic to those who used rural subjects in their writing given the nature of contemporary Irish and particularly Irish-speaking society, subject to intense economic and cultural pressures from outside which seemed to validate 'the conservatism, even the antiquarianism of many such writers . . .'[29]

Visiting Scholars and the Blasket Islands

When Hyde referred to the interest in Irish shown by continental scholars, those he had in mind included many of the pioneers – mostly Germans – of the study of the Old Irish language. Some of those who had learnt the medieval language came to Ireland to study modern Irish, and a number of them in their researches made collections of Irish texts, which often included folklore.*Thus, for example, the Danish linguist Holger Pedersen visited the Aran Islands in 1896 and made a collection of tales (which was not to appear in print for another century).[30]

Folklore, literature and Celtic studies came together in a particularly rich manner in the Blasket Islands off the west coast of Kerry.[31] In 1907 the Norwegian linguist Carl Marstrander (1883–1965) visited the island. He chose to go there instead of to Athens with the Norwegian Olympic team, for which he, a champion pole-vaulter, had been selected. He stayed for five months, spending two or three hours a day with Tomás Ó Criomhthain (1855?[32]–1937), learning modern Irish. He brought with him a newly published novel by Peadar Ó Laoghaire, *Niamh*, and as Muiris Mac Conghail puts it, '[i]t was a happy coincidence that Ó Criomhthain should be introduced both at the same time to the young Norwegian scholar and to the work of a writer in Irish who was to establish the direction for prose in modern Irish'.[33] Marstrander became a great friend to the islanders, who regarded him with the greatest affection, calling him *An Lochlannach*, 'the Viking'. According to Mac Conghail,

> Marstrander's decision to come to the Blaskets to learn Irish, his mastery of it in such a short time, his time spent working with the Island community and his friendship with Tomás and regard for the quality of Tomás's Irish, were all factors which convinced Tomás and the other Islanders that theirs was an important culture and that there was a future for the Island writer in Irish.[34]

Marstrander returned to Ireland to teach Old Irish and comparative philology at the School of Irish Learning in Dublin in 1910. One of his students was the young Englishman, Robin Flower (1881–1946), of the manuscripts

---

* More recent examples include the linguist Nils Holmer's study of the Irish of Co. Clare which included a volume of texts, most of which were folklore. Kenneth Jackson, also an eminent Celtic scholar, published a collection of folktales from the famous Blasket storyteller Peig Sayers (1873–1958) in *Béaloideas* in 1938 – he had gone to the island at the instigation of Flower. Heinrich Wagner, compiler of *the Linguistic Atlas and Survey of Irish Dialects*, in which a large number of short folklore texts appears, also published a separate volume on *The Oral Literature of Dunquin, Co. Kerry*.

department of the British Museum. The museum had an extensive collection of Irish-language manuscripts and Flower had been given the task of cataloguing them. He went to Dublin to perfect his Irish. Marstrander persuaded him to go to the Blaskets to learn from Ó Criomhthain, and his first visit in 1910 was to be the beginning of a life-long engagement with the island and its people, who called him Bláithín, an affectionate pun on his name ('little flower'). He spent his honeymoon there in 1911 and his ashes were later scattered there after his death. At the beginning he spent a couple of sessions per day with Ó Criomhthain, but eventually began to record Tomás's traditional knowledge.[35] 'We have to discuss what form my lessons are to take', he writes in *The Western Island* (1944); 'I want to practise myself in writing down the language from his lips. What is he to give me, isolated words and sentences, or tales and poems? The verdict falls for the tales . . .'[36]

The book includes much of the result. It is distinguished by a certain melancholy, a nostalgic mood. The last chapter, on the fairies, explains them as 'an image of man's unreconciled distrust of nature, and it was in the cities, which have devised a thousand ways of dissembling natural needs and natural fears, that men began to forget them'. But in the island, 'they will be gone in a few short years, I thought, for they have for a habitation the minds of the old men and women, and the young people no longer believe in them'. The preface ends with: 'The King is dead and Tomás and the greater part of that lamenting company, and all this that follows is the song we made together of the vanished snows of yesteryear'.[37]

Patrick Sims-Williams points to the gradual decline in the influence of Renan's 'elegiac regret for an ancient civilization'. He argues that the idea of 'an ancient culture which had reached a point of terminal decline' was destructive and points out that the literary revivals in Celtic languages since 1854 apparently contradict this. 'Perhaps Flower's view was that the compromises with modernity which the creation of a modern Irish literature necessitated were of a different order of magnitude from the unobtrusive (or only at this distance unobtrusive?) medieval assimilation of foreign influences, which he himself traced so assiduously'.[38]

Flower's folklore collections were large and important. His collection from Ó Criomhthain, *Seanchas ón Oileán Tiar*, appeared posthumously, in 1956, edited by Séamus Ó Duilearga, director of the Irish Folklore Commission (see below). He also recorded from Peig Sayers and from other Blasket islanders, as well as tales – as yet unpublished – in Inishmore in the Aran Islands in the early 1930s. The collections included various genres of folktales and songs, prayers and charms, riddles and proverbs as well as information on material culture and social history. He was a punctilious and careful collector, and innovative as well since he was using a recording machine, the ediphone, from 1929. Bo Almqvist considers that few scholars if any have given a better description of the context of storytelling, 'of the settings of the narration and of the way the performance influenced the audience'. Ó Duilearga looked on him as a 'guide and counsellor' and frequently visited him in London. Flower contributed an article to the first issue of *Béaloideas*, in 1927, and a collection of Blasket tales in the second volume in which, according to Almqvist, the storyteller Peig Sayers was first brought to the attention of a wider audience. In 1959, Ó Duilearga published a final collection of Flower's tales in *Béaloideas*, mainly from Sayers. Flower's tales had remained untranscribed in London, on more than two hundred ediphone cylinders, until Ó Duilearga arranged, on Flower's death, to have the cylinders sent *via* Dublin to the Dingle peninsula where the folklore collector Seosamh Ó Dálaigh transcribed them for the Folklore Commission. Most of them remain unpublished.[39]

Mac Conghail does not think that Flower, despite his regard for him, realized Ó Criomhthain's potential as a writer, and he sees the arrival of Brian Ó Ceallaigh (Bryan Kelly, 1889–1936) on the island in 1917 as helping to realize that potential. Ó Ceallaigh befriended Ó Criomhthain and persuaded him to write an account of his life and, introducing him to the works of Pierre Loti (*Pecheur d'Islande*) and Maxim Gorki, showed him 'that the lives of ordinary people, fishermen and Russian peasants, could be the stuff of literature'. Ó Ceallaigh was instrumental in getting *Allagar na hInisc* (1928), a journal of life in the island, and the classic autobiographical account *An tOileánach* (1929), published. Both works were edited by Pádraig Ó Siochfhradha.[40] They were translated into English as *Island Cross-Talk* and *The Islandman* respectively, the latter appearing in several other languages as well. Ó Criomhthain was a remarkable man. The youngest of eight children, he learnt to read and write English in school and earned a difficult livelihood hunting seals and fishing and endured much hardship, including the loss of all of his ten children but one to disease, accidents and emigration. According to one account, he was over forty when he learnt to read and write in his own language, using children's primers when weather conditions forced him to stay in a relative's house on the mainland (Irish had appeared on the schools' curriculum in the 1890s).

The context in which he could become a writer is well summarized by Mac Conghail. The change in attitude to the Irish language caused by the Gaelic League as well as the interest of scholars and language enthusiasts opened the island to a wider world and 'the village on the Great Blasket island was to become for a short and critical time a centre for those seeking both the living language and its culture'.[41] Tomás Ó Criomhthain's work is remarkable for its depiction of Blasket Island life from the inside. Gifted bearers of traditional culture like him were known to folklorists and linguists, but their knowledge, and their stories, were mediated by the scholars. Ó Criomhthain was the subject of his own narrative: the *seanchaí* wrote back. Undoubtedly his work derives from an awareness of the importance of his community and its disappearing way of life developed through his contact with the Gaelic League and particularly with sympathetic and selfless strangers such as Marstrander, Flower and Ó Ceallaigh. He comments towards the end of *An tOileánach*:

> I wrote exactly about a lot of our affairs so that they would be remembered somewhere and I tried to describe the mind of the people who were around me so that there would be an account of us left behind, because our like will not be again.[42]

Ó Criomhthain was the first and the most eminent of the Blasket Island writers, and this in a community which peaked at a population of 176 in 1916 before declining to 50 in 1947 and 20 in 1953, the year of the final evacuation to the mainland.[43] All of the Blasket writers are of interest to folklorists and ethnologists through their use of folklore and through their detailed depiction of the life of a folk society. The others included Muiris Ó Súilleabháin (1904–1950), author of the autobiographical work *Fiche Blian ag Fás* (1933, translated as *Twenty Years a-Growing*). This celebrated work owes much to the inspiration of the young English classicist, George Thomson (see Chapter 6), who had learnt modern Irish and came to the island at the suggestion of Robin Flower. There he became friends with Ó Súilleabháin and encouraged him in his desire to be a writer. E.M. Forster, in his introduction to the translation, also published in 1933, referred to the book as 'an account of neolithic civilisation from the inside'.[44]

Unlike Ó Criomhthain and Ó Súilleabháin, Peig Sayers (1873–1958) was illiterate in Irish, but she was a gifted storyteller who would win national and international recognition. From the mainland nearby, she married into the Blaskets. She was well-known to scholars such as Flower (who has a chapter of *The Western Island* devoted to her) and Kenneth Jackson, who recorded and published some of her stories. There are no less than three autobiographical accounts of her life, *Peig* (1936), since known to generations of Irish schoolchildren, and *Beatha Pheig Sayers* (1970, translated as *An Old Woman's Reflections*) dictated to her son Mícheál Ó Gaoithín (a noted storyteller, writer and poet), and *Machtnamh Seanmhná* (1939), dictated to Máire Ní Chinnéide.

Institutionalizing Folklore Studies

The legacy of the Gaelic League was instrumental in getting official support for the task of recording the folklore of Ireland, through the role of individuals who had been ideologically formed in the League and through the sympathetic attitude of the new Irish state to such an undertaking. The Swedish folklorist Carl Wilhelm von Sydow (see Chapter 2) played a role in encouraging Séamus Ó Duilearga and others in Ireland. He helped Ó Duilearga to visit folklore institutions in the Nordic countries in order to

study their methods. Von Sydow's study of the medieval Norse saga literature had made him aware of the importance of the Irish–Scandinavian
connection, though many would dispute the soundness of the Irish–Scandinavian parallels he made. He studied Irish under Marstander, teaching it at
Lund University in the 1920s.[45] Making his first visit to Ireland in 1920, he
met Peig Sayers and other storytellers on the Blasket Island and took many
photographs.[46] He also became friendly with Hyde and they later corresponded with each other in Irish. He managed to arrange a meeting with
Éamon de Valera in 1924, convincing him of the importance of recording
Ireland's folklore. Ó Duilcarga (James Hamilton Delargy, 1899–1980) was the
key individual in this regard. A native of the Glens of Antrim, he had moved
to Dublin as a child. He became interested in the Irish language and recorded
his first folk tales on holidays in Antrim. He studied in University College,
Dublin, and in 1923 was appointed assistant to Douglas Hyde (who had been
appointed professor of Modern Irish in 1909). He became lecturer in folklore
in UCD in 1934 (but was on secondment to the Irish Folklore Commission
from 1935) and held a chair of folklore from 1946 to 1969, though a department of folklore was not established there until 1971.[47]

The revival of the Irish language and the preservation of Irish folklore
were parallel undertakings. In that sense the creation of institutions for the
preservation of folklore can be seen as part of the 'Gaelicization' policy of
the new state. The forerunner of the Gaelic League, the Society for the
Preservation of the Irish Language, had achieved the concession of 'Celtic' as
a recognized subject for examination in the intermediate schools in 1878
and the teaching of Irish in primary schools (though outside school hours) in
1879. The Gaelic League managed to get Irish accepted as a full primary-
school subject in 1900 and it became the medium of primary school teaching
in Irish-speaking districts in 1904. After furious controversy, Irish was made
compulsory for matriculation in the National University of Ireland from
1913.The first Dáil, set up in 1919 in opposition to British jurisdiction after
the winning of a nationalist majority in the 1918 general election, instituted
a Department of the National Language. The new state implemented a
programme of promoting Irish in the schools and of preserving the Irish-
speaking districts, the Gaeltacht. This policy was supported both by the
Cumann na nGael governments of 1922–32 and the subsequent Fianna Fáil
governments of de Valera. The Gaelicization policy has been outlined by
Oliver MacDonagh as follows:

> First, the compulsory teaching of Irish in the schools was to produce in
> time – a very short time – a base of Irish speakers which would expand
> steadily as one age-group after another emerged from the system. This
> would be supplemented by state-subsidised Gaelic publishing, a state-
> subsidised Gaelic theatre, a large Gaelic component in the new radio
> service, 2RN, and similar intellectual and artistic supports, culminating in

an 'Irish Academy'. The National University was to be pressed to move in the same direction, with the ultimate objective of instruction in Irish at the tertiary as well as the lower levels of education. Secondly, the Gaeltacht areas were not merely to be kept alive and intact by economical and technical aid and bounties, but also to be used as recruiting grounds for Irish speakers to man the educational and law enforcement systems, the civil and armed services, and local government. To this end, a network of Gaeltacht secondary schools and colleges was planned. Correspondingly, the engineers, doctors, judges, lawyers, priests and others 'servicing' the Gaeltachts should themselves be Irish speakers. Finally, the public sector was to be used, so far as practicable, to accomplish the transformation. Preference should be given, for example, to native speakers for entry to the civil service. Irish should be used in official business wherever possible, and various public appointments were to depend upon competence in the 'language'.[48]

There has been much subsequent negative commentary on this policy, but it should be remembered that it was supported by the political representatives of the great majority of the population of a democratic state.

In 1925, Ó Duilearga attempted to found a folklore society along with Fionán Mac Coluim (1875–1966). The latter was a fellow Antrim man who, like Ó Duilearga, had moved south as a child. In London as a civil servant, eventually in the India Office, he became involved in a number of Irish cultural organizations, leading to a report being compiled on him by Scotland Yard. He was appointed as chief organizer of the Gaelic League in Munster, distinguishing himself through his dedication. He also began to collect folklore and folk songs, which he published in various Irish language organs. He represented the League in the United States where he raised funds. Back in Ireland he was assiduous in efforts to promote the Irish language in Irish-speaking districts.[49] At the end of 1926, as a result of a notice placed by Mac Coluim in the newspapers, a meeting was held attended by sixteen people, including Hyde and Pádraig Ó Siochfhradha (1883–1964). The purpose was to investigate the possibility of founding a folklore society. In the intervening period, Ó Duilearga had sought advice from the eminent Norwegian folklorist and Celtic scholar Reidar Christiansen on such a society. The 1926 meeting made proposals which were considered at another meeting on 11 January 1927, and at this second meeting the Folklore of Ireland Society (An Cumann le Béaloideas Éireann) was founded. It undertook to publish a folklore journal, and the motto of the society was printed on the journal's cover: '*Colligite quae superaverunt fragmenta, ne pereant*'. Ó Siochfhradha was elected president with Hyde as treasurer, Mac Coluim as one of the two secretaries and Ó Duilearga as editor of the journal and as librarian.[50] By the end of the 1930s the Society had about a thousand members.[51]

The first number of the first volume of the journal, *Béaloideas*, bore the date June 1927, and included contributions from Ó Duilearga, Hyde, Flower and Ó Siochfhradha. It opened with a bilingual four-page editorial from Ó Duilearga, in which he observed the timeliness of the founding of the society. Since 'the folklore that our ancestors had is dying rapidly along with the old people', if it is long more neglected 'there will be nothing useful left of the old native survivals [*sean-iarsmaí dúchais*], in the form of folklore and memory of old customs' He concedes that much is lost forever and that in ten years 'there will be such a large gap in the ranks of the old Irish speakers who are now alive and who have folk traditions [*sean-aimsireacht*]' that it will not be worth the effort of setting about the society's task. Nevertheless, there is still a rich heritage to be 'preserved for the nation' if the members do their utmost in the ten years to come. It is 'to save this valuable heritage from death' that the society was founded, to collect, publish and preserve for posterity the folklore of Ireland. He makes a case for the wider importance of this work: 'whatever Gaelic literature will be henceforth written in Ireland unless it is Irish [*Gaedhealach*] and unless its roots are grounded and fastened in the literature and folklore of Irish it will be something insipid and worthless'. He emphasized that the Irish were not alone, that there was interest 'in the life and folklore of the countryside' on the continent and that books were now been written in 'rural dialects' in countries where the educated respected folklore and local dialect: '[i]t is understood that there is some good in them . . . that they are living'. Thus the Irish could save their folklore and show the world that it was of value and worthy to be preserved. It could not be saved in its oral form alone. However, it could be written down and preserved 'for the people of Ireland so that it would find a new lease of life in the form of literature; and through the medium of print that it would again reach and provide intellectual fodder for Irish youth [*aos óg Clainne Gaedheal uile*]'. The Irish part of the editorial finishes with an appeal to the nation [*a Ghaedheala . . . Ná teipidh orainn!*] to support the aims of the society.

The English part of the editorial points out that in the previous forty years no concerted attempt had been made to collect 'that rich heritage of folklore which has been recognised by continental scholars to be of first-rate importance'. Ó Duilearga admitted the role of the Gaelic League in encouraging collections of folklore but the major part of these collections had been lost in the troubled years 1916 to 1922.* Arrangements had been made by Hyde to deposit the remainder in the National Library. Ó Duilearga paid tribute to various Irish-language periodicals which published folklore, especially to *An Lóchrann* in Munster, and also *An Stoc* in Connacht and *An t-Ultach* in Ulster. But many private collections still remained unpublished and he asked readers who possessed such collections to give them to the society for

---

* For example, the house of Fionán Mac Coluim was burned by the Black and Tans in 1920, with the loss of his book and manuscript collection [Breathnach and Ní Mhurchú, *Beathaisnéis a hAon*, p. 38].

publication '*do-chum glóire Dé agus onóra na hÉireann*' (for the glory of God and the honour of Ireland). The aim of the society 'is a humble one – to collect what still remains of the folklore of our country'. He scorned 'the nonsensical rubbish which passes for Irish folklore'. The society aimed to publish folklore in Irish with summaries in an international language and to compile a bibliography of Irish folklore. Already two large collections and several small ones had been sent to the society. He gave practical advice to collectors of folklore: the giving of detail on the informant and the provenance of collected material; the recording of material verbatim; the recording of 'calendar-customs, nature and plant-lore, folk-medicine, charms, prayers, beliefs and superstitions' in addition to folktales; the systematic collecting of place names (using maps and recording place-name lore) and personal names (giving the local pronunciation); and the forwarding of names and addresses of informants to himself. He finished his editorial with words of gratitude to the many benefactors of the society.[52]

The society quickly began to amass material donated by enthusiasts. By 1932 Ó Duilearga was able to announce that the society had two million words in its collection of folklore. But already the government, after continued representation, had given a small grant to establish the Irish Folklore Institute, with Ó Duilearga as its director, in 1930.[53] Further grants from private sources followed – from the Rockefeller Foundation in 1930 and the Carnegie United Kingdom Trust in 1931 – and it was possible to make collections as well as publishing three volumes. By 1935, some fifty thousand pages were in the possession of the Institute. In 1935 the government established Coimisiún Béaloideasa Éireann (the Irish Folklore Commission) 'with a small annual grant-in-aid for the purpose of collecting, cataloguing, and eventually publishing the best of what remained of Irish oral tradition'.[54] Ó Duilearga was appointed honorary director and Seán Ó Súilleabháin (1903–1996) became the archivist. The latter spent three months training in Sweden at the Dialect and Folklore Archive of Uppsala University and wrote a handbook for folklore collectors, *Láimhleabhar Béaloideasa* (1937), based on the Uppsala classification system. An enlarged version, co-dedicated to the people of Sweden and to the bearers of Irish traditional culture, was published as *A Handbook of Irish Folklore* in 1942.

The first full-time folklore collectors were appointed in 1935 and, according to Ó Súilleabháin's account,

> were men who had shown, by the work that they had done as part-time collectors for the society and the institute, interest in rural traditions and a capacity for acting as collectors. None of them was a university graduate; rather were they devoted men who knew their local Irish-Gaelic dialect well, had an intimate knowledge of country life, and a deep respect for the custodians of an ancient, orally preserved culture.[55]

Bo Almqvist adds that 'they were known to the people of the areas in which they worked' and thus 'would not be mistaken for tax collectors, gunmen on the run, or whatever else a stranger in an area can be mistaken for'.*[56] The number of collectors employed at any one time usually varied from seven to ten. All were men: no woman was ever employed as a full-time collector. They were generally sent to an Irish-speaking district, equipped with an ediphone recording machine. Recording was made on to the ediphone's wax cylinders (1,000 to 1,500 words each), and the material was transcribed into standard notebooks which were sent to the Commission in St Stephen's Green in Dublin, where they were bound in due course. In time most of the collectors had the use of a motor car, though the rationing of petrol during the 'Emergency' (1939–45) hindered their mobility. They kept a field diary of their daily activities, particularly valuable for the detailed descriptions of field-work and of individual informants.[57]

The American folkorist Richard Dorson spent a week in 1951 doing field-work in Kerry with Tadhg Ó Murchadha (who, along with Seán Ó hEochaidh in Donegal, was the first of the collectors appointed, in 1935). Dorson's remarks deserve to be quoted.

> The observer notices curiously how the rural families take for granted the visits of the folklore collector. He has become an institution like the priest and the postman, and receives a friendly welcome and often a high tea when he comes. The old men respond eagerly to his arrival, both from a glow of social pleasure and a sense of the value of his work and their contribution. The bonds of a fading language and a county kinship, the sanction of the government, and the backlog of many congenial interviews, all facilitated Tadhg Murphy's task . . . In former days the collectors had come from outside and above, from the educated, aristocratic, and professional class, to peer curiously in to the peasant culture beneath them. Now the collectors came from the ranks and spoke with their own people, not to publish curious books but to record their common legacy and to honor its carriers.[58]

Evidence enough of how close collectors were to their informants is the fact that many collected from members of their own families or neighbours. For example, Seán Ó Cróinín, the West Cork collector recruited by Ó Duilearga in 1937, collected songs from his mother, the famous singer, Bess Cronin.[59] In like manner Mícheál Ó Gaoithín, part-time folklore collector for the Commission, recorded tales from his mother, Peig Sayers.[60] Hundreds of others – 'teachers and school children, farmers and officials' – collected folklore in a voluntary capacity, it becoming 'something of a fashion', according to

---

* This is not a facetious observation. In Estonia in the early twentieth century folklore collectors were taken for rag-dealers or peddlars and one told of being taken for a German landlord or a spy. See Anu Kannike, '"Rahvuslik" rahvakultuur / "National"Folk Culture', *Pro Ethnologia* no. 2 (Tartu: Estonian National Museum, 1994), p. 22.

Caoimhín Ó Danachair. By the late 1930s, there were between 100 and 150 part-time collectors who were paid a little to cover their expenses.[61] Of the thousands who thus contributed in a part-time capacity during the lifetime of the Commission, Fionnuala Nic Suibhne estimates that not much more than one-eighth were female and of forty thousand or so informants, females constituted about six thousand.[62] The result of the intense work of collection manifested itself in the 68,000 manuscript pages lodged in the commission's archive in 1937–8, over 60 per cent the work of part-timers.[63]

Also in 1937–8, a scheme to record folklore with the help of schoolchildren was carried out with the cooperation of the Department of Education and the Irish National Teachers Organization. The Department issued a guidebook for the scheme to all the primary schools in the state – apparently there was an Irish-language and an English version.* The foreword to the booklet explained the project:

> The collection of the oral traditions of the Irish people is a work of national importance. It is but fitting that in our Primary Schools the senior pupils should be invited to participate in the task of rescuing from oblivion the traditions which, in spite of the vicissitudes of the historic Irish nation, have, century in, century out, been preserved with loving care by their ancestors. The task is an urgent one for in our time most of this important national oral heritage will have passed away for ever.[64]

The scholarly importance of the project, and hence the question of methodology, were also stressed, pointing out the need to record 'variants of the same story, tradition, belief, custom, etc., from every district in the country'. Thus scholars would be able to plot geographical distributions and make international comparisons. Customs and beliefs, which had come down from the Bronze Age as well as the Early Christian Period, would be able to 'throw light on our relations with the outside world during these two periods of our history'. Likewise, material of medieval origin. In addition,

> the social life of the country people – the historic Irish nation – is mirrored in what is known in Irish-speaking districts as seanchas and but little attention has been paid to this type of oral tradition in the past. Due to the lack of documentary evidence the story of the Irish countryman will never be known unless all this seanchas, in English and in Irish, in all its variants, is recorded from every townland in Ireland.[65]

A one-page list of instructions emphasized the identification of collectors and informants, and the value of every contribution, 'provided the material has been obtained locally'. It also stressed the necessity of locating exactly

---

* The Department's homologue in Northern Ireland declined to participate, although in 1955-56 a scheme modelled on that of 1937-38 was carried out under the auspices of the Committee on Ulster Folklife and Traditions and the Northern Ireland Ministry of Education.

the places mentioned in the pupil's contribution. The 'Subjects for Composi-tions' were in the form of a topic with a large number of specific questions about it.* It was a voluntary scheme to some extent. The circular issued by the Department of Education allowed schools in the cities of Dublin, Cork, Limerick and Waterford to opt out and left some ambiguity in other cases.

> It is appreciated that for historical and other reasons, some districts are relatively poor in folklore and that in some districts where folklore abounds the efforts of the pupils may be hampered by the apathy of the older people. It will be open to a teacher in such circumstances to make representations to the District Inspector for a modification or discontinu-ance of the scheme.[66]

The children were asked to collect folklore from family members and neigh-bours and to write it down in standard notebooks in school. The notebooks (of which there were some five thousand, amounting to half a million pages) were then returned to the Folklore Commission. Some six hundred of the teachers became correspondents of the commission, replying to over a hundred questionnaires on specific topics of folklore and traditional culture over the years.[67]

The so-called main collection of the commission covers much the same ground as the Schools' Collection, but much more comprehensively. Ó Súil-leabháin's *Láimhleabhar Béaloideasa* and *A Handbook of Irish Folklore* guided the collectors. The latter is a substantial volume with questions arranged thematically according to the following categories: 'Settlement and Dwelling', 'Livelihood and Household Support', 'Communication and Trade', 'The Community', 'Human Life', 'Nature', 'Folk Medicine', 'Time', 'Principles and Rules of Popular Belief and Practice', 'Mythological Tradition', 'Historical Tradition', 'Religious traditions', 'Popular Oral Literature' and 'Sports and Pastimes'. It was based on Ó Súilleabháin's own intimate knowledge of the archives and covered an encyclopaedic range. Altogether, by the late 1970s the archives (since 1971 in the care of the Department of Irish Folklore in University College, Dublin) had at least two million pages, a valuable

---

* The subjects were as follows: 'Hidden Treasure', 'A Funny Story', 'A Collection of Riddles', 'Weather Lore', 'Local Heroes', 'Local Happenings', 'Severe Weather', 'Old Schools', 'Old Crafts', 'Local Marriage Customs', 'In the Penal Times', 'Local Place-Names', 'Bird Lore', 'Local Cures', 'Home-Made Toys', 'The Lore of Certain Days', 'Travelling Folk', '"Fairy Forts"', 'Local Poets', 'Famine Times', 'Games I Play', 'The Local Roads', 'My Home District', 'Our Holy Wells', 'Herbs', 'The Potato-Crop', 'Proverbs', 'Festival Customs', 'The Care of our Farm Animals', 'Churning', 'The Care of the Feet', 'The Local Forge', 'Clothes Made Locally', 'Stories of the Holy Family', 'The Local Patron Saint', 'The Local Fairs', 'The Landlord', 'Food in Olden Times', 'Hurling and Football matches', 'An Old Story', 'Old Irish Tales', 'A Song', 'Local Monuments', 'Bread', 'Buying and Selling', 'Old Houses', 'Stories of Giants and Warriors' 'The Leipreachan [sic] or Mermaid', 'Local Ruins', 'Religious Stories', 'The Old Graveyards', 'A Collection of Prayers', 'Emblems and Objects of Value', 'Historical Traditions' and 'Strange Animals'.

collection of some twenty-five thousand photographs (Caoimhín Ó Danachair in particular was a gifted photographer) and thousands of recordings.[68] Some indication of the scale of the work can be gauged from the register of international folk tales known in Ireland, *The Types of the Irish Folktale*, prepared by Seán Ó Súilleabháin and Reidar Christiansen in 1963, which gave references to the 43,000 or so variants of these tales collected up to November 1956.[69] Research was also carried out by members of the commission's staff and published in scholarly journals at home – especially in *Béaloideas* – and abroad, as well as in monographs of which the most ambitious was *The Festival of Lughnasa*, a work of lasting importance by Máire Mac Neill (1904–1987). Ó Danachair's scholarship was supplemented by a number of works for the general public which were widely read.

Ó Duilearga's Vision of Irish Folklore

Ó Duilearga was the key figure in articulating the project of the commission. This he did in a rhetorical, Romantic style and with repeated echoes of Renan and Yeats. In this respect he contrasts with the other scholars of the commission. It is proposed to briefly look at some passages in three of Ó Duilearga's texts, which are, as always, distinguished by an elegant style and a powerful turn of phrase. Reading his writings, it is not difficult to grasp the great impact his words and ideas had on his interlocutors, inspiring a lasting affection for and loyalty to his name. The earliest is the text of a lecture in German on Irish folklore given in January and February 1937 in several German universities and published in the venerable German journal of Celtic Studies in 1943.

There he argued that the Irish folk tradition was in retreat from 'the new international urban culture', was richest 'where the Gaelic language is strongest, and [that] its keepers belong to the older generation'. Of fieldwork he wrote that 'in order to understand a people [*ein Volk*], one must not only speak their language but also live with them at home' and thus comprehend their tradition and the conditions under which they lived. He found that women were rarely tellers of the folktale, 'which is the preserve of the man'. The 250,000 pages lodged in the commission's archive by 1 January, 1937, he pointed out, were faithfully recorded from illiterate informants, for whom conversation, in place of reading, 'has become a fine art': '[f]or this lack of education every good folklore collector thanks God with a full heart'. He emphasized that the commission's staff treated the collected material reverentially and did not change or edit or touch it up in any way: ' . . .we consider ourselves not as creators or adapters, but as literary executors of earlier generations' and he argued that 'our manuscript collections are the embodiment of the past of a forgotten people'. He stressed the remarkable continuity in the Gaelic tradition from a medieval aristocratic culture. He explained that after the destruction of the native elite in the sixteenth and seventeenth centuries the common people saved 'in spite of all persecution some of the culture of the upper classes and admitted it into their age-old treasury of oral tradition'. Thus 'a large part of our medieval literature exists in oral form . . .' In a remarkable passage he articulated his view of Ireland to his German audience:

> Ireland sometimes reminds me of a lumber-room in an old house, where the accumulated odds and ends of centuries lie hidden and forgotten until one day the dust of the years is raised and the long-forgotten household accoutrements of an earlier world are revealed. In Europe there are only a few remaining corners left where the old world can find a free place. The storm and violence of modern life, the hustle and bustle of the big cities, the wail of the factory horn, the whirring of machines – the unbroken net of the busy industrial world has driven away and banished the old habits of living and of thinking. But in the far west of our remote island this insane nightmare is unknown and peace can find its refuge there.*

The Romantic feel of this passage is further emphasized by a description of the western abode of the storytellers, 'a wild, rocky, treeless, storm-lashed landscape by the Atlantic Ocean . . .' An account of his visit to a storyteller in Co. Cork echoes this.

> We beat a path which led us into a desert of mountain and bogland, and finally came upon a solitary house, where the mountain path stopped, as if it had considered that it was pointless to continue. Far and near an immense wilderness, brown mountain slopes and dark bog! And in the distance lay the sea. We continued on our way to the house of Ó Murachú, the blind storyteller, and turned ourselves towards the mountain. It was dusk, though there still lay over the landscape a weak reflection of light, in which we groped our way over boulders and heath. There was neither path nor trail, nor even a hint of one. At last my friend pointed ahead and I saw a long blue thread of smoke wind itself upwards.§

He gave an extended account of his friend, the storyteller Seán Ó Conaill, whose tales he was later to publish, and of storytelling evenings in that part of Co. Kerry. Sometimes the conversation turned to current affairs as some neighbour related a report read in a local newspaper, 'and one heard the

---

* This passage seems to reflect Yeats' comments on his collecting of folklore [Fairy and Folk Tales, p. 301]: this is cited in the previous chapter.

§ By way of comparison, the following is part of Crofton Croker's account [Researches in the South of Ireland, p. 277] of his visit to Gougane Barra in Co. Cork in 1813:

> For the last three miles, our road, or rather path, was up the side of steep acclivities, thence upon ranges of stone steps, over dreary mountainous swamps, and we were frequently obliged to quit the common track, in order to seek amongst the rushes for more secure footing. Large blocks of schistus rock lay scattered around, many of which at a little distance appeared like vast ruins: nor was there one tree or bush within view to destroy the appearance of entire neglect and desolation.

remarks and judgements of medieval men on modern European politics'. He told his audience that during much of the year his work brought him almost on a daily basis in contact with 'the poorest class [*Schicht*] in Ireland'.

> The more I live together with them the greater the high esteem and admiration I feel for them. Their fate is so hard: an incessant struggle with the stony, unproductive soil and the stormy Western Sea, to where harsh laws had banished their ancestors three hundred years ago. Today these poor farmers and fishermen are the only guardians of an ancient heritage. In their Gaelic language, which is their own, and in the rich tradition, which they have preserved, lies the key to the knowledge of an old world.[70]

'The Gaelic Storyteller', the Sir John Rhŷs memorial lecture to the British Academy in 1945, showed many of the same preoccupations: the continuity of the medieval Gaelic literary tradition in the oral tradition through the vicissitudes of Ireland's history, the interplay between the two, the loss of so much, and the antiquity of that tradition. In one passage he referred to Kuno Meyer (1858–1919), the great German scholar of the Celtic and particularly the Irish tradition, who,

> in a memorable phrase, has called the written literature of medieval Ireland, 'the earliest voice from the dawn of West European civilization'. In the unwritten literature and traditions of the Gaelic-speaking countryman are echoes out of the vast silence of a still more ancient time, of which hitherto the archaeologist has been the only chronicler.

Ó Duilearga spoke of the hero-tales still told by many Irish storytellers; and in listening to them 'one could bridge the gap of centuries and hear the voice of the nameless story-tellers and creators of the heroic literature of medieval Ireland'.

There is an affectionate account of Seán Ó Conaill, 'illiterate so far as unimaginative census-officials were concerned' but 'he was one of the best-read men in the unwritten literature of the people whom I have ever known'. He described visiting three nights a week during his holidays, and before sitting on a bag of salt to transcribe oral traditions, helping to clean the house, sweeping the floor, bringing in turf, lighting the lamp and chasing the hens out the half-door. He observed that one reason for the 'extraordinary popularity and appreciation' of oral tales was 'the aesthetic sensitivity and intellectual curiosity so marked in the older generation'. He also made an acute observation on one of the functions of storytelling as 'the oral "literature of escape"': 'for an hour or two the oppressed and downtrodden could leave the grinding poverty of their surroundings, and in imagination rub shoulders with the great, and sup with kings and queens, and lords and ladies, in the courts of fairyland'. He argued that 'the film is the modern folktale'.

He also knowledgeably commented on the Scottish Gaelic tradition, and the common basis it shared with the Irish. He demonstrated a comprehensive knowledge of the Gaelic literary tradition. Mentioning the recent acquisition by the National Library of a collection of Irish manuscripts previously in private ownership in England, he indicated that '[t]o these manuscripts of the literary tradition we hope in our time to see added the last Gaelic source available to the student of comparative ethnology, the collections of the Irish Folklore Commission, and the still unrecorded traditions of Ireland and Gaelic Scotland ... Irish literature, both written and oral, must be studied as a continuous whole'.[71] He pointed out the almost complete lack of research and commentary on the folklore collections. Irish oral traditions 'include contributions from the many ethnic elements which make up the Irish nation', but many 'contain unmistakable evidence of having belonged to a pre-Christian civilization, perhaps pre-Indo-European' and – probably reflecting the ideas of von Sydow – suggests that some of them 'may have been told in Ireland in Megalithic times'. The Irish wealth of folklore was due both to 'the ultra-conservative character of the Irish countryman' as well as to 'the peculiar circumstances of our historical and cultural development'. But it also had a strong assimilative capacity and made its own of many borrowed elements. He finished by underlining the pressing need to record 'the oral traditions of the peoples of the world' because soon the time will come 'when the sources of tradition will have dried up in the shifting sands of progress, and the voice of the story-teller and tradition-bearer will be stilled for ever'.

> In our own time and before our very eyes the last stronghold of an ancient civilization is slowly disintegrating and will soon pass away for ever. In the tradition of that old Gaelic world which stretches from Lewis and Uist to the coasts of Kerry there remains the tattered but still recognizable fabric of a culture which at one time belonged to the whole Atlantic area.

He points out that in Ireland English-speaking areas have by and large 'been left untouched [by the work of folklorists], and much valuable material still awaits the collector in these areas'.[72]

'The Gaelic Storyteller' is the best general account of the Irish storytelling tradition but, as Micheál Briody points out, it is hardly the definitive study.[73] On the other hand *Leabhar Sheáin Í Chonaill* (1948) is the definitive collection of the tales of a single Irish teller and a model of comparative commentary and annotation. It consists of the repertoire of folktales of Seán Ó Conaill (1853–1931), along with legends, *cante-fables*, traditions about festivals, songs and verses, children's games, prayers, charms and other information, along with a short autobiographical account dictated by Ó Conaill and an introduction and notes by Ó Duilearga – all writen in a simplified orthography adjusted to the phonology of the local dialect. The introduction informs us that he first visited Ballinskelligs in 1923 – to learn the local Irish – and sought out Ó Conaill at the suggestion of Fionán Mac Coluim. Between 1923 and 1931 he went there twelve times. Ó Conaill was already well accustomed to scholarly visitors, among them Mac Coluim and Pádraig Ó Siochfhradha, so that when Ó Duilearga began recording folklore, Ó Conaill shared his interest in the work and understood its importance. The recording sessions (almost all using pen and paper) were often visited by neighbours eager to listen, sometimes as many as a dozen were present in Ó Conaill's house.

Ó Conaill had a great love for his tradition and after the audience for his stories had disappeared he used to tell the stories aloud to himself when nobody was about. He never went to school and did not know English. The furthest he had gone from home was to Puck Fair in Killorglin, not much more than forty miles away, though he was brought to Killarney in 1928 in order to make recordings of his dialect. His memory was such that he was, according to Ó Duilearga, able to recount almost word for word a literary tale which had been read out to him twice more than fifty years ago.[74] When the Irish-language periodical *An Lóchrann* appeared (1907–1913), it was eagerly read by Ó Conaill's family, two of his children sending contributions to it. They read stories and songs from it and from *An Claidheamh Soluis* aloud to their father. Ó Duilearga in the introduction expresses his anguish at the death of the Irish language in that part of Kerry and the attendant loss of a wealth of tradition.

> The real importance of the living language that still lives on the lips of the old people of the Gaeltacht was not understood – and many people still do not understand it. When they are dead that will be the end of the Middle Ages in Western Europe, and the chain that is still a link between this generation and the first people who took possession of Ireland will be broken. A culture still lives among them that once belonged to the whole nation. It is a great shame [*feall*] that they do not get the respect and the honour that is due them.[75]

The commission can be seen as a continuation of the pre-independence nation building projects whose task was to define, preserve and renew the nation's cultural heritage. It was attached to the Department of Education and enjoyed the interest of Éamon de Valera, head of government for many of those years. It was wound up in 1971, its staff and holdings transferred to the newly established Department of Irish Folklore in University College, Dublin. John Wilson Foster sees the 'second generation' Irish folklorists of the period after the Anglo-Irish literary revival as

> mostly local men, Catholics, inhabitants of no Big House or Georgian terrace,* tutored by the Scandinavian pioneers – who have no personal system of belief to corroborate, no romantic image of a fey and credulous peasantry to project, little more desire than their contemporaries the New

---

* An ironic qualification to the above: the folklorists after the revival did inhabit a house in a Georgian terrace: number 86 St Stephens' Green, in which the Irish Folklore Commission was housed.

Critics to apply the anthropological method to texts. By the time they emerged, partly because they emerged, the Irish literary revival was finished.[76]

The commission's collection was a product of its time. The 'authentic' West of Ireland was the preferred research object for Irish folklorists, though all the leading folkloristic figures and the institutions were based in Dublin. Indeed, as we have noted, the folklore project of 1937–8, which was carried out through the schools, allowed Dublin and the other main cities to opt out. This myopia was not unique to folklorists. The West also attracted anthropologists from abroad (the discipline itself was established in Queen's University, Belfast from 1962 and in St Patrick's College, Maynooth from 1982) with most published monographs to date devoted to western rural communities. Urban anthropology and urban folklore research only began to develop in the 1960s.

The commission's preoccupation with pastness, with the countryside, with Irish-speaking districts, with male informants, with *Märchen* can all be faulted, but by standards that have subsequently arisen. They are the result of the philological orientation of contemporary folklore scholarship, the Romantic idea of the peasantry as a national *Mutterschicht*, the revivalist backgrounds of the folklorists, the unabashed sexism of the time* and the central place of the folktale in contemporary international scholarship. It can be shown that it did not consider its own influence on the tradition, nor the role of the collectors in providing an audience of sorts, as Clodagh Brennan Harvey has shown,[77] and on their choices of individual informants – but that would be to ask for a reflexive ethnography before its time. The scope and ambition of the work of the Folklore Commission was immense and the result an extraordinarily rich archive of international importance. It must be seen as one of the most important cultural projects in Irish history.

---

* For example, if a woman had been employed as a folklore collector, according to Civil Service rules she would have had to resign once she got married.

6. Folklore and Poverty

Folklore was distant from the observer, necessitating a journey outwards from the big cities, westwards towards the most remote, isolated and backward rural districts, and downwards, towards the poorest and most humble stratum of settled rural society. The social distance is obvious in the literature, yet is rarely commented upon except in the most superficial way. In fact poverty and isolation were necessary to the specificity of folklore since prosperity and integration of necessity involved the assimilation of modern values inimical to it. The key observers, that is those such as Yeats and Ó Duilearga who helped to shape the folkloric discourse in Ireland, took a strong position against the materialism of a modern urban, industrial world and a fatalistic view, coloured by a nostalgic Romanticism, of the inevitable decline of folklore communities. How could they come to grips with the poverty of the storyteller if it seemed to be the precondition of his or her art?

Those who idealized the Gaeltacht, the locus of Irish folklore *par excellence*, were aware that it was among the poorest parts of rural Ireland. Moreover, the best storytellers and the best speakers of Irish were among the poorest of its inhabitants. Already in 1891, the Congested Districts Board had been established to deal with the severe poverty of the West. As editor of *An Claidheamh Soluis* from 1903 to 1909, Patrick Pearse showed an awareness of the social realities of Irish-speaking communities and discussed problems such as tuberculosis in Connemara, poverty and emigration (although in his fiction, 'his creation of an idealized Irish-speaking West was a fully conscious aesthetic strategy'[1]). Irish-language periodicals wrote unsentimentally about rural depopulation, celibacy, late marriage and other problems of the West. The Gaelic League campaigned against emigration and had a question for the 1900 Oireachtas essay competition on 'Irish Emigration – Its Causes and Effects'. It seems to have been through the anti-emigration campaign that Pearse saw the necessity both for state intervention and the encouragement of self-reliance to eradicate poverty, 'a recognition that would of course in time evolve into the more fully developed if idiosyncratic socialism that won the respect and trust of James Connolly', as Philip O'Leary puts it.[2]

Douglas Hyde and Lady Gregory were aware of the poverty of those from whom they recorded their tales and songs. The narrators of the stories in *Beside the Fire*, according to Hyde, were 'to be found only amongst the oldest, most neglected, and poorest of the Irish-speaking population' while speakers of English 'either do not know them at all, or else tell them in so bald and condensed a form as to be useless'.[3] Hyde's most important source for *An Sgeuluidhe Gaedhealach* was Proinsias Ó Conchubhair, an inmate of the Poor House in Athlone, who sent him stories as he heard them from other inmates. Hyde commented on his unfortunate circumstances: 'How sad that the Poor House then was the best place to collect stories!'[4] Lady Gregory's *Poets and Dreamers* begins with her retelling of a conversation in Gort Workhouse between two women arguing about the worth of rival poets they had encountered in their childhood. Another chapter, 'Workhouse Dreams', is based on 'three happy afternoons' in a workhouse where she recorded a number of folktales, moved by the contrast 'between the poverty of the tellers and the splendour of the tales'. Of the tellers she wrote:

> It seemed as if their lives had been so poor and rigid in circumstance that they did not fix their minds, as more prosperous people might do, on thoughts of customary pleasure. The stories that they love are of quite visionary things . . . I think it has always been so to such poor people, with little of wealth or comfort to keep their thoughts bound to the things about them, that dreams and visions have been given. It is from a deep narrow well the stars can be seen at noonday . . .[5]

Famine was reported in the West as late as the 1920s. In 1922 the Executive Council of the Irish Free State sent seed potatoes and other relief to affected districts but similar reports in 1925 were rejected as exaggerations. Tim P. O'Neill points out that behind these and similar reports in the preceding decades 'lay the reality of a section of the western poor living on the edge of starvation . . .'.[6] All the Irish-speaking districts suffered from endemic emigration which threatened their viability in the most essential way. Ballinskelligs, Co. Kerry, where Séamus Ó Duilearga did much of his early field-work, had a population of 2,180 in 1841. By 1891, two years before the Gaelic League was founded, it had fallen to 1,550. In 1926, not long after the foundation of the Irish state, it was 923. In 1936, a year after the foundation of the Irish Folklore Commission, it was 796, and by 1971, the year after the commission was abolished, it had dropped to 452.[7] Emigration did not directly affect old people, who by and large were the best folklorists' informants. Emigration took away their loved ones, though remittances, on the other hand, often helped to keep whole communities afloat. It would be wrong to suggest that the problem did not concern the whole country;

indeed almost all Irish families were affected by emigration – the proportion of Irish-born people living abroad was 43 per cent in the early 1920s.[8] But emigration from the Gaeltacht, like that from the West in general, was particularly high, and its implications for the country which had rested its claim to independent nationhood on its Gaelic culture were particularly grave. Little wonder that folkloristic paeons to illiteracy, the Middle Ages and traditional rural life seemed to some in particularly bad taste.

Various writers recognized the relationship between folklore and underdevelopment and understood that to 'save' folklore was to preserve underdevelopment. Indeed D.P. Moran explicitly made that observation in 1905.[9] Sir William Wilde recognized that the creation of a modern society – 'the spread of education, and the introduction of railroads, colleges, industrial and other educational schools' – was one of the factors that was destroying traditional Irish agrarian society in the mid-nineteenth century. A similar observation was made by the anthropologist Roger Bastide about Europe in general and France in particular:

> It is curious to note that Folklore became a science just at the moment when it began to disappear in the west, and to disappear exactly after the transformations in the economic structure. M. Varagnac went as far as demonstrating that it was not military service nor even the development of the road network which provoked, in 1850, the disappearance, relatively quickly, of French folklore – but the introduction of mechanization in agriculture. Development kills folklore or, more exactly, does not allow it to subsist except in certain sectors of the population, more and more reduced, such as children, or societies of those 'natives of such and such a region' in the big cities . . .

But he also argues that misery killed folklore even faster than development since folklore depended on the existence of a folk community, 'organized and structured, capable of maintaining a tradition through time and of extending itself, spiritually, through renovation, from one generation to the next'. But 'where misery goes so far as to make the destiny of a man equal to that of a simple animal, hemming him into despair and passivity, there folklore will not exist'.[10]

At the turn of the twentieth century, there were two notions of the Ireland of the future, one industrial and primarily associated with the nascent Sinn Féin party and the labour movement, the other agrarian, primarily associated with cultural revivalism and particularly with the Anglo-Irish writers of the literary renaissance. The latter view was most potently formulated by Yeats, for whom Ireland was the ideal place for the renewal of literature, being poor, uncorrupted by commercialism, and shaped by a history that had developed qualities of imagination and heroism in the people. Maurice Goldring argues that, unlike the Gaelic revivalists who saw themselves at the service of Irish-speaking communities whose voices they tried to make heard, Yeats, Lady Gregory and, to a lesser extent, Synge, 'showed simply that they were capable of vibrating in harmony with the peasant world and its culture'. He holds that there was no dialogue there, just a fundamentally egoistic use by the writers of the poetic spectacle the peasant offered. 'Misery for them was never poverty, and transformed itself into rich tapestries'. As has been memorably expressed in a Brazilian context, 'Intellectuals are the ones who like misery; the poor prefer luxury'.[11] Goldring grants that the engagement of a literary movement with the peasant way of life was neither new nor particularly Irish, but contends that, despite the great gulf between the 'myth' of a rural civilization and the social reality, the myth dominated not only literary life, but political and religious life in Ireland as well. He exemplifies that in the writings of figures as diverse as D.P. Moran, Michael Collins and Æ (George Russell).

Reading the Blasket autobiographies, he argues that the picture they gave of rural life was very different. The islanders lived in closed and isolated communities, subject to a hostile environment and fearing the outside world. 'Natural events, storms, bad weather, bad harvests, were neither more nor less explicable than famines, emigration, evictions, wars and uprisings . . .. Blessed ignorance or resigned acceptance, catastrophes come and go, caused by unknown powers, results of fate . . .' He instances Tomás Ó Criomhthain's resignation at the deaths of his family, understood as God's will; the islanders' view of a shipwreck as a blessing, since its cargo allowed them to feed themselves, and of war as good, since it brought them other such cargoes; and their rebellion never going beyond 'brutal revolt', such as pelting tax collectors with stones. He points out that in the autobiographies 'the culture of these people only arrives at expression when it comes into contact with strangers'.

The attraction of such communities for the writers of the Irish literary renaissance, who felt themselves marginalized by the materialism of Europe, was the strength of the oral poetic tradition and the magical powers of poets and poetry. 'In the rural society of the West of Ireland, they saw their ideal live, the image of the Ireland that they wished to fashion: a rural society led by a new aristocracy, the aristocracy of the mind'. Goldring concludes that they engaged only with a small portion of the peasantry, that which was the most isolated and thus whose economic development was the most retarded. He makes the point that the social position of the writers, who were mostly landowners or related to landowners, explains 'their repugnance at accepting the evolution of the rural world'. Because it did not accept change, the 'myth' did not engage with the peasants who organized themselves in the Land League (to the detriment of the interests of certain writers who were landowners). And it rejected the religion of the peasants, concentrating on their 'paganism' rather than on their Catholicism. The myth, then, could not function among the peasants themselves because it was fundamentally hostile to their interests. Instead it worked among the urban intellectuals and middle classes, who were to direct the new state. Goldring points out that ruralist ideologies were particularly influential in countries that industrialized late, where the values of liberal capitalism had a slender base, where the middle classes defined themselves negatively against industry and the proletariat, were hostile to capitalism and to socialism, and where late entry into global economic competition, as in Ireland, led to a reactive defence of traditional values. Industrial progress then could be seen as a betrayal of traditional ideals.[12]

There was no strong alternative to nationalism on the Left. The rural proletariat had been in terminal decline since the Famine of the 1840s and the subsequent haemorrhage of emigration,* while the only significant industrial region, around Belfast, had an ethnically divided workforce. The Labour Party did not stand in the elections of 1918 in which Sinn Féin triumphed. During the War of Independence, Republican forces were used on occasion to quash land agitation, in response to which the Dáil Ministry of Home Affairs expressed the concern '[t]hat the mind of the people was being diverted from the struggle for freedom by a class war . . .'.[13]

De Valera's vision of Ireland in the decades after forming his government in 1932 was favourable to the project of the folklorists. Gearóid Ó Crualaoich has shown that this vision originated in Romanticism and in the ideals of Young Ireland and the Gaelic League. Referring to the mode of thinking which 'sees the Irish peasant as really a type of aristocrat-in-disguise', he argues that the 'rhetorical denial of true "peasant" status to Irish rural society' goes 'hand in hand with a tacit acquiescence in the use of a largely "peasant" model for thinking about and managing social and economic development in the years of de Valera's ascendency'. The achievement of peasant proprietorship 'had little effect on the nature of rural society or the structures of agriculture' while emigration safely released the excess population. Thus rural life seemed to be lived 'to a pattern that was unbroken since time immemorial, while a new metropolitan elite could, since the revolution, maintain a seemingly benign form of the old structural ascendency over the "liberated" countryside'.

> Here was indeed a source of that 'truly Irish' order of things that was so important a part of the national dream. Cleared of its Big Houses – in reality or by selective vision – the hinterland of the essentially pre-industrial Irish market towns was at once the source of economic self-sufficiency, in all but a few instances where imported frugal luxuries were not to be decried, and also the heartland of moral and social values bearing testimony to the spirituality and selflessness of the Irish people.

---

* Figure cited by Caoimhín Ó Danachair are revealing. In 1841 there were 736,838 'cottier labourers' and 471,062 farmers. In 1911, the respective figures were 129,638 and 383,167 and in 1971, 35,569 and 181,627. Caoimhín Ó Danachair, 'Cottier and Landlord in Pre-Famine Ireland', *Béaloideas* nos 48–9 (1980–1), pp. 164–5.

He contends that 'the conception of a folk or peasant-type society' was central to de Valera's (and Fianna Fáil's) political philosophy from 1932 to 1959, making 'it easier for both leader and party to get on with the "real" job of manifesting and reinforcing Irish sovereignty while leaving Irish society relatively unaltered'.[14]

The Englishman George Derwent Thomson (1903–1987) developed an interest in Ireland and Irish through his mother, whose father was Irish. Like many others, he was entranced by the small community of the Blasket Island, but he tried to understand it within its specific historical and social context. He first visited the Blasket in 1923 – on Robin Flower's recommendation – to learn Irish, and befriended a young islander, Muiris Ó Súilleabháin, who became his teacher. He persuaded Ó Súilleabháin not to emigrate to America, but to join the newly formed Irish police force, and encouraged him to write a classic autobiographical account (see Chapter 5). A life-long Marxist and a brilliant classical scholar, Thomson felt that he had found the key to understanding the Homeric poems in the Blaskets, teaching him 'what it is like in a pre-capitalist society', where the traditions of the islanders, 'especially their poetry, date from a time when social relations were profoundly different from those in which I have been brought up'.[15] He described the storyteller Peig Sayers as 'a woman from the Middle Ages' whose mind was so taken with the traditional world that 'she scarcely understood that it was disappearing'. Tomás Ó Criomhthain was also a man from the Middle Ages, but he understood that the world was changing, 'and not for the better', writing his accounts so that that the old world would be remembered.

Thomson argues that we should not lament the passing of that old world because of its terrible hardships, and asks whether poverty was the reason why it survived so long. A harsh nature, infertile land, small fishing boats, the paying of rent to landlords all made the islanders' lives difficult. He points out that 'unless there was a lot of wealth going to a few people, there would be no accumulation of money', and that was the *sine qua non* of the industrial revolution: '[a]s long as mechanized industry was being established in the cities, the poverty of the countryside was a historic necessity'.[16] In the Middle Ages, Thomson recounts, international trade and the circulation of money declined, money falling out of circulation in many rural areas, such as the Irish-speaking parts of Ireland. Thus, to describe the life of the Blaskets as medieval was simply to say that it took no part in the great developments that have happened in Western Europe since the Middle Ages. The Blaskets had monetary connections with the outside world, paying rent to landlords, buying goods from shopkeepers in Dingle and receiving remittances from relations in America. But within the island, the only money that circulated was for dowries. Money did not influence the islanders' relationships with one another since '[t]here was neither master nor servant among them'. They were bound to each other by kinship and marriage ties, lived within a short distance of each other, 'every man of them a Jack-of-all-trades, while they hunted and fished in co-operation . . .' All strangers who visited were treated equally. 'They did not think any less of [a stranger] for being poor, nor think more of him for being rich'. If they were to praise him, they described him as 'noble and humble (*uasal agus íseal*)'.

The socio-economic processes which destroyed the Blasket community were doing the same all over the world, according to Thomson. Those who would control it were the 'the poor simple people in every country who are both backward and cultured as were the people of the Blaskets'. And when they would be in control, 'backwardness will be completely ended and civilization will leap ahead'.[17] He tried to make his own contribution to that in Ireland. Concerned at the decline of Irish-speaking districts, he argued that they could only be saved by giving employment to their inhabitants. In Galway (where he taught Greek through Irish in the university from 1931 to 1934 and translated Greek works into Irish), he organized extramural lectures for Gaeltacht people on topics that concerned their culture and daily life, but received no support from the College authorities. He admitted many years later that his efforts to save 'the culture of the Irish-speaking peasantry' were unsuccessful because 'you cannot raise the cultural standards of a people without raising their economic standards . . .'[18]

Ironically, the Irish state was built on the symbolic values of a 'deep' Ireland located in the Gaelic western fringes but the physical struggle to achieve that state was won elsewhere. In the War of Independence the most active areas were neither the traditional agrarian west nor the rich eastern counties. Cavan and the province of Munster, excluding its most westerly and Irish-speaking county, Kerry, were the most active, in regions where farms were above subsistence level, towns were well developed and a stratum of strong farmers existed, as Tom Garvin shows. Munster was a core area, in contributions to the Gaelic League and in origins of the revolutionary leadership from 1900 to 1923.[19] The Gaeltacht was an atypical part of Ireland. The region most remote from Dublin and metropolitan culture, cultural elements survived there which had disappeared from other parts of the country: the Irish language, heroic tales and lays, timber-framed canvas-covered boats (*currachaí* or *naomhóga*), traditional costume (as in the Aran Islands). The land was by and large extremely limited in potential use, a high proportion of it consisting of hills, mountains and bog. Irish-speaking districts were characterized by subsistence farming and were incapable of sustaining a significant population of farm labourers. The idealization of a region with very limited social stratification as a model for the nation helped to elide the social divisions that were very clear elsewhere in the country.

Ó Cadhain's Critique of Folklore Studies

Another intellectual who appreciated the culture of the Gaeltacht but insisted on situating it within the contemporary social and political reality was Máirtín Ó Cadhain (1905–1970), the most important prose writer in Irish in the twentieth century. He was born into a family of storytellers in Connemara. 'I was squeezed from the world of folklore, a world that changed little in a thousand years'. Trained as a teacher in Dublin, qualifying in 1926, he was soon teaching at home in Connemara. In 1930, he was one of three teachers who, in response to the Department of Education's offer of a 10 per cent raise in recognition of the special status of the Gaeltacht, replied that the money should be given to the people of the Gaeltacht. Around the same time, he was active in groupings formed to further the interests of the Gaeltacht, Cumann na Gaeltachta, which campaigned to reclaim the lakes from the private ownership of landlords, and Muintir na Gaeltachta, which lobbied the government to grant some of the rich lands acquired from land-lords in Co. Meath to Gaeltacht people. This successful campaign led to the settlement of Irish-speakers from Connemara in Rathcarn.

Ó Cadhain was active in the Gaelic League and joined the Irish Republican Army 'to liberate my people, the rural poor'. His links with the IRA cost him his job in 1936, after which he moved to Dublin. There he wrote, organized and taught for the Gaelic League, was recruiting officer for the IRA and a member of its Army Council. Arrested in 1939, he was imprisoned for a brief period. In 1940, he gave the oration at a Republican funeral and was interned without trial until July 1944 in the Curragh. There he taught Irish, read (in many languages), wrote, translated the *Red Flag* and the *Internationale* into Irish and gave lectures on social philosophy, on the radical political thinker and land reformer James Fintan Lalor (1807–1849), on the socialist thinker and revolutionary James Connolly (1868–1916) 'and perhaps a little of Marx'. But in a debate he opposed the motion 'That communism is the only form of government that guarantees social justice', asserting that '[a]s a matter of fact Stalin is the world's greatest capitalist, and Russia – the first attempt at Communism – the greatest slave state of history!' After a number of casual and poorly paid labouring jobs, he secured a post as a translator in the civil service in 1947, representations having been made on his behalf to de Valera, pointing out the benefit to the cause of the Irish language. In 1956 he was appointed lecturer in Irish in Trinity College Dublin and became Professor of Irish there in 1969.[20]

His political commitment, particularly to the language and to the Gaeltacht, was a constant in his life, and helps to explain his lack of sympathy with any sort of Gaelic and folkloristic scholasticism that offered nothing to Gaeltacht people. A lecture he gave in 1949, 'Why is literature in Irish not growing?' ('*Tuige nach bhfuil Litríocht na Gaeilge ag Fás?*'), was a caustic critique of scholars' attitudes to the language and to the Gaeltacht.

> The University, the Institute* and the Folklorists would love if there were
> nine or ten more dialects to be messing around with. They would be
> delighted if there were no one in the Gaeltacht able to write or read, or
> they were only able to read and write English. That would leave their
> sounds, their words, their grammar, their folklore as pure as is so dear to
> scholarship . . . The Irish language does not belong to cranks [*cantalóirí*],
> nor to professors nor to the Gaeltacht. It belongs to the people [*cine*]. It is
> as the language of a people [*teanga chine*], and not as the language of
> professors or of a couple of remote districts that it is destined to live.[21]

As an eight-year old, he tried to write down a Fenian tale. He published a
list of proverbs in the newspaper *An Stoc* in 1928. Among other folklore
items, he published stories about saints collected from his father and mother
in *Béaloideas* in 1930, and other collections in the same journal in 1933, 1935
and 1936. Indeed it was mostly folklore he published until 1938.[22] Folklore
had a great influence on his imagination, as in his description of a journey to
the Soviet Union in 1959.

> I went east to Kirghizia, a Soviet republic in central Asia . . . I was think-
> ing of the folktales of my youth. This was the Eastern World. This was my
> journey to the well at the world's end, going along under the belt of the
> jet! These horses each of which had the hammer and sickle on its
> haunches were the cavalry of the Emir of Bokhara, of the Golden Horde
> . . . They were also the slim brown steeds in the stories of my father and
> my grandfather . . .[23]

He gave a perceptive and characteristically truculent lecture on folklore
to Cumann na Scríbhneoirí (the Writers' Club) in 1950, its publication
causing a good deal of controversy.[24] It deserves to stand as an important
text on Irish folklore, deliberately provocative as it is. In it he recounted how
folklore was the only learning that most of his neighbours had and that he
knew many long folktales and other traditional lore before he knew English;
indeed his earliest memory was of listening to his grandfather telling stories
to an old neighbour.

> It was long after that that I understood that my grandfather was an 'active
> carrier of tradition' and that the neighbour was only a 'passive carrier'.
>   One day my grandfather was telling a story: a long story about 'the
> twelve sons of a King and a Queen'. Suddenly the 'passive carrier' thought
> he would break out as an 'active carrier'.
>   'It was not like that at all', he said, as he smiled in a satisfied way to
> himself; 'Indeed it was not. You are going astray . . . Wait a while now and
> I will tell you what the youngest son did . . .'

---

* The School of Celtic Studies in the Dublin Institute for Advanced Studies (founded in
1940).

'When the sons of valour are telling stories Let the sons of the hags be silent' [*Nuair a bhíos clann na gaisce ag inseacht scéil,/ Bíodh clann na gcailleach i sost a mbéil*], said the 'active carrier', fidgeting on the stool.

His ironic use of von Sydow's notions of 'active' and 'passive carrier of tradition' in English in the anecdote is indicative enough of an ironic stance towards folklore scholarship. Discussing what 'folklore' meant, he quoted the German folklorist Lutz Mackensen's advice to the folklorist 'to go out among the people and live the life of the peasants in the country, the fisherman on the shore, and the workmen of the towns', mischievously adding that Professor Ó Duilearga was known to sweep the kitchen in Kerry (a reference to the latter's account of the prelude to a storytelling evening in Seán Ó Conaill's house).

Probably every country in the world has its societies and journals of folklore, but in Ireland that is not enough, he contended. Whatever culture goes with the Irish language, and the language itself, are completely under its sway. 'To say it in another way, the cultivation of Irish is only a branch of folklore'. A biting passage refers to the Day of Judgement:

> There will be many folktales and much folklore on that day, every 'passive carrier of tradition' will be an 'active carrier', and Indo-European Man [a reference to the philology of Celticists] will be giving a full account of himself. I am certain that there will be as many stories of gods and stories of men [*an oiread déscéalaíochta agus daonscéalaíochta*] as will kill any folklorist, but it is likely that only one Ediphone will be allowed. Is the only thing that the Gaels of the twentieth century will be able to put on that Ediphone, that they collected a couple of million pages of folklore?

He explained how he understood folklore, that it is 'a constant thing', that it is being born before our eyes here in Dublin, in London, in New York', that new versions of old things are always appearing, that every urban trade has its own folklore. He excoriated the language movement's preoccupation with 'old' traditions: 'We are a people for whom every old thing is important – good or bad'.

> There is no craft but an old craft. There is no learning but the learning of old unlearned people.* It was almost all folklore in *An Lóchrann* and in *An Stoc*. Hence, it is now said that they were the two best Irish newspapers ever. The importance of the Gaeltacht is not that Irish can be learnt there. Nor that Irish can sprout out from there to the rest of the country. Little chance. There 'the old customs are practised'. It is there above all that folklore is. The Gaeltacht is only a branch of folklore.

Ó Cadhain questioned the usefulness of folklore again and again: 'Despite [Wolfe] Tone not having any folklore he brought two fleets to Ireland'. He

---

* Ó Duilearga had referred to Seán Ó Conaill as 'one of the best-read men in the unwritten literature of the people whom I have ever known' (see Chapter 5).

castigated folklorists 'because of the smell of winding sheets and open graves: because of the "death", "death hanging", "death in the sky", that is felt everywhere folklore and Gaelic learning are carried on". He traced this constant lament for the expiring Gaelic culture through Ó Duilearga, Robin Flower and Ernest Renan. As for Flower's wistful comments on the departure of the fairies from the Blaskets, Ó Cadhain retorted that so much dust had been raised building roads and new houses in his own district in the previous twenty years that few fairies could be left, and that electricity would get rid of the remainder! He quoted a newspaper account of an exhausted Irish-speaking youth who barely spoke English found wandering in the English town of Wigan and exclaimed: 'The end of the Middle Ages in Wigan, in South Boston, in the Bowery . . . Did these lamenters for the Middle Ages [*éagmaiseoirí na MeánAoiseanna*] ever open their small gentle mouths to advance this residue of the Middle Ages as a people?'. 'That is the sin that is crying out to God: the Delargian lament [*an t-olagón duileargúil*], the medieval dirge that is sucking every drop of hope from the people'. He argued that Connemara has changed more in his own time than in a thousand years. 'The Middle Ages have gone forever . . . It is Ireland's curse that not enough machinery is whirring around it . . .'*

Many of the barbs in the lecture are directed at Ó Duilearga's writings, and indeed folklorists in general are unjustly tarred by the Romantic-scouring brush he aims at him. Quoting Ó Duilearga's editorial in the first issue of *Béaloideas*, in which he argued that any future Gaelic literature which was not rooted in Gaelic literature and folklore would be worthless, Ó Cadhain asked how people wrote literature elsewhere in Europe without folklore. He argued that the importance of folklore lay in preserving that of it which remained as a 'live wire', transmitting 'the electricity of humanity through the complex of our mechanical lives', and thus 'active' people such as Æ and his like were more important than folklorists. He pointed out that everywhere in the Gaelic world, from the Hebrides to the Aran Islands, new verses were being composed, but that very little of these compositions got into print. 'More than any other aspect of folklore, of oral literature, this belongs completely to the people, and that is the secret of its perpetuity'. He found folklorists showing no interest in it. He admired the use that Yeats, Lady Gregory and Synge made of folklore. Of Yeats:

> Folklorists do not treat today of the folklore collecting he and Gregory did, nor of the collections he printed. He went fluttering from them to the ancient tales of the gods until he felt intuitively the bond between the two kinds, until he composed tales of the gods himself. He went fluttering to India and China, to mysterious oratories, and occult knowledge, and

---

* This is certainly a rejoinder to Séamus Ó Duilearga's 'wail of the factory horn, the whirring of machines – the unbroken net of the busy industrial world [that] has driven away and banished the old habits of living and of thinking' (see Chapter 5).

hidden philosophies of the Middle Ages. But he always returned to the forgotten legends of Knocknarea, to the bankrupt leprechauns of Lissadell, to the ragged fairies of the Burren, to embroider them in poetry, to coax their ancient secrets from them.

What he appreciated was the imaginative and creative use made of folklore. Living on in Yeats's art, it transcended the dead 'logarithms, paradigms and glosses' of the scholars.*

Gramsci, Hegemony and the Subaltern

Another intellectual who was 'squeezed out' of the world of folklore was the Sardinian Antonio Gramsci (1891–1937). Born into an impoverished family, he was a hunchback as the result of a childhood accident and as such the object of fear and persecution. His own background can help to explain the centrality he attached to the question of the impoverished South in Italian politics as well as 'the importance of understanding a backward, subordinate folk culture'.[25] Gramsci's interest in folklore can be traced to his background. His home district was 'riddled with witch-craft, spell-casting and belief in the supernatural'.

> The Gramsci children were reared to a knowledge of were-wolves, blood-sucking demons and other terrors of night-time. By day as well they learned the legendary Sard landscape and its archaic tongue, from older relatives or the itinerant story-tellers who passed through Sorgono and Ghilarza.

'The first adult ambition' of 'Antonu Su Gobbu' writes Tom Nairn, 'before he became the Italian revolutionary, Antonio Gramsci, was to rediscover this fabulous world, and justify it through scholarship'. Nairn argues that he is the most important Western Marxist.

> But it cannot be without some significance that he was also a product of the West's most remote periphery, and of conditions which, half a century later, it became fashionable to call 'Third World'. No comparable western

---

* Ó Cadhain was not the first writer to criticize the work of the folklorists. In 1939 the poet Patrick Kavanagh (1904–1967) published an article in the *Irish Times* under the heading 'Twenty-three tons of Accumulated Folk-Lore – Is it of any Use?'

> Folk-Lore collecting like its modern sister, mass-observation is an attempt by sentimental science to do without the poets who are now starving to death . . . Not only is this stuff culturally useless, it is definitely harmful. Let Dr Deleargy (*sic*) say what he may, this weighty collection is a rubbish heap that sooner or later will have to be destroyed . . . Supposing the money that is being spent – or should I say wasted? – on dead things was spent to keep cigarettes in the mouths of poets, there would be a hope that April might wake green beauty in Ireland's thought . . .

Kavanagh, like Ó Cadhain, showed the artist's disdain for the pedantry of the scholar, but also used the folk culture of his own background to enrich his writings. Ó Catháin and Uí Sheighin, *A Mhuintir Dhú Chaocháin, Labhraigí Feasta!*, p. xxii.

intellectual came from such a background. He was a barbed gift of the backwoods to the metropolis, and some aspects of his originality always reflected this distance.[26]

In 1911, as the winner of a scholarship, he began his studies in the University of Turin. He became an activist in the Italian Socialist Party around 1913 and began writing journalism for a socialist newspaper from 1914. He was elected to the central committee of the newly founded Italian Communist Party in 1921 while editor of *Ordine Nuovo*, one of the party dailies. In 1921 he went to Moscow, and later to Vienna, to work for the Comintern. Elected a deputy in the Italian Parliament in 1924, he returned to Italy. Despite his parliamentary immunity, he was arrested in 1926 and detained, first in prisons and, as his health deteriorated, in clinics. He was released conditionally, to hospital, in 1934 and died there in 1937, a few days after he was given unconditional release. From 1948 his *Prison Notebooks* began to be published, in a definitive edition in 1975, and have since been translated into many languages.[27]

Gramsci's writings on folklore, which he called by the borrowed word (*folclore*) are scanty. In his own words, he sought 'a more cautious and precise assessment of the forces acting in society', and the observations on folklore may be seen as a contribution towards that. He called for a critical analysis of popular culture because he argued that ideas could have the weight of a material force. He was both critical of popular ideology and at the same time felt solidarity with subaltern social classes. He wished to see a new culture arise among the people, which would bridge the divide between modern culture and folklore. In that sense folklore was incapable of bringing that situation about and had to be superseded. One of the key elements of his thought was the connection between the people and the intellectuals and specifically their negative relationship in the Italian context. In letters to his family he showed a deep interest in Sardinian dialect and folklore and often asked specific questions about local usage.[28]

We have a fascinating account of the events that followed the sending of a Sardinian brigade to crush the striking workers of Turin in 1917. The socialists decided to circulate a leaflet among the soldiers asking them to support the workers. Gramsci rejected the first three drafts of the leaflet, but accepted the fourth with some changes. He advised against the use of the words 'brothers' and 'class' because, for Sardinian peasants, Turin workers were *signori* and not brothers, and a 'class' was only known from school. He suggested referring to 'rich' and 'poor' because the 'rich' forced shepherds

---

* Cf. the French law of 1849 on the press portrayed popular literature as dividing society into two classes, the rich – represented as tyrants – and the poor – as victims – and thus exciting envy and hatred. The first study of French popular literature was at the instigation of the minister of the police: Paul Nisard's *Histoire des livres populaires et de la littérature de colportage* (1854). See de Certeau, Julia and Revel, 'La beauté du mort', pp. 45–46, 51–52.

and miners in Sardinia and workers in Turin to work.* It was essential to make the soldiers know this because their officers had told them that these 'signori' – the Turin workers – were striking and manning barricades to betray the soldiers fighting at the front. They had to be informed that these workers were striking because they had no bread and wanted an end to the war, just what the shepherds and miners of Sardinia wanted. The leaflet, in Italian and in Sardinian (translated by Gramsci), was circulated in the soldiers' barracks. Through Sardinian workers, contact was made with the soldiers and at a meeting the latter were surprised to find a Sardinian 'professor' defending the workers. Many of these Sardinian soldiers returned to Turin as workers after the war.[29]

For Gramsci the basic problem of hegemony was not *how* a new group came to power, but how they came to be accepted, not just as rulers, but as guides that most people looked up to, exercising a moral leadership. By hegemony, Gramsci does not mean dominance as such, but rather the leadership which a particular group, a social class or a part of it, exercises in society through the winning of influence over other groups. Before gaining state power, before which hegemony cannot be completely achieved, the group must be able to give intellectual and moral leadership, and hegemony rests primarily on that. A hegemonic group, in other words, is hegemonic because it has gained the consent of other groups to its leadership of society. It may use coercion as a last resort in order to maintain its dominant position, though the more coercion there is the less the hegemony. The term subaltern is used to refer to the groups who are not hegemonic, and means lacking in autonomy, being subject to the hegemony of another group.[30] The nature of hegemony presupposes that the ruling group in society has taken account of the interests of the other groups. It has been argued that the strongest element in hegemony is the ruling group's ability to go beyond its own narrow and selfish interests. Its strategy is to ensure that its own interests can become the interests of other groups as well so that the whole of society, the whole nation, seems to share a common purpose. In other words it 'universalizes' its own interests.

Hegemony can present itself as an interchange of services between different social classes. Néstor García Canclini argues that if the people are not to be seen as a submissive mass it must be admitted that their dependence is due in part to the fact that some of their needs are able to be fulfilled through 'hegemonic action'. He gives the example of peasant and indigenous migrants to the cities of Latin America whose local culture (language, customs and beliefs) does not help them to accommodate to urban life. From mass culture they get the necessary information to function in the city. Thus television, which in one way can be seen as an agent of hegemony, in another way is a 'manual of urbanity', which 'indicates how to dress, eat and express one's feelings in the city'.[31]

Hegemony is won through a politics of alliances with other groups, that must open up a national perspective to the whole of society. So a hegemonic class manages to combine a national perspective with its own class interests so as to achieve national leadership. This is what Gramsci means by the concept of 'national-popular'. It does not refer to any specific cultural content. Creating a national-popular culture 'would mean confronting and overcoming the same obstacles (dialects, folklore, local particularisms) as the formation of a national language'. It would not mean imposing the first term on the second in the series of oppositions he establishes in his writings between language and dialects, between philosophy and common sense (or folklore), between high culture and popular culture, intellectuals and people, party and masses. Rather it would mean 'to construct an educative alliance between them' since hegemony involves an educational relationship.[32] What distinguishes the bourgeoisie from previous ruling classes is that it is not closed, unlike the aristocracy, to which entry was possible only by birth. Instead it represents itself as being in continuous expansion and capable of absorbing the entire society. Hegemony then has cultural, political and economic implications and is not to be understood simply as a particular dominant social class using the state for its own interests; indeed it can be said that 'all domination is strengthened insofar as it ceases to be so by converting itself into hegemony'.[33]

Gramsci sees two realms within the state, political society, which is the state apparatus of administration, law, services, and so forth, and civil society. This latter consists of all those organizations that are usually called private, from political parties, trade unions and the media to religious and cultural organizations. Civil society is crucial for the concept of hegemony. It is the voluntary sector of society, the realm of consent, whereas political society is that of coercion and intervention, most visible through the role of the police and armed forces. The modern state he defines as 'hegemony armoured by coercion', and he dates it from around 1870, with the beginning of the organization of the masses into politics for the first time. The state needs the consent of the governed in order to function properly, but it educates that consent. The culture of the popular classes was of concern because 'the constitution of a whole new social order around capital required a more or less continuous, if intermittent, process of re-education'.[34] In this sense the school has a positive educational function and the courts a repressive and negative educational function. He points out that the state has its own conception of life and the duty of spreading it 'by educating the national masses'. Thus it 'competes with and contradicts other implicit and explicit conceptions', of which folklore is one, and it must be 'overcome'. Referring to the proposition that folklore should be taught in teacher training schools, he insists that for the teacher to know folklore 'means to know what other conceptions of the world and life are actually active in the intellectual and moral formation of young people, in order to uproot them and replace them with conceptions which are deemed to be superior'. Indeed this has already been the case, folklore being 'under systematic bombardment, from the elementary schools to . . . the chairs of agriculture'. Folklore should not be considered 'an eccentricity, an oddity or a picturesque element', but should be taken very seriously.

> Only in this way will the teaching of folklore be more efficient and really bring about the birth of a new culture among the broad popular masses, so that the separation between modern culture and popular culture of folklore will disappear. An activity of this kind, thoroughly carried out, would correspond on the intellectual plane to what the Reformation was in Protestant countries.[35]

Gramsci received permission to write in prison in January 1929 and began work on the first Notebook in February. The plan of work lists sixteen 'principal arguments', of which 'The concept of folklore' is the seventh.[36] The key passage in which he defines folklore is complex, and deserves to be quoted in full.

> Folklore should . . . be studied as a 'conception of the world and life' implicit to a large extent in determinate (in time and space) strata of society and in opposition (also for the most part implicit, mechanical and objective) to 'official' conceptions of the world (or in a broader sense, the conceptions of the cultured parts of historically determinate societies) that have succeeded one another in the historical process. (Hence the strict relationship between folklore and 'common sense', which is philosophical folklore.) This conception of the world is not elaborated and systematic because, by definition, the people (the sum total of the instrumental and subaltern classes of every form of society that has so far existed) cannot possess conceptions which are elaborated, systematic and politically organized and centralized in their albeit contradictory development. It is, rather, many-sided – not only because it includes different and juxtaposed elements, but also because it is stratified, from the more crude to the less crude – if, indeed, one should not speak of a confused agglomerate of fragments of all the conceptions of the world and of life that have succeeded one another in history. In fact, it is only in folklore that one finds surviving evidence, adulterated and mutilated, of the majority of these conceptions.

At first glance Gramsci's references to folklore seem undoubtedly negative. Alberto Cirese has given a close reading of Gramsci's text, which is the basis for the following discussion.[37] First of all, Gramsci contextualizes folklore 'in the framework of a nation and its culture', but opposed to official conceptions of the world. As a conception of the world and life, it is characteristic of certain strata of society, namely the 'people', who may be understood as 'all the subaltern and instrumental classes in every society that has existed up to now', and hence a heterogeneous group. Folklore must be understood as a reflection of the conditions of their cultural life. Cirese outlines Gramsci's fundamental proposition in the following terms:

> Folkloric conception is to official
> as subaltern social class is to hegemonic
> as simple intellectual category is to cultured
> as unorganic combination is to organic
> as fragmentary internal organization is to unitary
> as implicit mode of expression is to explicit
> as debased content is to original
> as mechanical opposition is to intentional
> as passive conflict is to active.

This list of negative qualities, he argues, comes 'by deduction from the very concept of "people"' since, as Gramsci writes, 'the people . . . *cannot* possess elaborated and systematic conceptions which . . . are politically organized and centralized'. Cirese adds that '[e]laboration, systematicness and centralization are in fact expressions of hegemony (even if not only of hegemony), which is precisely what those classes which are still subaltern lack'.

He finds a certain tension here, but references to folklore in other of Gramsci's writings moderate some of the above. Speaking of 'popular morality', Gramsci notes a particular tenacity in its conceptions, stronger and more effective than those of 'official morality'. And they are not necessarily the *'gesunkenes Kulturgut'* of the official culture which he elsewhere suggests. Indeed he speaks of

> that mass of beliefs and opinions on the subject of one's "own" rights which are in continual circulation amongst the popular masses, and are for ever being reviewed under the pressure of the real conditions of life and the spontaneous comparison between the ways in which the various classes live.

Some, 'the fossilized reflections of the conditions of days gone by', are conservative and reactionary, but others consist of

> often creative and progressive innovations, spontaneously determined by the forms and conditions of life as it is developing, which go against, or merely differ from, the morality of the ruling strata of society.

This points to the oppositional value of folklore, and, as Cirese says, 'the way is opened to a recognition of its ability both to produce its own autonomous culture and to select products handed down from above for its own, opposing, ends'. Hence folklore can provide a spontaneous form of 'the spirit of cleavage', which Gramsci elsewhere defines as the progressive acquisition of a class instinct. Gramsci tends to establish 'a constant relationship between cultural phenomena and the social groups by which they are conveyed'. His notion of spontaneous conceptions of the world is backed up again and again by reference to concrete social situations.

Thus he points out that everyone is automatically involved in a social group or groups, and that 'in acquiring one's conception of the world one always belongs to a particular grouping which is that of all the social elements which share the same mode of thinking and acting'. This grouping may consist only of dispersed and isolated individuals or a concrete social group: one's village, for example. The conception of the world that is dominant there may be heterogeneous in origin, but is born from a cultural activity which is socially internal to the group. He notes 'the frequent affirmation made by Marx on the "solidity of popular beliefs" as a necessary element of a specific situation', and compares them to 'material forces'. What he calls 'spontaneous philosophy', or 'common or popular philosophy', he sees as being proper to everyone. It is in language and in folklore since 'even in the slightest manifestation of any intellectual activity whatever . . . there is contained a specific conception of the world'.

The observations on folklore are few in Gramsci's writings, but much of his work has implications for popular culture in general. Hegemony is the key concept, so that hegemonic culture and subaltern cultures are inescapable notions in studying culture within the state. The notion of subaltern denies the autonomy of the 'folk', thus standing firmly against the Romantic notion, and sees it as the product of a historical process, firmly within the framework of the state and in an unavoidable relationship with a hegemonic culture. And folklore cannot be understood outside of this context. The notion of the subaltern, too, is larger than the folk, because the Romantic notion referred to the peasantry only. Folklore, then, in Gramsci's formulation, is part of the culture of subaltern groups. They may be very different from one another, and their culture is very heterogeneous in origin, consisting of elements generated from within the group as well as elements borrowed from hegemonic groups, but what all these groups have in common is that they do not exercise hegemony. Thus the 'popular' does not reside in any inherent quality: it is a question of position.

Gramsci's work has influenced many scholars working on folklore and popular culture. In particular we mention Ernesto de Martino, Alberto Cirese and Luigi M. Lombardi Satriani. Lombardi Satriani has defined folklore as part of a mental heritage that is stable, collective and specific to the under-privileged, and 'hence culturally subaltern', classes of a society.[38] In folklore, he identifies four levels of challenge to the dominant culture. The first is immediate challenge with implicit or explicit rebellion against the status quo: here he gives the example of folk songs which make a clear opposition, pre-political though it may be, between rich and poor, lords and commons, strong and weak. The second is immediate challenge with implicit or explicit acceptance of the status quo: here he finds a text, for example, where the division between rich and poor is pointed out, but it leads back to God and the inevitability of poverty. The third is implicit challenge ('or by position'): here are phenomena – such as beliefs, practices and artefacts – which, by their otherness and their very presence, are an implicit opposition to the dominant order. In the last level, acceptance of the hegemonic culture, he finds three categories. The first are hegemonic cultural phenomena shared with popular culture – examples being the oppression of women or the notion that authority is necessary. The second are products of the hegemonic culture successively passed on to popular culture – such as some of the peasant material culture of the South of Italy which derives from that of the bourgeoisie of the end of the nineteenth century. The third are products of the hegemonic culture elaborated for and imposed on popular culture. He finds here a huge field since it includes much of the products of industrial society, such as popular prints, clothing and furniture. He also identifies various themes in folklore which fulfill 'anaesthetizing functions' (*funzione narcotizzante*): the necessity of contenting oneself with one's lot; the need to have patience; fatalism; the necessity of authority; ignorance being better than knowledge; the merits of being attached to one's own district. He gives various examples from Italian folklore.[39]

García Canclini finds Lombardi Satriani's analysis too extreme, arguing that '"anaesthetizing" or "challenging" qualities are too easily attributed to cultural phenomena that are neither one nor the other, but a combination of experiences and representations whose ambiguities correspond to the unresolved nature of contradictions among popular sectors'. He contends that Lombardi Satriani treats domination and challenge 'as if we are dealing with two phenomena foreign to each other, whose existence came before both cultures became part of a single social system'.[40] His point, argued elsewhere, is that the key issue is not whether folklore survives, disappears or is dominated by the hegemonic culture, but how it interacts with it. As an example he argues that

> often, the only alternatives created by the subaltern sectors are magical techniques, through which they try to control 'risk' and domination. Since socio-economic backwardness, hunger, unemployment, the lack of medical assistance, etc., make them live in 'permanent risk', popular groups tend to dehistoricize reality in order to exorcize risk.[41]

He points to the popular need 'to hold history, to repeat security even though this creates a process of exploitation and domination'. Hence 'the overcoming of the most critical situations (serious illnesses, death, catastrophes, etc.) is obtained through the dehistoricization of their processes', through the use of magical techniques. He refers to De Martino's observation that the continuity of subaltern traditions can perpetuate domination.[42] Paulo Freire in Brazil came to similar conclusions about subaltern groups and their 'quasi-adherence' to objective reality. If the explanation for adversity 'lies in a superior power, or in men's own "natural" incapacity, it is obvious that their action will not be orientated towards transforming reality, but towards those superior beings responsible for the problematical situation, or towards that presumed incapacity'. The response, therefore, will be magico-religious.[43]

Research on the folktale (*Märchen*) has considered many of these issues. As an art form its origins are very ancient. The common people always cultivated it. In it they expressed the manner in which they understood the social order as well as their needs and aspirations, 'either affirming the dominant social values and norms or revealing the necessity to change them'. In this way, the folktale adapted to changes in the social order. When written down in the eighteenth and nineteenth centuries, it still retained many archaic features but by and large reflected late feudal conditions. Jack Zipes argues that the folktales recorded by the Grimm brothers deal with 'exploitation, hunger and injustice familiar to the lower classes in pre-capitalist societies'. The magic in the stories reflects their wish to change the world. Looking at a number of the Grimms' tales, he finds the initial situation characterized by its apparent hopelessness.

This hopelessness derives from the objective social circumstances of the agrarian lower classes. They were isolated in their work and in their abode and able to resist growing exploitation only imaginatively, through the utopian solution of the folktale.

> As pre-capitalist art form, the folk tale presents, in its partiality for everything metallic and mineral, a set and solid, imperishable world. This imperishable world can be linked to concepts of medieval patriarchalism, monarchy and absolutism . . . The world of the folktale is inhabited largely by kings, queens, princes, princesses, soldiers, peasants, animals and supernatural creatures, rarely by members of the bourgeoisie. Nor are there machines nor signs of industrialization. In other words, the main characters and concerns of a monarchistic and feudal society are presented, and the focus is on class struggle and competition for power among the aristocrats themselves and between the peasantry and aristocracy. Hence the central theme of all folk tales: 'might makes right' . . . .. There is no mention of another world. Only one side of characters and living conditions is described. Everything is *confined to a realm without morals*, where class and power determine social relations. Hence, the magic and miraculous serve to rupture the feudal confines and represent metaphorically the conscious and unconscious desires of the lower classes.[44]

It is not difficult to see why the folktale should continue to be a living art form in those regions in which market relations and literacy were weakest. We know from the historical evidence that it was not these regions that were to the forefront of political struggles. Those who lived in the world of folklore were least able to confront the objective political and socio-economic conditions that repressed them. On the other hand, the short humorous tales (*Schwank-Märchen*) of the urban working classes at the dawn of the capitalist era are much more optimistic in tone, dealing with active journeymen and workers who are able to make up for their weakness through resourcefulness and wit.

Popular Culture between Populism and 'Miserabilism'

The exclusion of sections of the population from full participation in national life, through poverty, unemployment, homelessness, emigration and illiteracy troubled George Thomson, and others. Ó Cadhain was aware of the official idealization of the Gaeltacht on the one hand and the official inability to do anything significant about its socio-economic problems on the other. He saw only too well the similarity between folklore and populism. The opposing perspectives of Séamus Ó Duilearga and Ó Cadhain reveal a fault line in the approach to popular culture which has appeared almost everywhere that an interest in the popular has been cultivated. Claude Grignon and Jean-Claude Passeron see the debate on popular culture departing from a 'class ethnocentrism', which is 'a spontaneous practice of description which precedes every scientific enterprise of analysing a society or a culture'. The first break with this attitude is towards cultural relativism. This 'credits popular cultures with the right to have their own meaning' but, in contradistinction to the study of distant or past cultures, it has to artificially attribute autonomy to them, since 'it must . . . treat dominated cultures as if they were not so'. The second break questions this autonomy and refuses to ignore the relationships of force and the unequal interaction between the social classes of the same society which are part of a 'legitimate cultural order' in a class society. The debate, thus, oscillates between a populism based on the autonomy of popular culture and a '*misérabilisme*' which sees popular culture as inescapably slotted into a legitimate social order. Where 'the populist marvels at discovering the symbolic treasures in a popular culture . . . the bourgeois like the *misérabiliste* sees only penury . . .'[45]

Renato Ortiz sees the two poles of the debate in similar terms. If popular is considered synonymous with the people, then there is an 'intimate association between popular culture and the national question . . .' that transcends 'the restrictive inflection of class', which is the other way of seeing the popular. This latter perspective contrasts popular culture with that of the elite and attributes 'to its concrete manifestations the potential to construct a new society'.[46] Antonio Augusto Arantes sees the two perspectives in terms of a denial that popular forms contain any kind of knowledge on the one hand and an assertion of the role of popular culture in resisting class domination on the other.

> The first [perspective] refers in general to aspects of technology (work techniques, healing procedures, etc.) and of 'knowledge' of the universe, while the second emphasizes artistic forms of expression (oral literature,

> music, theatre, etc.); the one tends to think in terms of events in the past, as something which was or soon will be replaced; and the other thinks of them in the future, glimpsing in them the signs of a new social order . . .[47]

This is a form of the distinction between a more prosaic 'folklife' and a more poetic, and symbolically richer, 'folklore'.

García Canclini calls the proponents of the two approaches the inductivists and the deductivists. He places their origins in different disciplinary and ideological positions, the inductivist in culturalist North American anthropology and in populism, the deductivist in sociology, communications studies and education and with a strong Marxist flavour.[48] The inductivists' point of departure is the intrinsic nature of those properties supposedly pertaining to the popular classes, their genius, the creativity that other sectors have lost, their resistance. The deductivists define popular culture 'from the general to the particular', in terms of mode of production, dominant class, ideological apparatus, imperialism, and so forth. He argues that, from the 1960s and 1970s, many writers have analysed popular culture in terms of 'manoeuvres of domination', and have attributed to social agents such as the media a monopoly of power, and have over-estimated the influence of the dominant sectors on popular culture. He points out that for decades folklore and anthropology were the only disciplines dedicated to the study of the popular and, because of their restricted object of study, they identified it with the traditional, the peasant or the indigenous. Their studies,

> very sensitive to the specificity of every group, tend to mark the *difference* without explaining the *inequality* which confronts them and links them to other sectors. They intend to dissimulate the distances between unequal cultures with the doctrine of cultural relativism, affirming that all are valuable in their own way.

Referring to Latin America, he contends that this 'relativist pseudo-egalitarianism' was used in indigenist politics, which, ostensibly preserving the traditions of indigenous groups, in reality institutionalized their marginalization. He argues that folklore goes further than anthropology in its 'traditionalism':

> Not only does it limit the popular to peasant and indigenous manifestations, but it also reduces research – except in Gramscian writers and in a few others – to the collection of objects and the description of their formal values. Therefore the majority of the texts on craftwork, festivals and traditional music catalogue and exalt popular products without situating them in the logic present in social relations. They limit themselves . . . to listing and classifying those pieces . . . which stand out by their resistance or indifference to change.

This conception of the popular has been influential in universities, state institutions such as museums and in the mass media. It appears in folk music and dance troupes, 'showing the product and hiding the social process which engendered it, selecting that which is most adaptable to the "Western" aesthetic and eliminating the signs of poverty or of conflicts which gave rise to the songs and the dances'.[49]

The notion of folklore was predicated on the recognition of cultural difference: folklore belonged to the 'others'. Even when the premises of folklore scholarship were to be questioned, particularly in the 1960s, the emphasis on marginality remained, though re-politicized. Of the change in orientation of North American folkloristics at that time, Roger D. Abrahams points out a particular emphasis on studying subaltern groups such as Blacks and Hispanics.[50] Lombardi Satriani's writings in the 1960s on folklore as a 'culture of challenge' were influential, as he recently reflected, in part because of the presence of a new sub-culture of politicized youth at the time.[51] If folklore is only subaltern culture, then folklorists avoid studying the culture of hegemonic groups. After all, the specializations of the humanities and the social sciences have always been devoted to that. The problem is that from the second half of the twentieth century, there has been a de-linking of social class and form of culture. There are subaltern and hegemonic groups, but is there a subaltern or hegemonic culture? After all, the same culture industries serve all social groups and, to a significant extent, members of all social groups consume some of the same cultural products: Irish traditional music and rock and roll, soap operas and Hollywood blockbusters, televised sporting events, romantic and detective novels, pornography. The next chapter will discuss, among other questions, the coming together of folk, popular and elite culture in the culture industries and will consider how social differences are reproduced through different ways of consuming them.

7. From Folklore to Popular Culture … and Beyond?

The concept of folklore came to terms with the social conditions that were irrevocably transforming it with difficulty. Associated with a mode of exis-tence radically different from that of the city, it seemed to imply more than isolation and backwardness; it also implied independence. 'Oral' and 'tradi-tional', it was implicitly or explicitly opposed to the world of reading and writing. But in fact the growing proximity to each other of the 'oral' and the 'literary' is a feature of the development of all modern societies. A stratum of popular culture that has its origins in learned culture has existed in Europe for centuries. It can be traced to classical or Biblical sources and to medieval and early modern science, literature and theology. The three great religions long established in Europe rest on scriptures and the mediation of literate groups. From the city Christianity had spread out to the recalcitrant countryside (*pagus* in Latin, whence *paganus*, a pagan). The influences on popular culture from outside greatly increased with the rise of capitalism, industrial society and the growth of literacy. It was in this context that the notion of 'folklore' appeared, retreating before the commercialization and mechanization of agriculture, the centripetal force of the industrial cities, the building of roads and railways, the extension of education. A 'literature of confutation' had long inventoried popular errors, but increased literacy made new 'errors' accessible to the people, as a market reached through the medium of a popular literature, and hence a new cause for official concern. Literacy meant the ability to read the Bible, but also *The Rights of Man* and chapbook fiction.

The decline of the peasantry in industrial capitalism motivated folklore studies during the nineteenth century. The intensification of that in the second half of the twentieth century* without a doubt problematized the field of folklore studies, but in the same way the growth of a tertiary sector

---

* The following figures are for agrarian employment as a percentage of the economically active population in select countries *c.* 1990 and on the eve of the Second World War (in brackets): Belgium 2 per cent (17 per cent); France 5 per cent (36 per cent); Germany

and the decline of the industrial proletariat has from the 1960s made a specifically class-based urban popular culture an elusive object.* The gradual breakdown of the congruence between social class and culture in the second half of the twentieth century made previously unquestioned notions of 'high', 'folk', 'popular', and 'mass' culture problematical since they no longer corresponded to specific social sectors.[1] The intense cultural circulation of today makes the notion of the folk untenable and suggests either a backdating of the notion of folklore to cultural elements specific to the peasantry at a time when that was possible, or a reinterpretation of the term. Indeed since the Second World War and in particular since the 1960s, the growing contradictions within these earlier notions of folklore and popular culture have led to much soul-searching among scholars and to new research orientations.

From Folk to Masses

The relationship between folklore and popular literature is part of a wider relationship between a residual agrarian world and its partial reconstitution in a modern state. The second half of the nineteenth century heralded a period of immense social change in much of Europe and North America, which was to continue and to intensify in the twentieth century. The modernization of agriculture, the concomitant destruction of the traditional agrarian world, industrialization and urbanization – through internal and international migration – happened on an unprecedented scale. Millions of ordinary people could no longer be defined within a traditional social structure and they began to participate in politics for the first time. The changing relationship between the two 'ordering systems' which have co-ordinated everyday life in the modern era – agrarian popular culture in late feudal society and urban popular culture in the age of industrial capitalism – did not simply involve the replacement of the former by the latter. Rather a complex of 'synchronisms, overlappings, and transformation processes' developed,

---

3 per cent BRD and 10 per cent DDR (26 per cent); Netherlands 4 per cent (21 per cent); Sweden 3 per cent (29 per cent); United Kingdom 2 per cent (6 per cent); Finland 8 per cent (57 per cent); Ireland 13 per cent (48 per cent); Portugal 17 per cent (49 per cent). See Göran Therborn, *European Modernity and Beyond. The Trajectory of European Societies 1945–2000* (London, Thousand Oaks and New Delhi 1995), pp. 66–7.

* For example, the following figures give the percentages of the population in selected European countries working in industry in 1987 and in 1960 (in brackets): Belgium 25.8 per cent (46.7 per cent); France 27.2 per cent (39 per cent); Germany 38.9 per cent (47.6 per cent); Netherlands 23.6 per cent (42.7 per cent); Sweden 29.1 per cent (43.9 per cent); United Kingdom 26.7 per cent (47.6 per cent). The trend was masked in some countries by late industrialization: Finland 31 per cent (31.5 per cent); Ireland 27.1 per cent (23.1 per cent); Portugal 31.3 per cent (27.8 per cent). See Emmanuel Todd, *L'Invention de l'Europe*, new edition (Paris: Seuil, 1996), pp. 561–8 ('La fin du prolétariat').

which, in Wolfgang Kaschuba's words, 'served to create a complicated amalgam, an interlacing and juxtaposition of elements from popular culture and workers' culture in the nineteenth century'.[2] Maurice Goldring has reminded us that in the city we can learn what became of the peasants, whose 'culture has been filtered in a new way of life', and he argues that it is in the cities 'that one can find the values and the mentalities that the weight of a peasant civilization has imprinted on modern Ireland.[3] Stuart Hall has argued that the starting point for the study of the basis of popular culture and of the transformations it underwent must be the 'more or less continuous struggle over the culture of working people, the labouring classes and the poor' during this period of transition.[4]

The old negative view of the common people was renewed by bourgeois fears of the destabilization of the social order through urbanization, industrialization and democratization. With the decline of rural life, the popular classes of the city became more frightening than those of the countryside. Fear of the city and reverence for the countryside, disdain for urban popular culture and an interest in folklore – two sides of the same coin – were then validated by Romantic ideas. Foreign observers had already noticed the levelling of the population in North America, since the eighteenth century in speech, and the nineteenth century in clothing. They found it difficult to discern differences in status, class or ethnic origin by the outward appearance or behaviour of the individual, as opposed to the obvious hierarchies and distinctions of European society.[5] The urban industrial population of the nineteenth century came to be defined through the notion of social class. In the context of social levelling, the notion of 'mass society' appeared, and the United States became the first such society.

A democracy of the masses was a democracy of the lowest common denominator, leading to an averaging-out of culture, inevitably downwards, and, in accordance with this pessimistic prognosis, mass-produced culture was to be attacked from the Left and from the Right. 'Masses' has been both a derogatory term in conservative thought and a positive term in socialist thought. By the sixteenth century, 'vulgar' (from Latin *vulgus*, presumably a cognate of *folk*) had lost the more positive connotations evident in *Vulgate* (from *vulgare*, to make public). In the sixteenth and seventeenth centuries, 'multitude' had the same derogatory connotation. It was to be replaced by 'mob' (an abbreviation of *mobile vulgus,* the unstable crowd) in the eighteenth century. 'Mob' in turn came to specify an undisciplined crowd in the early nineteenth century while 'masses' was taken up to refer to the general 'common people', a usage given a special impetus at the time of the French Revolution. 'Masses', then, Raymond Williams shows to have two different connotations, as 'the modern word *for many-headed multitude* or *mob*: low, ignorant, unstable', and as 'a description of the same people but now seen as a positive or potentially positive social force'.[6]

The closing decades of the nineteenth century saw a new scholarly interest in crowds and especially in their delinquency. Criminal anthropology, which developed an interest in folklore, was largely Italian in its origins. Cesare Lombroso, one of its founders, wrote of how he had solved the problem of the nature and origin of the criminal, concluding that 'the characteristics of primitive men and inferior animals seemed to be reproduced in our era'. Crowd psychology was pioneered by three conflicting claimants, Scipio Sighele (*La folla delinquente*, 1891), Henry Fournial (*Essai sur la psychologie des foules*, 1892) and Gustave Le Bon (*Psychologie des foules*, 1895). Le Bon, whose work was the most influential of the three, saw the crowd as akin to an inferior form of evolution – which he compared to the savage, the woman and the child. He considered the crowd to be distinguished by impulsiveness, irrationality and a mental unity, to the extent that it was easily influenced and manipulated. The masses wished to reduce society to a primitive communism, which was the human condition before civilization. The notion of the equality of human beings was the cause of the evils of society, and he seems to have been preoccupied by the threat of organized labour (trade unions were legally recognized in France in 1884).

Gabriel Tarde (1843–1904) broke with the xenophobic basis of Le Bon's notions and was an important influence on the development of the social sciences. He argued that the crowd belonged to the past and that the new possibilities of communication facilitated by the press, the railway and the telegraph had helped to constitute publics, which were the social groups of the future. The public represented the mental unity of a group which was separated physically, and yet its units, individuals, could simultaneously belong to several publics. Society progressively is divided into publics which transcend religious, social, economic and political divisions, and, because of the logic of the forms of communication which make publics possible, they gradually transcend national borders.[7]

The development of new social classes in modern European societies as a result of industrial capitalism created individuals whose social and cultural experience was not reflected in an indigenous high culture which was barely accessible to them. Newly urbanized individuals were to be especially receptive to American popular culture, the products of which were already widely available in the 1930s, and particularly after the Second World War. The notion of 'Americanization' revived elite fears of the destabilizing influence of low-brow popular culture, particularly on the heels of the cataclysmic social changes that followed the First World War. From the 1920s on, fears were expressed in various European countries about the nefarious influence of jazz and American films, and the young were seen as most at risk. Fr Peter Conefrey's campaign against jazz and dance halls in Co. Leitrim in the 1930s explicitly linked them to communism.[8] After the Second World War, American consumerism was commonly identified as a danger, with housewives, teenagers and the working class seen as the groups most threatened.[9] A Danish scholar, Søren Schou, explains why American popular culture appealed so much to Europeans.

> American films, magazines, and books told us about a life many of us were going to live, an urban or suburban life. In Denmark, daily existence was changing for many people as we left our agrarian past and approached a new status as an industrial nation ... American popular culture became a guide during this mental transformation; the American big city fiction helped us to adjust to changing times. One could say that it was instrumental in bringing about the 'mental' modernisation of Denmark. But it should be emphasised that the modernisation occurred in a specific, American form not strictly inherent in the process of modernisation itself.[10]

A similar point has been made about the million of peasant and indigenous migrants to the cities of Latin America in the twentieth century. Ignorant of urban life, the mass media taught them how to behave in the city and provided cultural forms that articulated their experience.[11]

The fear of 'Americanization' was fundamentally an elite's fear of losing its role as cultural and moral gate-keeper.[12] Indeed elite opposition to American popular culture helped to give it an anti-establishment value in youth culture (which developed after the Second World War). Americanization has been portrayed as a threat to various national cultures in the twentieth century. But American popular culture also helped to unify society, it has been argued, by offering a way of life which was valid for all social classes. In effect the polemics about Americanization belonged to the same discourse as those about mass culture. American influence tended to be linked to new media technologies, and hence was associated with the 'media panics' which have inevitably followed their appearance.

If fears about the influence of new media such as cinema, photography, television, video, the Internet, and about the 'culture industry' in general, have recurred in the twentieth century, these were prefigured by polemics about print and the spread of radical ideologies through it.[13] 'From the advent of mass-circulation fiction and magazines to film and television, comics and cartoons, the introduction of a new mass medium causes strong public reactions whose repetitiveness is as predictable as the fervour with which they are brought forward', concludes Kirsten Drotner. Media panics are both an attempt 'to re-establish a generational status quo that the youthful pioneers seem to undermine' and part of a cultural struggle by elites whose status as cultural arbiters is being undermined by modernization.[14] Later critics of 'Americanization' had similar motivations. A factor in media panics can also be the fear of a national elite or aspiring elite of the 'denationalization' of the young by a foreign culture industry. This clearly was part of Douglas Hyde's argument for the 'de-anglicization' of Ireland.

There is a long European tradition of seeing America as a kind of utopia as well as a crass materialistic country. The allure of the USA as the land of freedom and prosperity is much older, and appealed particularly to non-elite groups. George Thomson wrote of the Blasket Islanders living on remittances from their children in the United States, 'and consequently that country came to be associated in their minds with the Elysium of Irish mythology . . . which was also located beyond the Atlantic . . .'.[15] The USA was the 'Land of Liberty', as the song had it, the Land of Milk and Honey, and the first modern nation: the model for modernity. The dominance of American cultural forms is a complex process and has been closely connected to the global projection of US political and economic power. American culture was deliberately cultivated, for example, under military occupation in post-war Germany and Italy.[16] Americanization is a form of globalization, which in turn has largely been given its characteristic political, economic and cultural shape today by the USA. But the logic of capitalism itself has always been global.

Walter Benjamin, in his famous text from 1936, 'The Work of Art in the Age of Mechanical Reproduction', discussed the extent to which the media do not just transmit but transform their content. He observed that 'the technique of reproduction detaches the reproduced object from the domain of tradition' and reactivates it for the perceiver in his or her own situation, leading to 'a tremendous shattering of tradition . . .' This process was at its most powerful in film. 'Its social significance, particularly in its most positive form, is inconceivable without its destructive, cathartic aspect, that is, the liquidation of the traditional value of the cultural heritage.' But the media compensate for this loss with the offering of a new form of belonging, which comes from belonging to a mass audience. Benjamin saw the liberating potentialities offered by new technologies. Film and photography, by their reproducibility, broke with the traditional singularity of the work of art that had so facilitated its development of a 'sacred aura', as he called it. Film and photography thus were particularly open to ordinary people. Benjamin saw media technology as having the potential to free art by removing it from bourgeois control and making it widely available.

Horkheimer and Adorno's concept of a 'culture industry' is first found in a text from 1944, influenced both by the authors' experiences of totalitarianism under National Socialism and, after their leaving Germany, of mass democracy in the United States. Their notion of an all-powerful culture industry envisaged ordinary people deprived of any cultural autonomy in an industrial system that not only regulates work, but regulates leisure too, and which produces commodities for the market along with the desire for them. Mass culture thus was part and parcel of the industrial system. It was a culture produced *for* rather than *by* the masses. In contrast, North American commentators, from the 1940s, tended to see mass culture in a much more positive way. Mass culture affirmed democracy because the culture produced in the mass media was a culture of the masses. It was the most important socializing agent in society, integrating the majority of the population into a mass society while at the same time greatly increasing the choices open to the individual, who could find his or her own lifestyle. It allowed an unprecedented communication and cultural circulation between the different levels of society.

These two opposing perspectives on mass culture – the 'apocalyptic' and the 'integrative' ('*apocalittici e integrati*'), as Umberto Eco terms them – have since become familiar.[17] The notion of mass-mediated culture has been usefully applied since the 1970s to all forms of culture disseminated through the mass media irrespective of their origin, whether in elite, folk, popular or mass culture. In this sense, all culture when transmitted through the mass media becomes popular culture.[18]

Globalization

Americanization is a form of globalization, and both are products of the transformations in communications which are central to the experience of modernity. David Harvey speaks in terms of a 'space-time compression':

> . . . the history of capitalism has been characterized by speed-up in the pace of life, while so overcoming spatial barriers that the world sometimes seems to collapse inwards upon us. The time taken to traverse space and the way we commonly represent that fact to ourselves are useful indicators of the kind of phenomena I have in mind. As space appears to shrink to a 'global village' of telecommunications and a 'spaceship earth' of economic and ecological interdependencies . . and as time horizons shorten to the point where the present is all there is . . . so we have to learn how to cope with an overwhelming sense of *compression* of our spatial and temporal worlds.

Inevitably, a loss of identity with place and a loss of historical continuity ensue. The golden age of museums and of folklore-collecting are examples of attempts to re-establish continuity through the re-articulation of significant cultural elements in new forms ('the invention of tradition').[19]

From the mid-twentieth century on, telecommunications, rapid international transportation and computerization have undermined the spatial basis of tradition – and of community – in an absolute way.[20] Community today may not be tied to a specific place, the population of which may be constituted by members of a variety of different communities, publics if one will. The 'average exoticism' of daily life in towns and villages today (in Hans Magnus Enzensberger's depiction) exemplifies the de-spatialization of community where the person who is a curiosity in a particular locality can no longer be judged as odd but simply as a member of a different community.

> Market towns in Lower Bavaria, villages in the Eiffel Hills, small towns in
> Holstein are populated by figures no one could have dreamed of only thirty
> years ago. For example, golf-playing butchers, wives imported from Thai-
> land, counter-intelligence agents with allotments, Turkish Mullahs,
> women chemists in Nicaragua committees, vagrants driving Mercedes,
> autonomists with organic gardens, weapons-collecting tax officials,
> peacock-breeding smallholders, militant lesbians, Tamil ice-cream sellers,
> classics scholars in commodity futures trading, mercenaries on home
> leave, extremist animal-rights activists, cocaine dealers with solariums,
> dominas [*sic*] with clients in top management, computer freaks commut-
> ing between Californian data banks and nature reserves in Hesse,
> carpenters who supply golden doors to Saudi Arabia, art forgers, Karl May
> researchers, bodyguards, jazz experts, euthanasists and porno producers.
> Into the shoes of the village idiots and the oddballs, of the eccentrics and
> the queer fish, has stepped the average deviationist, who no longer stands
> out at all from millions like him.[21]

Ulf Hannerz speaks of the constitution of 'a global ecumene, a single field
of persistent interaction and exchange between cultures'.[22] He argues that
'[t]he entities we routinely call cultures are becoming more like subcultures
within this wider entity . . .'.[23] A consequence of this is that the nation state's
integrative capacity has been weakened everywhere in a process that
Helmut Hartwig calls a 'declassing of the centre'. The 'compressed centre'
has historically been created 'through national, social and cultural processes
of feedback', and it is in relation to it that people developed a sense of
belonging to and participation in society, sharing meanings and goals. But
today globally organized processes in the media, in the economy and in
society as a whole have 'emptied' the centre of its traditional meanings.[24]
The democratic state has more and more sought non-cultural and non-ideo-
logical foundations for its power and become largely indifferent to
programmes of cultural conformity. The separation of the nation and the
state is thus seen by Zygmunt Bauman as a pronounced present-day
tendency, what he calls the 'privatization of nationality'. Culture has become
a part of the private domain and has had a resurgence in the form of 'a
powerful demand for pronounced, though symbolic rather than institutionalized, ethnic distinctiveness'. He sees ethnicity as creating less antagonism
than before because of the fluidity of present-day cultural boundaries and
the state's indifference to cultural and ethnic pluralism within its borders.[25]

Globalized cultural references are today a part of consumer society. Renato
Ortiz speaks of an 'international-popular culture' being constituted in the
world. Celebrities, images and situations are made known through magazines, television and film, creating an 'international-popular memory',
especially among the youth. Because this culture is not specific to place and
because of its global extent, it cannot reflect only the perspective of a
restricted group or place but must attain all nations and social classes. It can

only do this by avoiding referring to the conflicts of the world, by encouraging forgetfulness: in order to ensure a permanent present, 'the international-popular memory must expel the contradictions of history . . .'.[26]

Relocating Tradition

Part of the tradition/modernity problematic rests on a notion of a pre-modern era which was unchanging. Hence the last glimpses of an earlier world seen by Romantics in Europe as industrial society was consolidated or by ethnographers in Africa and Asia as colonial regimes were normalized seemed to suggest an infinite placid sea on the eve of the storm. Edmund Leach contends that, since we understand better than before how culturally destructive colonialism was in Africa, the oppositions traditional/post-traditional and tribal/detribalized there have been understood in terms of before and after European colonial influence, thus downplaying the role of non-European influences in social change and indeed of the ethnographers themselves.[27] In the same way, Robin Flower saw the Blasket Island's 'unobtrusive . . . medieval assimilation of foreign influences' as having more integrity than the necessary 'compromises with modernity' he witnessed himself,[28] which he was a part of and which he had little interest in recording.

The end of tradition is based on the ideal notions of a past completely dominated by tradition and of a present and future completely antithetical to it. In this frame, de-traditionalizing processes are salient since they explain how we have come to the present juncture. A contrasting perspective is to query the ideal notions and argue that the past was never as dominated by tradition nor the present as free of it as we like to presume. If that is the case, we must accept, along with de-traditionalization, the continuity and construction of traditions. Indeed people in all societies live and have always lived between conflicting demands of traditional values and individual desires.[29] Michael Kearney points out that the shifting polarities of anthropology over time – primitive and civilized, traditional and modern and underdeveloped and developed – have blinded us to the in-between status of today's peasant, commonly a migrant who does not correspond to any of these categories.[30] Timothy Luke insists that seeing the end of tradition is now itself a tradition, and that it exists 'as a set of practices, a constellation of beliefs, and a mode of thinking that we inherit from Rousseau, Marx, and Weber'. We escape the dichotomies of tradition and modernity by looking at spatial rather than temporal transformations, Luke argues, since the understanding of traditional practices has conventionally been tied to the notion of tradition being anchored to place.[31]

Lauri Honko's comparison of tradition to a store, 'only some parts of which are in use at any given time, the other parts simply waiting to be activated (memory culture) or gradually vanishing'[32] is a useful way of conceiving of the dynamism of tradition and the constantly provisional nature of its death. Honko sees 'the first life of folklore' as 'the natural, almost imperceptible existence of folklore in the folklore community'. There is no concept of folklore; it is 'neither noticed, recognised or emphasised'. The folklore of the community is discovered by strangers and the self-consciousness brought in by the 'external discoverers of folklore' inevitably changes the way in which the community sees its own culture and heritage. There is a continuity of form, but the cultural item in question will now carry additional meanings, national, or indeed commercial.[33] Richard Handler has observed such a process in the politically charged late 1970s in Québec. City dwellers went to the countryside in search of cultural authenticity (rather as generations of Irish people went to the Gaeltacht). In the country the visitors stayed with local families as paying guests, and helped to give them a consciousness of their own distinctiveness. Handler describes 'a transition between unconscious folkways and objectified "tradition"'.[34] The Blasket Island literature was motivated by the 'external discoverers of folklore', but there the discourse was not monopolized by them, allowing individuals such as Tomás Ó Criomhthain to find a modern voice which would outlive the imminent death of his community.

Notions of 'the invention of tradition' (in the context of folklore), of 'folk-lorism(us)', defined as folk culture presented at second hand, and of 'fakelore' (a self-evident term coined by the American folklorist Richard Dorson), seem to imply the lack of some defining property of authenticity. Honko suggests the term 'the second life of folklore' to refer to folklore material being used 'in an environment that differs from its original cultural context'. He makes a convincing case for the rejection of more negative notions in order 'to try to restore the research value of events in the second life of folklore to something approaching their indisputable cultural value'.[35] The 'second life' of folklore is everywhere around us. It is in vernacular references in architecture or interior design, in personal adornment, in marketing strategies for goods (a folkloric reference suggesting tradition, authenticity and naturalness), in staged performances of song and dance, in the display cases of museums, in the plots of cartoons, novels and films. It has become a part of the post-modern landscape.

An important point about the 'second life' of folklore is that it can refer to folklore products mediated by the culture industries or the market in general. As such, it is often independent of popular creativity. Tellingly, on the occasion of an exhibition of folk art in Stockholm's Kulturhuset in 1992–3, Beate Sydhoff, the director, could write of the subject of the exhibition:

> We have assigned it the role of a concept from the old rural society and set it in the mould of an antiquated relic primarily of the last century. Alternately idealised and commercialised, it has emerged from these 'transformations' in the shape of specific objects or ornaments destined

mainly for the mass tourist market. Any connection with 'the people' has long since disappeared, not because of any disinterest on their part, but rather that they have gone on to create quite different things. A gulf has arisen between the conception of folk art and the reality of folk, or popular creativity.[36]

The exhibition covered a wide variety of aspects of popular creativity, from home decoration, subcultural aesthetics, types of popular music and naïve art to the continuing reference to folk art as an inspiration to present-day artists.

García Canclini contends that modernity does not suppress traditional culture, but in fact develops and transforms it for at least four different reasons:

> (a) the impossibility of incorporating the entire population into urban industrial production; (b) the need of the market to include traditional symbolic structures and goods in the mass circuits of communication in order to reach even the popular layers least integrated into modernity; (c) the interest of political systems in taking folklore into account with the goal of strengthening their hegemony and legitimacy; (d) continuity in the cultural production of the popular sectors.

He shows that there have never been as many artisans or popular musicians in Latin America as today. Their products have both a 'first' and a 'second life', supporting traditional functions and providing employment for indigenous people and peasants but also developing new functions, such as attracting tourists and urban consumers, who 'find signs of distinction in folkloric goods and personalized references that industrialized goods do not offer'. Traditional festivals and the production and sale of craftsmanship now are no longer the exclusive property of popular groups, but government ministries, private foundations, private companies, and radio and television also play their part in organizing them. Thus 'the popular is not defined by an a priori essence' but by the various strategies used by popular groups, by folklorists, anthropologists, museologists, sociologists, communications specialists, politicians and the media: 'Folk or traditional cultural facts are today the multidetermined product of actors that are popular and hegemonic, peasant and urban, local, national, and transnational'.[37]

Consumption and Culture

In a world where the majority lives in cities, where the largest employment sector in the richer countries is neither agriculture nor industry, where there is an unprecedented amount of cultural circulation and where it is no longer possible to 'hold' economic and cultural processes within the boundaries of the state, where do we look for folklore and popular culture? If we reject the notion of folklore and popular culture as having an inherent quality, but accept that its specificity derives from its position within a socio-economic system, then we can begin by looking at how we discern cultural difference within society today. The notion of 'distinction' is used by Pierre Bourdieu to refer to behaviour that distinguishes a person from what is 'common' or 'vulgar'. 'The profit of distinction', he asserts, 'is the profit that flows from the difference, the gap, that separates one from what is common.' Art is not equally accessible to all since, to understand it, a specific competence is needed that is not equally distributed. Those who possess the intellectual instruments for making sense of art, however, secure 'profits of distinction' for themselves and 'the rarer these instruments are the greater the profits' – for example in the appropriation of avant-garde works of art. He seems to see the popular classes as having a passive role in strategies of distinction, as the negative against which the other classes define themselves, so that in that sense he rejects the notion of a popular culture. The instruments for understanding art, philosophy, science and so forth are 'cultural capital'. With an educational system, cultural capital has the conditions for its full realization. One kind of capital can be converted into another. For example, economic capital can be converted into nobility by good deeds, social work and philanthropy. Some people's interests are best served by the 'revaluing of cultural capital with respect to economic capital'. The reproduction of a dominant class 'depends to a large extent on the transmission of cultural capital' which has the property of being apparently natural and innate, and allows members of the dominant class to feel themselves essentially superior.[38]

From the middle of the twentieth century on, the linkage of 'high' and 'popular' culture to specific social groups has tended to fall away. High culture today is cultivated by a fraction of the upper social classes while the popular products of the culture industries – television soap operas, films, popular music and so forth – are consumed by the majority of all social classes. A particularly good example of that was the pop star, Elton John, playing to the assembled masses of the British establishment at the funeral of Princess Diana in Westminster Abbey in 1997. In modern democratic societies there is mass access to consumer products. In the absence of a high and a popular culture based on separate social classes – in fact they are mediated by the same culture industries – consumption has become the means by which spheres of distinction are established. Industrial production since the 1970s has tended to supersede the Fordist model of standardized and centralized mass production and moved to a system of 'flexible accumulation' which has encouraged the individualization of consumption.[39] The cultural products on offer today derive from high, folk, popular, and mass culture. 'Just as the abrupt opposition between the traditional and the modern does not work, so the cultured, the popular, and the mass-based are not where we are used to finding them', contends García Canclini. He argues that these changes have lessened the traditional cultural advantages of elites since there is more cultural circulation between 'the cultured' and 'the popular', and an undermining of the pretensions to originality and uniqueness (largely a nineteenth-century development, as Bourdieu has shown us) of elite art.[40]

Towards New Readings of Folklore and Popular Culture

Wolfgang Kaschuba points out that European folklorists and ethnologists previously attached great importance to the notions of tradition and continuity and showed little interest in cultural innovation and social change. He argues that this is evidence of 'its particular sociopolitical role as a "science of legitimation" of conservative values'.[41] But it was inevitable that the profound transformations in Western society since the Second World War and above all since the 1960s, outlined above, would force a rethinking both of the fields of folklore and popular culture and of the research approaches to them. From the 1950s and 1960s, research into 'traditional' culture has reoriented itself in many ways.

The continued decline of traditional rural life forced scholars to reconsider the traditional object of their research, the folk. The sociologist Henri Menras foretold the end of peasant society in 1967 (and argued twenty years later that his prognosis had been correct and that 'in one generation France has seen a thousand year civilization, constitutive of itself, disappear').[42] Intense urbanization all over the world meant that popular culture was less and less constituted by peasant and 'traditional' communities. One of the problems of the peasant concept, pointed out by Michael Kearney, was that it was an anthropology of 'unitary objects'. But peasants today are commonly migrants for whom participation in informal economies is characteristic, and they must be looked at as 'complex subjects' who 'do not conform to the classic categories of rural society, being neither peasant nor proletarian, neither farmer nor petty merchant, and neither rural nor urban'.[43]

The mystification of the folk had become suspect after the Second World War for political reasons anyway, particularly in those countries in which folklore was compromised by too great an identification with nationalist aims. Similarly, anti-colonial struggle from the 1950s against the 'good guys' of the Second World War helped to undermine the fundamental racism of evolutionist notions of the primitive in anthropology and at the same time offered powerful readings of the colonial condition from the inside by writers such as Franz Fanon and Albert Memmi.[44] The work of these writers was extremely influential, marking turning points in the growing self-awareness of the colonial world. But it also contributed to a new conscientization and sensibility in Western Europe and North America, influencing the student revolts and the counter-culture of the 1960s.

The concept of youth culture derived from the expansion of education in the richer countries after the Second World War, thus helping to separate youth as a discrete social category. The new social movements* came into their own from the 1960s and, spurred by student activism, helped to create a new sensitivity to issues of power in society. They informed new and powerful readings within the established university disciplines. Thus feminism, the black civil rights movement, the anti-apartheid movement, the gay rights movement, the Green movement, all helped to shape a new public discourse. Counter-cultural tendencies, notably among the hippies, consciously rejected the logic of Western modernity and showed a receptiveness to folk and indigenous culture, not as part of some national essence, but as alternatives to Western culture and as repositories of non-materialistic values. Lyndon Johnson's reason for not running for re-election for the presidency of the United States in March 1968 vividly portrays the turbulent social forces of the time: 'I felt that I was being chased over the edge by rioting blacks, demonstrating students, marching welfare mothers, squawking professors and hysterical reporters'.[45]

There was a change in orientation of North American folklore research at the time. Individuals entered the field 'because of a political commitment to particular peoples, ones identified in the public mind with either a marginal or a minority status', according to Roger Abrahams, helping to re-direct the discipline towards 'discovering the expressive systems of groups hitherto excluded from the distribution of political power, especially blacks and hispanics'.[46]

From the 1970s, feminist readings began to inform folklore research and anthropology.[47] There had always been women folklorists and anthropologists, although, as we have pointed out, there were no women among the full-time folklore collectors of the Irish Folklore Commission (and hence we know very little about female storytelling in Ireland[48]). The fact that men's activities tend to dominate in the public arenas and women's in the more private ones, as Claire Farrer points out, meant that much of social life was invisible to the male researcher.[49] Women have always been the subject of research, nevertheless, whether as gifted singers and storytellers recorded by folklorists, or as an essential part of the classic anthropological field of kinship and marriage. Speaking of anthropology, Henrietta Moore shows that there was an initial realization from the 1970s on of a three-tiered bias in the representation of women in anthropological writing. This included the individual bias imported by the male ethnographer, the bias inherent in the society under scrutiny and the underlying bias inherent in gender relations in Western society. 'The main problem was not, therefore, one of empirical study, but rather one of representation'.[50]

---

* A social movement is defined as 'a collective attempt to further a common interest, or secure a common goal, through collective action outside the sphere of established institutions'. See Anthony Giddens, *Sociology* (Cambridge: Polity Press, 1989), p. 624.

There was a new engagement of folklore scholarship with the social sciences, a shift from a diachronic 'literary historical' focus on text to a synchronic socio-linguistic stress on context, pioneered above all in the United States.[51] Instead of being understood as a collection of specific cultural elements, folklore was now envisaged as a process of communication. The key word was performance. Folklore was artistic communication in small groups. Because it was process that characterized folklore, the diachronic notion of tradition lost importance. At the same time, there was a decisive shift to the study of folklore in urban environments.

The lively debate about *Volkskunde* in Germany after the Second World War was particularly intense in the 1960s and led to a break with the traditional orientations of the discipline: the so-called *Abschied vom Volksleben*. Kaschuba sums up the results:

> The 'Abschied' gradually opened up new perspectives for the subject, without totally losing sight, thematically and methodically, of the old shores. And this seems to me characteristic for European ethnology to this day: its oscillation between historical and present-day orientations without finding a final and fixed balance, its scepticism towards the traditions of our discipline which have been frequently challenged but not entirely got rid of, its permanent search for possible methods of approaching the horizons of everyday life which always orientate themselves afresh in an interdisciplinary way and get lost occasionally in this process.[52]

In Ireland, folklore courses were only established in the universities in the 1970s. The Department of Irish Folklore was set up under Bo Almqvist in University College, Dublin in 1971 to succeed the Irish Folklore Commission, and a de facto folklore department, formally attached to the then Department of Irish History, was established under Gearóid Ó Crualaoich in University College, Cork in 1977. Though the latter institution taught initially only through Irish, its engagement with the social sciences and particularly with anthropology from its inception marked the first break with the approach that had dominated Irish folklore studies in the South since the Gaelic Revival.

Preserving Folklore

Folklore archives helped to chronicle plebeian aspects of national, regional and local culture and contain a wealth of traditional knowledge – strategies for building or cultivation suited to local conditions, the names and properties of the flora and fauna of a locality, cures for locally known ailments of humans and animals, an incredibly detailed knowledge of the physical environment, down to the names of rocks and fields and the traditions attached to them. Some of this traditional knowledge is still alive, but it is disappearing everywhere in the world, the shrinking evidence for a former biological and cultural diversity. While the desirability of sustaining the planet's biolog-ical diversity is now generally acknowledged, less so is its cultural diversity, despite the fact that the latter is a facet of the former and that neither can be sustained by the same mindset which undermined them in the first place. If underdevelopment itself is a recent concept, the supposed lacks it implied have long motivated state and private (often landowners') intervention in agrarian societies – Michael Kearney points out that peasants were the main target of 'developmentalism'.[53]

Underdevelopment began with the coining of the word by President Truman on 20 January, 1949. 'On that day, two billion people became under-developed', insists Gustavo Esteva, which meant that, from then on, 'they ceased being what they were, in all their diversity, and were transmogrified into the inverted mirror of others' reality . . .'[54] Development theorists have shown us how the condition of 'underdevelopment' was created by 'devel-opment', how ignorance was defined in terms of the absence of diplomas, professional teachers and registered schools, how ill-health was understood in terms of independence from medical services, hospitals and drugs, how poverty was defined by the World Bank in 1948 in terms of a country's Gross National Product (average per capita income of less than $100 = poverty).

Traditional peasant and tribal cultures are endangered almost every-where, though there are grassroots movements in Africa, Asia and Latin America resisting the developmental mindset.[55] Similarly, in Western coun-tries there are groups striving for alternative strategies to share the world, not just with the rest of humanity, but with all the other life forms of the planet. In Ireland and in Western Europe generally we are witnessing the demise of the small farmer and of a rural society that is not an extension of the suburbs. The documentation of much of traditional culture will continue – Western pharmaceutical companies are scouring the Third World in search of traditional cures that they can patent and market; various state agencies and private companies will investigate communities in order to govern them better or to better exploit their natural or labour resources; museologists,* anthropologists, folklorists, sociologists, historians will collect artefacts, document traditional social organization and record performances, customs and beliefs, often as a salvage operation. Folklore and popular culture does not disappear, indeed is constantly being created, but less and less offers alternatives to modernity from an experience outside of it. This, clearly, is a loss of cultural diversity, and the loss of a bank of traditional strategies for coping with adversity.

UNESCO approved an international recommendation on the safeguarding of folklore and traditional culture at its General Conference in Paris in

---

* The Ulster Folk and Transport Museum also plays an important role in preserving native breeds of animals – such as the famous Kerry Cow – which are on the brink of extinction as a result of generations of scientific farming.

November 1989. Representatives of fifty-two countries and observers from nine international organizations attended the conference; additionally, eight countries sent their comments. In total seventeen countries in Europe, fifteen in Asia, fourteen in Africa and fourteen in the Americas were represented. Among the issues considered were the logistical ones of training, documentation and international cooperation, the rights of communities over material recorded from their own traditional culture, and the question of the exploitation of traditional culture, for commercial or for other reasons. According to Lauri Honko, president of the special committee which investigated the matter, the primary concern of the recommendation was 'the creation of an adequate infrastructure for folklore work and preservation, an infrastructure which will allow for the recycling of folklore both inside and outside its original context, thus permitting larger numbers of people to become shareholders in values inherent in folklore'. He points out that the international consensus of the recommendation 'provides for ethical codes and checks against parochial or over-nationalistic attitudes'. Folklore, he maintains, 'should be allowed to flourish where it is dynamic, and to be remembered, maybe even revived, in contexts that may not be the most original but which lend it new and fuller meaning'. The document defined folklore somewhat conservatively as follows:

> Folklore (or traditional and popular culture) is the totality of tradition-based creations of a cultural community, expressed by a group of individuals and recognized as reflecting the expectations of a community in so far as they reflect its cultural and social identity; its standards and values are transmitted orally, by imitation or by other means. Its form[s] include, among others, language, literature, music, dance, games, mythology, rituals, customs, handicrafts, architecture and other arts.

The recommendations were wide ranging, and were covered by various headings. The 'identification of folklore' included making national and international registers of folklore institutions, recording and cataloguing folklore and coordinating the various systems of doing so, as well as the creation of a standard international 'typology of folklore'. The 'conservation of folklore', while pointing out that living folklore, because of its changing nature, cannot necessarily be directly protected, called for the effective protection of 'folklore that has been fixed in a tangible form'. Recommendations included the establishment of national folklore archives and museums (or sections within existing museums), the representation of folklore in the appropriate contexts, the harmonizing of recording and archiving methods, the training of specialists and the provision of access to folklore materials through making copies available on a regional basis. The 'preservation of folklore' referred to the teaching and study of folklore in the curriculum, 'taking into account not only village and other rural cultures but also those created in urban areas by diverse social groups, professions, institutions, etc., and thus promoting a better understanding of cultural diversity and different world views, especially those not reflected in dominant cultures'; guaranteeing the right of access of communities to their own folklore 'by supporting their work in the fields of documentation, archiving, research, etc., as well as in the practice of traditions'; the establishment of national co-ordinating bodies; the provision of 'moral and economic support for individuals and institutions studying, making known, cultivating (or holding) items of folklore; and the promotion of scientific research'.[56]

Closing Remarks

If the 'folk' who crystallized in European consciousness from the end of the eighteenth century were in a sense an imaginary community, they nevertheless made possible the 'imagined community' which is the nation to a number of previously stateless ethnic groups. National identity is built partly on fiction, but so too is personal identity since the process of identity formation of necessity is a rhetorical stance of difference. Is it necessary to know the myths we live by? Perhaps not, but we should know the myths we research with. The complicity of scholarship with nationalist or imperialist projects is nothing new, though we should beware of projecting present-day professional concerns or to dead scholars. The present disciplinary divisions of the universities, and the professional specializations associated with them, for example, are scarcely a century old.

It is necessary to deconstruct the work of previous scholarship in order to understand it in all its complexity and to ensure that the pitfalls of a new generation of scholars have at least the merit of being new. The interdisciplinarity of much research on culture today has opened up many new perspectives of which folklore research should be particularly well placed to take advantage, being much less encumbered (if that is the right word) by a canonical scholarly literature (there being no folkloristic equivalent to Weber or Malinowski). At the same time, if the somewhat clichéd postmodern demise of metanarratives is true, folklore research already has the advantage of never having had one and, historically, of coming into being to oppose that of the Enlightenment. Its stress on the importance of cultural difference, the value of traditional knowledge and the desirability of sustaining them suffered from the lack of any concrete programme of action and from a surfeit of wistfulness, but can nevertheless be appreciated today from a postmodern and post-developmentalist perspective which has cut the notion of progress down to size.

The future of folklore scholarship seems to be the maintenance of its decentred academic tradition along with wider and deeper international cooperation and continued drawing on other disciplines. The local denominations of folklore, folklife, ethnology and a number of more localized terms will persist as will as the continued use of a variety of research languages, including Irish. This seems to be the guarantee of a variety of research perspectives and conclusions drawn from specific local traditions. This seems the appropriate place to call for a closer relationship between the two ethnological traditions that have long worked in Ireland, folklore and anthropology. The overlaps are obvious: Haddon working in the Aran Islands and on the Torres Straits expedition, Jeremiah Curtin recording myths in Kerry and among native Americans, the same communities as the fields of both folklorists and anthropologists.*

International cooperation has greatly increased in folklore studies and ethnology. Within Europe, the post-1989 dispensation has greatly intensified relations between the former East and West. At the same time, as the UNESCO meeting in Paris in 1989 showed, folklore is seen in every continent as a value to be cherished, and professional bodies such as the International Society for Folk Narrative Research have increasingly organized their conferences outside of the traditional European strongholds of folklore scholarship.

Folklore archives, one of the primary sources for folkloristic and ethnological research, contain large amounts of material recorded by and from non-elite groups in society. The positivistic élan behind most folklore collection has, in many ways, benefited research. Free of overtly theoretical constructs (though based on theoretical premises), new analyses can depart from the same rich data on which old analyses were based. Besides the value of the data itself, two particularly humanistic aspects to the folklore archive should be stressed: its legitimation of the culture of subaltern agrarian communities and its preservation of traditional knowledge, which may yet be understood as a resource in re-thinking the human world which our notions of progress constantly endanger.

---

* For example, the West Clare of Conrad M. Arensberg, *The Irish Countryman. An anthropological study* (Prospect Heights, Illinois: Waveland Press, 1988 [1937]), the South West Galway/North West Clare of Robert Cresswell, *Une communauté rurale de l'Irlande* (Paris: Institut d'Ethnologie, Université de Paris and Musée de l'Homme, 1969), the Inisheer of John C. Messenger, *Inis Beag. Isle of Ireland* (New York: Holt, Rinehart and Winston, 1969), the Tory Island of Robin Fox, *The Tory Islanders. A people of the Celtic fringe* (Cambridge: Cambridge University Press, 1978), the Dingle Peninsula of Nancy Scheper-Hughes (*Saints, Scholars, and Schizophrenics. Mental Illness in Rural Ireland* (Berkeley, Los Angeles and London: University of California Press, 1979); the South West Donegal of Lawrence J. Taylor (*Occasions of Faith. An Anthropology of Irish Catholics* (Dublin: Lilliput Press, 1995).

Notes and References

Introduction

1 Antonio Gramsci, *Selections from Prison Notebooks*, ed. and trans. by Quintin Hoare and Geoffrey Nowell Smith (London: Lawrence and Wishart, 1971), p. 188.
2 *Le Petit Robert* (Paris: Le Robert, 1983), p. 800.
3 Tom Garvin, 'North referendums will end Dev's bid to undo 1921 Treaty', *The Irish Times*, 14 May, 1998.
4 Gearóid Denvir, 'An Béal Beo: Filíocht Bhéil Chonamara Inniu' in Gearóid Denvir, *Litríocht agus Pobal. Cnuasach Aistí* (Indreabhán, Conamara: Cló Iar-Chonnachta, 1997), p. 264.
5 Mícheál Ó Conghaile, *Gnéithe d'Amhráin Chonamara Ár Linne* (Indreabhán, Conamara: Cló Iar-Chonnachta, 1993), pp. 7, 10, 12, 13, 26, 30, 34, 47.
6 Denvir, 'An Béal Beo: Filíocht Bhéil Chonamara Inniu', p. 278.

1: The End of Tradition

1 Raymond Williams, *Keywords*, revised and expanded edition (London: Fontana, 1988), pp. 319–20.
2 David Gross, *The Past in Ruins. Tradition and the Critique of Modernity* (Amherst: University of Massachusetts Press, 1992), pp. 8–18.
3 Gross, *The Past in Ruins*, pp. 21–3.
4 Gross, *The Past in Ruins*, pp. 23–5.
5 Benedict Anderson, *Imagined Communities* (London and New York: Verso, 1983), p. 187. Perhaps 'no longer existed' is not appropriate. 'New' places established through colonization may be seen as a continuation, but in a new land: Atholl represented an Irish expansion into Pictland (*Athfhódla*, 'New Ireland') as Castilla la Nueva represented a Castilian expansion into formerly Moorish territory.
6 Juan José Sebreli, *El asedio a la modernidad*, 8th edition (Buenos Aires: Editorial Sudamericana, 1995), p. 73.
7 Gross, *The Past in Ruins*, pp. 28–30.
8 Luigi M. Lombardi Satriani, *Antropologia culturale e analisi della cultura subalterna*, 2nd edition (Milano: Biblioteca Universale Rizzoli, 1997), pp. 141–2.
9 Gross, *The Past in Ruins*, pp. 30–3; Robert Muchembled, *Culture populaire et culture des élites dans la France moderne (XVe–XVIIIe siècle)*, 2nd edition (Paris: Flammarion, 1991), pp. 225–6; Antonio Gramsci, *Selections from Prison Notebooks*, ed. and trans. Quintin Hoare and Geoffrey Nowell Smith (London: Lawrence and Wishart, 1971), p. 54.

10   Mikhail Bakhtin, *Rabelais and his World*, trans. Hélène Iswolsky (Bloomington: Indiana University Press, 1984), p. 33.

11   Muchembled, *Culture populaire et culture des élites*, pp. 342–3.

12   Peter Burke, *Popular Culture in Early Modern Europe*, revised edition (Aldershot: Scolar Press, 1994), pp. 270–1.

13   Bonnie Anderson and Judith Zinsser, 'Women in the Salons' in Stuart Hall and Bram Gieben (eds), *Formations of Modernity* (Cambridge: Polity Press, 1992), p. 60.

14   Hall and Gieben, *Formations of Modernity*, p. 6; Néstor García Canclini, *Hybrid Cultures. Strategies for Entering and Leaving Modernity*, trans. Christopher L. Chiappari and Silvia L. López (Minneapolis and London: University of Minnesota, 1995), pp. 11–13; Gross, *The Past in Ruins*, pp. 40–42.

15   Polanyi, Karl, *Origins of Our Time. The Great Transformation* (London: Victor Gollancz Ltd, 1945), pp. 41, 47, 49, 62, 77–8.

16   Gross, *The Past in Ruins*, pp. 34–47.

17   Eugen Weber, *Peasants into Frenchmen. The Modernization of Rural France 1870–1914* (London: Chatto and Windus, 1977), p. 471.

18   Williams, *Keywords*, pp. 208–9.

19   Björn Hettne, *Development Theory and the Three Worlds*, 2nd edition (London: Longman, 1994), pp. 49–50, 161.

20   See Michael Kearney, *Reconceptualizing the Peasantry. Anthropology in Global Perspective* (Boulder, Colorado and Oxford: Westview Press, 1996).

21   Karl Marx and Frederick Engels, 'Manifesto of the Communist Party' in Karl Marx and Frederick Engels, *Selected Works*, Vol. 1 (Moscow and London: Foreign Language Publishing House and Lawrence and Wishart Ltd, 1951), pp. 36, 42; Hettne, *Development Theory and the Three Worlds*, p. 51; Anthony Giddens, *Sociology* (Cambridge: Polity Press, 1989), p. 278.

22   Anthony Giddens, *Durkheim* (Glasgow: Fontana/Collins, 1978), pp. 22–33; Lidia Girola, 'Durkheim y el diagnóstico de la modernidad' in Gina Zabludovsky (ed.), *Teoría sociológica y modernidad* (México: Plaza y Valdés, 1998), pp. 37–50; Giddens, *Sociology*, p. 692; Michel Panoff and Michel Perrin, *Dictionnaire de l'ethnologie* (Paris: Payot, 1973), p. 22.

23   Williams, *Keywords*, p. 76; Rafael Farfán, 'F. Tönnies: la crítica a la modernidad a partir de la comunidad' in Zabludovsky, *Teoría sociológica y modernidad*, pp. 191, 195–7, 205 *et seq.*; Ferdinand Tönnies, *Community and Association*, trans. and supp. Charles P. Loomis (London: Routledge and Kegan Paul Ltd, 1955), *passim*.

24   Hettne, *Development Theory and the Three Worlds*, p. 51; Giddens, *Sociology*, pp. 127, 278, 486–7, 708–9, 712–14; David Held, 'The Development of the Modern State' in Hall and Gieben, *Formations of Modernity*, pp. 114–15, 189–90, 198, 220–1, 250–2, 261.

25   See J.S. Donnelly and Kerby A. Miller (eds), *Irish Popular Culture 1650–1850* (Dublin: Irish Academic Press, 1998) *passim*.

26   Joseph Lee, *The Modernisation of Irish Society 1848–1918* (Dublin: Gill and Macmillan, 1989), pp. 8–9.

27   Niall Ó Ciosáin, *Print and Popular Culture in Ireland, 1750–1850* (London: Macmillan, 1997), pp. 27–31.

28   W.R. Wilde, *Irish Popular Superstitions* (Dublin: Irish Academic Press, 1979), pp. 9–11, 14–15.

29   Douglas Hyde, *Language, Lore and Lyrics. Essays and Lectures*, ed. with a preface and introduction Breandán Ó Conaire (Dublin: Irish Academic Press, 1986), p. 157.

30   Giuseppe Cocchiara, *Storia del folklore in Europa* (Torino: Boringhieri, 1971), p. 34.

31   Jean Poirier, *Histoire de l'ethnologie*, 2nd edition (Paris: Presses Universitaires de France, 1974), p. 14. The work is *Histoire philosophique et politique des établissements et du commerce des Européens dans les deux Indes*.

32 Antoni Mączak, *Viaggi e viaggiatori nell'Europa moderna*, trans. Renzo Panzone and Andrzei Litwornia (Roma-Bari: Editori Laterza, 1994), pp. 407–32.

33 Julio Caro Baroja, *La aurora del pensamiento antropológico* (Madrid: Consejo Superior de Investigaciones Científicas, 1983), pp. 78–82.

34 Cocchiara, *Storia del folklore in Europa*, pp. 33 *et seq.*, 135 *et seq.*; Renato Ortiz, 'El viaje, lo popular y el otro' in *Otro territorio. Ensayos sobre el mundo contemporáneo*, trans. Ada Solari (Buenos Aires: Universidad Nacional de Quilmes, 1996), pp. 27–46.

35 James Clifford, 'On Ethnographic Authority' in *The Predicament of Culture. Twentieth-Century Ethnography, Literature, and Art* (Cambridge, Mass. and London, England: Harvard University Press, 1988), p. 26.

36 Claude Lévi-Strauss, *Structural Anthropology 2*, trans. Monique Layton (Harmondsworth: Penguin, 1978), p. 35.

37 Hermann Bausinger, *Volkskunde ou l'ethnologie allemande*, trans. Dominique Lassaigne and Pascale Godenir (Paris: Éditions de la Maison des sciences de l'homme, 1993), pp. 19–20.

38 Cocchiara, *Storia del folklore in Europa*, pp. 135–7.

39 Tzvetan Todorov, *Les morales de l'histoire* (Paris: Bernard Grasset, 1991), p. 32; Cocchiara, *Storia del folklore in Europa*, pp. 139–40.

40 Cocchiara, *Storia del folklore in Europa*, pp. 138, 140–3; Bausinger, *Volkskunde*, p. 20.

41 Cocchiara, *Storia del folklore in Europa*, pp. 154–5; Burke, *Popular Culture in Early Modern Europe*, p. 10; Claire O'Halloran, 'Irish Re-creations of the Gaelic Past: The Challenge of Macpherson's Ossian', *Past and Present*, no. 124, August 1989, pp. 69 et seq.

42 Malcolm Chapman, *The Celts. The Construction of a Myth* (New York: St Martin's Press, 1992), p. 127.

43 Cocchiara, *Storia del folklore in Europa*, p. 158.

44 Chapman, *The Celts*, p. 121.

45 Cocchiara, *Storia del folklore in Europa*, pp. 162–7.

46 Cocchiara, *Storia del folklore in Europa*, pp. 162–7.

47 Cocchiara, *Storia del folklore in Europa*, pp. 188–9.

48 Bengt Holbek, *On the Comparative Method in Folklore Research. NIF Papers No. 3* (Turku: Nordic Institute of Folklore, 1992), p. 6; Burke, *Popular Culture in Early Modern Europe*, p. 14.

49 Isaiah Berlin, *Vico and Herder. Two Studies in the History of Ideas* (London: The Hoggarth Press, 1976) p. 145.

50 Berlin, *Vico and Herder*, pp. 153, 174, 186 et seq.

51 Denys Cuche, *La noción de cultura en las ciencias sociales*, trans. Paula Mahler (Buenos Aires: Ediciones Nueva Visión, 1999), pp. 12–15.

52 Norbert Elias, *The Civilizing Process*, trans. Edmund Jephcott (Oxford UK and Cambridge USA: Blackwell, 1994), pp. 4–5, 7–8, 13, 15, 16, 24–6.

53 Williams, *Keywords*, pp. 87 et seq.

54 Berlin, *Vico and Herder*, pp. 157–63, 181–2, 184.

55 H.G. Schenk, *The Mind of the European Romantics* (Oxford, New York, Toronto and Melbourne: Oxford University Press, 1979), p. 16.

56 Berlin, *Vico and Herder*, pp. 181–3.

57 Berlin, *Vico and Herder*, pp. 165–9, 180.

58 Antonio Gramsci, *Letteratura e vita nazionale* (Roma: Editori Riuniti, 1991), p. 123; Sebreli, *El asedio a la modernidad*, p. 160.

59 Wolfgang Brückner, 'Histoire de la Volkskunde. Tentative d'une approche à l'usage des Français' in Isac Chiva and Utz Jeggle (eds), *Ethnologies en Miroir. La France et les pays de langue allemande* (Paris: Éditions de la Maison des sciences de l'homme, 1987), p. 226; Berlin, *Vico and Herder*, p. 180.

60   Jennifer Fox, 'The Creator Gods: Romantic Nationalism and the En-genderment of Women in Folklore' in *Journal of American Folklore*, no. 100 (1987), pp. 565 et seq.

61   Brückner, 'Histoire de la Volkskunde', p. 226 – the citation is from Hermann Bausinger.

62   Cocchiara, *Storia del folklore in Europa*, pp. 194–5.

63   Brückner, 'Histoire de la Volkskunde', p. 225.

64   Cocchiara, *Storia del folklore in Europa*, p. 197.

65   Clarissa Campbell Orr, 'Romanticism in Switzerland' in Roy Porter and Mikuláš Teich (eds), *Romanticism in National Context* (Cambridge: Cambridge University Press, 1988), p. 134.

66   Schenk, *The Mind of the European Romantics*, pp. xxi, 13–14.

67   Porter and Teich, 'Introduction', p. 3; Renato Ortiz, *Românticos e folcloristas* (São Paulo: Olho d'Água, 1992), p. 17.

68   Schenk, *The Mind of the European Romantics*, pp. xxii, 3, 6–7, 9, 13–14, 15, 18, 21.

69   Schenk, *The Mind of the European Romantics*, pp. 22–6. Eighteenth-century republican thought in England – though not in Scotland – and in North America tended to be hostile to capitalism, seeing its potential for corruption, and seeking 'a lost or at least endangered communitarian society'. Colonial pamphlets in the 1770s were opposed to commerce and took pride in the agrarian nature of America. See Thomas Bartlett, 'The Burden of the Present: Theobald Wolfe Tone, Republican and Separatist' in David Dickson, Dáire Keogh and Kevin Whelan (eds), *The United Irishmen. Republicanism, Radicalism and Rebellion* (Dublin: The Lilliput Press, 1993), p. 3.

70   Sebreli, *El asedio a la modernidad*, p. 87.

71   Schenk, *The Mind of the European Romantics*, pp. 34, 37.

72   Chapman, *The Celts*, pp. 130–1.

73   Joep Leerssen, *Remembrance and Imagination* (Cork: Cork University Press, 1996), pp. 157 et seq., 190.

74   Joep Leerssen, *Mere Irish and Fíor-Ghael. Studies in the Idea of Irish Nationality, its Development and Literary Expression prior to the Nineteenth Century*, 2nd edition (Cork: Cork University Press, 1996), pp. 289 et seq.; Chapman, *The Celts*, pp. 205–7.

75   Ernest Renan, *The Poetry of the Celtic Races, and other Studies*, trans. with introduction and notes William G. Hutchison (London: Walter Scott, Ltd: n.d. [Introduction dated Sept. 1896]), pp. 2–3; see also Patrick Sims-Williams, 'The Medieval World of Robin Flower' in Mícheál de Mórdha (ed.), *Bláithín: Flower. Ceiliúradh an Bhlascaoid* 1 (Dingle: An Sagart, 1998), pp. 75–6.

76   Renan, *The Poetry of the Celtic Races*, pp. 4–5, 7.

77   Matthew Arnold, *On the Study of Celtic Literature* (London: Smith, Elder and Co., 1867), pp. 14, 105, 109.

78   Chapman, *The Celts*, pp. 214–17.

79   Schenk, *The Mind of the European Romantics*, pp. 44, 92–3, 95–6.

80   Schenk, *The Mind of the European Romantics*, pp. 17, 187 et seq., 202.

81   Jesús Martín-Barbero, *Communication, Culture and Hegemony*, trans. Elizabeth Fox and Robert A. White (London, Newbury Park, New Delhi: Sage, 1993), pp. 6–7.

82   Ortiz, *Românticos e folcloristas*, pp. 18, 19, 20.

83   Martín-Barbero, *Communication, Culture and Hegemony*, p. 11.

84   Julia Kristeva, *Étrangers à nous-mêmes* (Paris: Gallimard, 1988), p. 261.

85   Porter and Teich, 'Introduction' to *Romanticism in National Context*, p. 3; Campbell Orr, 'Romanticism in Switzerland', p. 134; Stephen Bann, 'Romanticism in France' in Porter and Teich, *Romanticism in National Context*, pp. 240, 252.

86   Bann, 'Romanticism in France', p. 252.

87   Chapman, *The Celts*, pp. 125, 128, 134, 136–8.
88   Patrick Rafroidi, *L'Irlande et le romantisme* (Paris: Éditions Universitaires, 1972), p. 13.
89   Tom Dunne, 'Haunted by history: Irish Romantic writing 1800–1850', in Porter and Teich (eds), *Romanticism in National Context*, p. 70; Leerssen, *Remembrance and Imagination*, pp. 31 et seq.
90   Dunne, 'Haunted by history', pp. 71, 72.
91   Leerssen, *Remembrance and Imagination*, pp. 37–8, 49.
92   John Hutchinson, *The Dynamics of Cultural Nationalism. The Gaelic Revival and the Creation of the Irish Nation State* (London: Allen and Unwin, 1987), p. 97.
93   D. George Boyce, *Nationalism in Ireland*, 2nd edition (London and New York: Routledge, 1991), pp. 169–70.
94   Dunne, 'Haunted by history', pp. 88–9.
95   Hettne, *Development Theory and the Three Worlds*, pp. 164–5.
96   Sebreli, *El asedio a la modernidad*, pp. 121, 221–3.
97   Sebreli, *El asedio a la modernidad*, pp. 25, 75.

2: Towards a Concept of Folklore

1   Jacques Revel, *A invenção da sociedade*, trans. Vanda Anastácio (Lisboa and Rio de Janeiro: Difel and Bertrand Brasil, 1990), pp. 78–80.
2   The term is that of Alberto M. Cirese, *Cultura egemonica e culture subalterne*, 2nd edition (Palermo: Palumbo, 1979), p. 126.
3   Giuseppe Cocchiara, *Storia del folklore in Italia* (Palermo: Sellerio, 1981), pp. 16–17.
4   Revel, *A invenção da sociedade*, p. 84.
5   See Cocchiara, *Storia del folklore in Europa, passim*, and the standard introduction of Stith Thompson, *The Folktale* (Berkeley, Los Angeles and London 1971: University of California Press, 1971).
6   Cirese, *Cultura egemonica e culture subalterne*, pp. 126–7.
7   Raymond Gillespie, 'Popular and Unpopular Religion: A View from Early Modern Ireland', in Donnelly and Miller, *Irish Popular Culture 1650–1850*, p. 31.
8   Gearóid Ó Crualaoich, 'The "Merry Wake"' in Donnelly and Miller, *Irish Popular Culture 1650–1850*, pp. 173–6; Seán Ó Súilleabháin, *Irish Wake Amusements*, trans. author (Cork: Mercier Press, 1967), pp. 146–54.
9   Diarmuid Ó Giolláin, 'The Pattern' in Donnelly and Miller, *Irish Popular Culture 1650–1850*, p. 214.
10   Revel, *A invenção da sociedade*, p. 82.
11   Jean Cuisenier and Martine Segalen, *Ethnologie de la France* (Paris: Presses Universitaires de France, 1986), p. 6; Nicole Belmont (edition and introduction), *Aux sources de l'ethnologie française. L'Académie celtique* (Paris: Éditions du CTHS, 1995), pp. 9–10.
12   Bausinger, *Volkskunde*, pp. 12–16, 18.
13   Cirese, *Cultura egemonica e culture subalterne*, pp. 126–7.
14   Mats Rehnberg, 'Folkloristiska inslag i olika tidevarvs idéströmningar kring det egna landet' in Lauri Honko (ed.), *Folklore och Nationsbyggande i Norden* (Åbo: Nordiska Institutet för Folkdiktning, 1980), pp. 21–2.
15   Leerssen, *Remembrance and Imagination*, pp. 68–9.
16   William A. Wilson, *Folklore and Nationalism in Modern Finland* (Bloomington and London: Indiana University Press, 1976), pp. 9–10; Rehnberg, 'Folkloristiska inslag i olika tidevarvs idéströmningar kring det egna landet', pp. 17 et seq.; Jouko Hautala, *Finnish Folklore Research 1828–1918* (Helsinki: Finnish Society of Sciences, 1968), pp. 12–13.

17   Richard Dorson, *The British Folklorists* (London: Routledge and Kegan Paul, 1968), pp. 1–10.
18   Dorson, *The British Folklorists*, pp. 13–18.
19   Mączak, *Viaggi e viaggiatori nell'Europa moderna*, pp. 407–32.
20   Cirese, *Cultura egemonica e culture subalterne*, p. 246.
21   Revel, *A invenção da sociedade*, pp. 94–5.
22   Cuisenier and Segalen, *Ethnologie de la France*, p. 6; Belmont, *Aux sources de l'ethnologie française*, pp. 9–10.
23   Bausinger, *Volkskunde*, pp. 23–4.
24   Robert Welch (ed.), *The Oxford Companion to Irish Literature* (Oxford: Clarendon Press, 1996), p. 98.
25   Constantia Maxwell, *The Stranger in Ireland. From the Reign of Elizabeth to the Great Famine* (Dublin: Gill and Macmillan, 1979), pp. 20 et seq., 68 et seq.
26   Maxwell, *The Stranger in Ireland*, pp. 163 et seq.; 189 et seq.
27   Cited in Christopher Morash, 'Introduction', in W.M. Thackeray, *The Irish Sketchbook* (Dublin: Gill and Macmillan, 1990), p. xiii.
28   A good selection of these writings is in Diarmaid Ó Muirithe, *A Seat Behind the Coachman. Travellers in Ireland 1800–1900* (Dublin: Gill and Macmillan, 1972).
29   Bausinger, *Volkskunde*, pp. 24–5.
30   Bausinger, *Volkskunde*, p. 25.
31   Brückner, 'Histoire de la Volkskunde, p. 224.
32   Belmont, *Aux sources de l'ethnologie française*, pp. 9–11, 13, 17, 19, 26–37. The memoir is on pp. 39–51.
33   Revel, *A invenção da sociedade*, pp. 93–4.
34   Belmont, *Aux sources de l'ethnologie française*, pp. 15–16.
35   Cirese, *Cultura egemonica e culture subalterne*, pp. 132–3, 246–7.
36   Alan Gailey, 'Folk-life Study and the Ordnance Survey Memoirs' in Alan Gailey and Dáithí Ó hÓgáin (eds), *Gold Under the Furze. Studies in Folk Tradition* (Dublin: The Glendale Press, 1982), pp. 150–64; Paul Ferguson, 'Ordnance Survey' in S.J. Connolly (ed.), *The Oxford Companion to Irish History* (Oxford: Oxford University Press, 1998), pp. 415–16; Leerssen, *Remembrance and Imagination*, pp. 100 et seq.
37   Leerssen, *Remembrance and Imagination*, p. 102.
38   Brian Friel, John Andrews and Kevin Barry, 'Translations and A Paper Landscape: Between Fiction and History', *The Crane Bag* vol. 7, no. 2, p. 119.
39   See Stiofán Ó Cadhla, 'Mapping a Discourse: Irish *Gnosis* and the Ordnance Survey 1824–1841' in *Irish Journal of Anthropology* vol. 4 (1999), pp. 84–109. It was not possible to take this into account in the writing of this section.
40   Gailey, 'Folk-life Study and the Ordnance Survey Memoirs', *passim*.
41   Niall Ó Ciosáin, 'Boccoughs and God's Poor: Deserving and Undeserving Poor in Irish Popular Culture' in Tadhg Foley and Seán Ryder (eds), *Ideology and Ireland in the Nineteenth Century* (Dublin: Four Courts Press, 1998), pp. 93 et seq.
42   Schenk, *The Mind of the European Romantics*, p. 164.
43   Ortiz, 'El viaje, lo popular y el otro', pp. 27–36.
44   Bausinger, *Volkskunde*, pp. 17–20, 38–9, 44; Jack Zipes, *Fairy tales and the Art of Subversion. The classical genre for children and the process of civilization* (London: Heinemann, 1983), p. 47; Cocchiara, *Storia del folklore in Europa*, pp. 251–2, 256–7; Linda Dégh, 'Folk Narrative' in Richard M. Dorson, *Folklore and Folklife. An Introduction* (Chicago and London: University of Chicago Press, 1972), pp. 54–5.
45   Burke, *Popular Culture in Early Modern Europe*, p. 4; Brückner, 'Histoire de la Volkszkunde', pp. 226–7; Cocchiara, *Storia del folklore in Europa*, p. 249, 258–9; Elfriede Moser-Rath, 'Deutschland' in Kurt Ranke (ed.), *Enzyklopädie des Märchens* Band 3 (Berlin and New York: Walter de Gruyter, 1981), pp. 526–7; Bausinger, *Volkskunde*, pp. 41–2.

46   Thompson, *The Folktale*, pp. 369, 371.
47   Thompson, *The Folktale*, pp. 370 et seq.; Bausinger, *Volkskunde*, pp. 44–6; Linda
      Dégh, 'Folk Narrative', p. 55.
48   Thompson, *The Folktale*, p. 379.
49   Moser-Rath, 'Deutschland', pp. 523–5; Thompson, *The Folktale*, pp. 370 et seq.
50   The letter, dated 22 August, 1846, is reproduced in Alan Dundes, *The Study of
      Folklore* (Englewood Cliffs, NJ: Prentice Hall, 1968), pp. 4–5; Dorson, *Folklore and
      Folklife: An Introduction*, p. 1.
51   Ó Danachair, 'The Progress of Irish Ethnology, 1783–1982', *Ulster Folklife* vol. 29
      (1983), p. 5.
52   Williams, *Keywords*, pp. 136–7.
53   Cuisenier and Segalen, *Ethnologie de la France*, pp. 8–9.
54   Williams, *Keywords*, pp. 236–7.
55   Burke, *Popular Culture in early Modern Europe*, p. 8; Williams, *Keywords*, p. 237.
56   Cuisenier and Segalen, *Ethnologie de la France*, p. 15; Cirese, *Cultura egemonica e
      culture subalterne*, p. 61.
57   Poirier, *Histoire de l'ethnologie*, p. 20.
58   Panoff and Perrin, *Dictionnaire de l'ethnologie*, p. 99.
59   Lucy Mair, *An Introduction to Social Anthropology*, 2nd edition (Oxford: Clarendon
      Press, 1972), p. 8.
60   Åke Hultkrantz, 'The Concept of "Folk": in Sigurd Erixon's Ethnological Theory' in
      Hermanna W.M. Plettenburg (ed.), *Erixoniana. Contributions to the Study of European
      Ethnology in memory of Sigurd Erixon* 1 (Arnhem: Rijksmuseum voor Volkskunde
      'Het Nedelands Openluchtmuseum', 1970), p. 18; G. de Rohan-Csermak, 'La contri-
      bution erixonienne à la théorie ethnologique' in Plettenburg, *Erixoniana*, pp 11–17;
      Sigurd Erixon, 'Ethnologie régionale ou folklore' in *Laos* 1 (1951), pp. 9–19.
61   Don Yoder, 'Folklife Studies in American Scholarship' in Don Yoder (ed.), *Ameri-
      can Folklife* (Austin and London: University of Texas Press, 1976), p. 4.
62   Pertti J. Anttonen, 'Profiles of Folkore 2: Department of European Ethnology Lund
      University, Sweden', *NIF Newsletter* (Turku: Nordic Institute of Folklore) no. 2,
      1993, p. 3.
63   Cuisenier and Segalen, *Ethnologie de la France*, pp. 25, 37–9.
64   Seathrún Céitinn, *Forus Feasa ar Éirinn* 1 (London: Irish Texts Society, 1902), pp. 4, 6.
65   Céitinn, *Forus Feasa* II (London: Irish Texts Society, 1908), p. 324.
66   See the discussion in Roslyn Blyn-LaDrew, 'Geoffrey Keating, William Thoms,
      Raymond Williams, and the Terminology of Folklore: "*Béaloideas*" as a
      "Keyword"', *Folklore Forum* vol. 27, no. 2, pp. 5–37.
67   Dorson, *The British Folklorists*, pp. 1–18.
68   Richard M. Dorson, *Folklore and Fakelore* (Cambridge, Massachusetts and
      London, England: Harvard University Press, 1976), pp. 81, 108–9.
69   Michèle Simonsen, *Le conte populaire français* (Paris: Presses Universitaires de
      France, 1981), p. 21.
70   Hautala, *Finnish Folklore Research*, p. 63.
71   'The Devolutionary Premise in Folklore Theory' in Alan Dundes, *Analytic Essays in
      Folklore* (The Hague, Paris and New York: Mouton, 1975), pp. 16–27; Bausinger,
      Volkskunde, pp. 105–6.
72   Edward B. Tylor, *Primitive Culture. Researches into the Development of Mythology,
      Philosophy, Religion, Art, and Custom* (London: John Murray, 1871), p. 1.
73   Both cited in George W. Stocking, Jr, *After Tylor. British Social Anthropology
      1888–1951* (London: The Athlone Press, 1996), pp. 6, 8.
74   Tylor, *Primitive Culture*, pp. 40–1; See Ortiz, *Románticos e folcloristas*, pp. 29–31;
      Cocchiara, *Storia del folklore in Europa*, pp. 405 et seq.; Cuisenier and Segalen,
      Ethnologie de la France, p. 16.

75 Ortiz, *Românticos e folcloristas*, pp. 32–4; Bausinger, *Volkskunde*, p. 48; Cuisenier and Segalen, *Ethnologie de la France*, p. 16.

76 I.M. Lewis, *Social Anthropology in Perspective* (Harmondsworth: Penguin Books, 1976), p. 37.

77 Ortiz, *Românticos e folcloristas*, pp. 36–8.

78 Tylor, *Primitive Culture*, pp. 38–9.

79 Ortiz, *Românticos e folcloristas*, p. 38.

80 George W. Stocking, Jr., *Race, Culture, and Evolution. Essays in the History of Anthropology* (Chicago and London: University of Chicago Press, 1982), p. 225.

81 Stocking, *After Tylor, passim*.

82 Stocking, *After Tylor*, pp. 98 et seq.

83 Stocking, *After Tylor*, pp. 104–373.

84 Rosemary Lévy Zumwalt, *American Folklore Scholarship. A Dialogue of Dissent* (Bloomington and Indianapolis: Indiana University Press, 1988), pp. xi–xii, 1.

85 Lévy Zumwalt, *American Folklore Scholarship*, pp. 5–6.

86 Stocking, *Race, Culture, and Evolution*, pp. 201, 221, 223 et seq.; Cuche, *La noción de cultura en las ciencias sociales*, pp. 25 et seq.

87 Stocking, *Race, Culture, and Evolution*, p. 152; Carmelo Lisón Tolosana, *Ensayos de antropología social* (Madrid: Ayuso, 1978), pp. 235 et seq.; Stocking, *After Tylor*, p. 180.

88 Hautala, *Finnish Folklore Research 1828–1928*, pp. 64, 70.

89 Richard M. Dorson, 'Introduction. Concepts of Folklore and Folklife Studies' in Dorson, *Folklore and Folklife. An Introduction*, pp. 8 et seq.; Thompson, *The Folktale*, pp. 430 et seq.; Simonsen, *Le conte populaire français*, pp. 43 et seq.; Michael Chesnutt, 'The Demise of Historicism in Nordic Folktale Research' in Chesnutt (ed.), *Telling Reality. Folklore Studies in Memory of Bengt Holbek* (Copenhagen and Turku: Dept of Folklore, University of Copenhagen and Nordic Institute of Folklore, 1993), pp. 234–53.

90 Hautala, *Finnish Folklore Research*, pp. 88, 139 et seq.; Thomson, *The Folktale*, pp. 430 et seq.

91 Montserrat Iniesta i Gonzàlez, *Els gabinets del món. Antropologia, museus i museologies* (Lleida: Pagès 1994), p. 102.

92 Kevin Danaher, 'Introduction' to T. Crofton Croker, *Researches in the South of Ireland* (Dublin: Irish Academic Press, 1981), p. vi.

93 Roland Schaer, *L'invention des musées* (Paris: Gallimard/Réunion des Musées Nationaux, 1993), p. 96.

94 Iniesta i Gonzàlez, *Els gabinets del món*, pp. 109–10.

95 Bjarne Stocklund, 'How the Peasant House Became a National Symbol. A Chapter in the History of Museums and Nation-Building' in *Ethnologia Europaea* no. 29, vol. 1 (1999), pp. 6–9.

96 See Iniesta i Gonzàlez, *Els gabinets del món*, pp. 117–18.

97 Schaer, *L'invention des musées*, p. 96–97; Iniesta i Gonzàlez, *Els gabinets del món*, pp. 116–17.

98 Iniesta i Gonzàlez, *Els gabinets del món*, pp. 116–17.

99 Tony Bennett, *The Birth of the Museum. History, Theory, Politics* (London and New York: Routledge, 1995), pp. 115–16.

100 Iniesta i Gonzàlez, *Els gabinets del món*, p. 58.

101 Heiki Pärdi, 'Estonian National Museum – a Symbol of Estonian People and a Museum', *Pro Ethnologia* no. 2 (1994), pp. 39–49.

102 Bennett, *The Birth of the Museum*, pp. 109–110.

103 E.E. Evans, 'The Early Development of Folklife Studies in Northern Ireland' in Alan Gailey (ed.), *The Use of Tradition* (Cultra: Ulster Folk and Transport Museum, 1988), pp. 91–6; Alan Gailey, 'Creating Ulster's Folk Museum' in *Ulster Folklife* no. 32 (1986), pp. 54–77.

104 A.T. Lucas, 'The National Folk Life Collection' in Patricia Lysaght, Anne O'Dowd and Bairbre O'Flynn (eds), *A Folk Museum for Ireland* (Dublin: [no publisher], 1984).

105 Ann Kanike, '"Rahvuslik" rahvakultuur/"National "Folk Culture', *Pro Ethnologia* no. 2 (1994), pp. 23–24.

106 Barbara Kirshenblatt-Gimblett, 'Objects of Ethnography' in Ivan Karp and Stephen D. Lavine (eds), *Exhibiting Cultures. The Poetics and Politics of Museum Display* (Washington and London: Smithsonian Institution Press, 1991), pp. 388 et seq.

107 Bausinger, *Volkskunde*, p. 296.

108 Stuart Hall, 'Notes on Deconstructing "the Popular"' in Raphael Samuel (ed.), *People's History and Socialist Theory* (London, Boston and Henley: Routledge and Kegan Paul, 1981), p. 236.

109 García Canclini, *Hybrid Cultures*, p. 137.

110 Eric R. Wolf, *Peasants* (Englewood Cliffs, New Jersey: Prentice-Hall, Inc., 1966), p. 2.

111 Robert Redfield, 'Peasant Society and Culture' in *The Little Community/Peasant Society and Culture* (Chicago and London: University of Chicago Press, 1960), pp. 20–1, 36–7.

112 Kearney, *Reconceptualizing the Peasantry*, pp. 4, 34–5, 38–9, 50.

113 Redfield, 'Peasant Society and Culture', pp. 41 et seq.

114 Kearney, *Reconceptualizing the Peasantry*, pp. 50–2.

115 Gearóid Ó Crualaoich, 'The Primacy of Form: A "Folk Ideology" in de Valera's Politics' in J.P. O'Carroll and John A. Murphy (eds), *De Valera and His Times* (Cork: Cork University Press, 1986), p. 52.

116 Isac Chiva, 'Les revues ethnologiques en Europe: richesses et paradoxes' in Christiane Amiel, Jean-Pierre Piniès and René Piniès (eds), *Au miroir des revues. Ethnologie de l'Europe du Sud* (Carcassonne and Paris: Garae/Hesiode and Ent're-vues, 1991), p. 204.

117 Klaus Roth, 'European Ethnology and Intercultural Communication' in *Ethnologia Europaea* no. 26, vol. 1 (1996), pp. 3–5.

3: Folklore and Nation building

1 Leerssen, *Remembrance and Imagination*, p. 37.

2 Roberto Schwarz, 'Brazilian Culture: Nationalism by Elimination', trans. Linda Briggs in Roberto Schwarz, *Misplaced Ideas. Essays on Brazilian Culture* (London and New York: Verso, 1992), p. 1.

3 José Joaquín Brunner, *Cartografías de la modernidad* (Santiago [de Chile]: Dolmen Ediciones, n.d.), pp. 160–2.

4 E. Bradford Burns, *A History of Brazil*, 3rd edition (New York: Columbia University Press, 1993), pp. 328–30.

5 Elias, *The Civilizing Process*, pp. 22–3.

6 Cited in Joan Prat, 'Historia' in Joan Prat, Ubaldo Martínez, Jesús Contreras and Isodoro Moreno (eds), *Antropología de los Pueblos de España* (Madrid: Taurus Universitaria, 1991), p. 14.

7 Alan Dundes, 'Nationalistic Inferiority Complexes and the Fabrication of Folklore: A Reconsideration of Ossian, the *Kinder- und Hausmärchen*, the *Kalevala*, and Paul Bunyan' in Reimund Kvideland and Torunn Selberg (eds), *1: The 8th Congress for the International Society for Folk Narrative Research* (Bergen: [no publisher], 1984), pp. 155–71.

8 Renato Ortiz, *A moderna tradição brasileira*, 5th edition (São Paulo: Editorial Brasiliense, 1994), p. 161.

9 See Ortiz, *Românticos e folcloristas*, p. 68.

10 See Joseph Ruane, 'Colonialism and the Interpretation of Irish Historical Development' in Marilyn Gulliver and P.H. Gulliver (eds), *Approaching the Past. Historical Anthropology through Irish Case Studies* (New York: Columbia University Press, 1992), pp. 293–323.

11 Michael Hechter, *Internal Colonialism* (London and Henley: Routledge and Kegan Paul, 1975), p. 73.

12 Sir William Wilde, *Irish Popular Superstitions* (Dublin: Irish Academic Press, 1979 [1852]), p. 27.

13 Ngũgĩ wa Thiong'o, *Decolonising the Mind. The Politics of Language in African Literature* (London, Nairobi and Portsmouth N.H.: James Currey/EAEP/Heinemann, 1986), p. 111.

14 Ngũgĩ, *Decolonising the Mind*, p. 12.

15 Anu Kanike, '"Rahvuslik" rahvakultuur/"National" Folk Culture', p. 21.

16 Paul F. Saagpakk, *Eesti-Inglise Sõnaraamat/Estonian-English Dictionary*, 2nd Edition (Tallinn: Koolibri, 1992), *s.v. 'saks'*.

17 Fredrik Barth, *Ethnic Groups and Boundaries. The Social Organization of Cultural Difference* (Bergen-Oslo/London: Universitets Forlaget/George Allen and Unwin, 1969), p. 31.

18 Ilmar Talve, *Suomen kansankulttuuri* (Helsinki: Suomalainen Kirjallisuuden Seura, 1980), p. 296; Mart Laar, Lauri Vahtre and Heiki Valk, *Kodu lugu 1* (Tallinn: Loomingu Raamatukogu 40/41, 1989), p. 88.

19 Billy Ehn, Jonas Frykman, Orvar Löfgren, *Försvenskningen av Sverige* (Stockholm: Natur och Kultur, 1993), p. 13.

20 Barth, *Ethnic Groups and Boundaries*, pp. 10–11, 24–5.

21 Alberto M. Cirese, 'Alterità e dislivelli interni di cultura nelle società superiori' in Alberto M. Cirese (ed.), *Folklore e antropologia* (Palermo: Palumbo, 1972), pp. 38–9.

22 C.A. Ferguson, 'Diglossia' in Pier Paolo Giglioli (ed.), *Language and Social Context* (Harmondsworth: Penguin, 1972), p. 236.

23 Julia Kristeva, *Étrangers à nous-mêmes* (Paris:Gallimard, 1988), p. 262.

24 Michel de Certeau, Dominique Julia and Jacques Revel, 'La beauté du mort' in Michel de Certeau, *La culture au pluriel* (Paris: Seuil, 1993), pp. 48–51.

25 Ju. M. Lotman, 'On the Metalanguage of a Typological Description of Culture', *Semiotica* vol. 14, no. 2 (1975), pp. 101–5.

26 Diarmuid Ó Giolláin, 'Myth and History. Exotic Foreigners in Folk-belief', *Temenos. Studies in Comparative Religion presented by Scholars in Denmark, Finland, Norway and Sweden* vol. 23 (1987), pp. 74–5.

27 Lauri Honko, 'Studies on tradition and cultural identity: An introduction' in Lauri Honko (ed.), *Tradition and Cultural Identity* (Turku: Nordic Institute of Folklore, 1988), p. 11.

28 Ju. M. Lotman, 'The Dynamic Model of a Semiotic System', *Semiotica* vol. 21, nos 3/4 (1977), p. 198.

29 Honko, 'Studies on tradition and cultural identity: An introduction', pp. 9–11.

30 See Anthony D. Smith, *National Identity* (London: Penguin, 1991), p. 40; Miroslav Hroch, 'From National Movement to Fully-formed Nation: The Nation-building Process in Europe' in Gopal Balakrishnan (ed.), *Mapping the Nation* (London and New York: Verso, 1996), p. 79; David Held, 'The Development of the Modern State' in Hall and Gieben (eds), *Formations of Modernity*, pp. 87–8.

31 Ernest Renan, 'What is a Nation?' in Omar Dahbour and Micheline R. Ishay (eds), *The Nationalism Reader* (New Jersey: Humanities Press, 1995), pp. 150, 154; Guy Hermet, *Histoire des nations et du nationalisme en Europe* (Paris: Éditions du Seuil, 1996), pp. 129–33.

32 Jürgen Habermas,'The European Nation-State – Its Achievements and Its Limits' in Balakrishnan, *Mapping the Nation*, pp. 284, 287.

33   Ernest Gellner, 'The Coming of Nationalism and Its Interpretation: The Myths of Nation and Class' in Balakrishnan, *Mapping the Nation*, pp. 138–39; Hroch, 'From National Movement to Fully-formed Nation', pp. 79–80.

34   Hroch, 'From National Movement to Fully-formed Nation', p. 80.

35   Ernest Gellner, *Nations and Nationalism* (Oxford UK and Cambridge UK: Blackwell, 1983), pp. 35, 61.

36   Hroch, 'From National Movement to Fully-formed Nation', p. 84.

37   Hroch, 'From National Movement to Fully-formed Nation', pp. 80–5.

38   Ernesto Laclau, *Politics and Ideology in Marxist Theory* (London: NLB, 1977), p. 175.

39   Aleksander Loit, 'Die nationalen Bewegungen im Baltikum während des 19. Jahrhunderts in vergleichender Perspektive' in Aleksander Loit (ed.), *National Movements in the Baltic Countries during the 19th Century. Acta Universitatis Stockholmiensis Studia Baltica Stockholmiensia 2* (Stockholm: Centre for Baltic Studies University of Stockholm, 1985), p. 63.

40   Hroch, 'From National Movement to Fully-formed Nation', p. 80.

41   Peter Alter, *Nationalism*, trans. Stuart McKinnon-Evans (London, New York, Melbourne, Auckland: Edward Arnold, 1989), pp. 28 et seq.

42   Partha Chatterjee, 'Whose Imagined Community?' in Balakrishnan, *Mapping the Nation*, p. 217.

43   Pertti J. Anttonen, 'Nationalism, Ethnicity and the Making of Antiquities as a Strategy in Cultural Representation', *Suomen Antropologi. Journal of the Finnish Anthropological Society*, no. 1 (1994), p. 33.

44   García Canclini, *Hybrid Cultures*, pp. 123, 130.

45   Ephraim Nimni, *Marxism and Nationalism* (London and Boulder, Colorado: Pluto Press, 1991), pp. 26–7.

46   Nicholas Mansergh, *The Irish Question 1840–1921*, 3rd edition (London: George Allen and Unwin Ltd, 1975), pp. 96, 99.

47   Löfgren, 'Rational and Sensitive', pp. 51 et seq., p. 74.

48   Loit, 'Die nationalen Bewegungen im Baltikum während des 19. Jahrhunderts in vergleichender Perspektive', p. 66.

49   Diarmuid Ó Giolláin, 'Colonialism in the Eastern Baltic? The Estonian and Finnish Cases' Unpublished paper given to the Conference of the Anthropology Association of Ireland, St Patrick's College, Maynooth, 1996.

50   Toivo Raun, 'The Estonians and the Russian Empire, 1905–1917', *Journal of Baltic Studies* vol. XV, nos 2/3, p. 138.

51   David Kirby, *The Baltic World 1772–1993. Europe's Northern Periphery in an Age of Change* (London and New York: Longman, 1995), p. 268.

52   Oskar Loorits, 'Eesti rahvaluuleteaduse tänapäev', *Õpetatud Eesti Seltsi Kirjad 1. Vanavara vallast* (Tartu: Õpetatud Eesti Selts, 1932), pp. 7–8.

53   Uku Masing, 'Esten' in Kurt Ranke (ed.), *Enzyklopädie des Märchens 4* (Berlin and New York: Walter de Gruyter, 1984), p. 480; Eduard Laugaste, *Eesti rahvaluule*, 3rd edition (Tallinn: Valgus, 1986), pp. 112–13.

54   Laugaste, *Eesti rahvaluule*, p. 117; Loorits, 'Eesti rahvaluuleteaduse tänapäev', p. 8.

55   Richard Viidalepp, 'Auhindadest ja auhindamisest', *Rahvapärimuste Selgitaja* II nr. 1 (8 [1940]), pp. 84–5.

56   Richard Viidalepp, *Valimik muistendeid Koolide Kogumisvõistluselt 1939. Eesti Rahvaluule Arhiivi Toimetused 10* (1939), p. 11.

57   William A. Wilson, *Folklore and Nationalism in Modern Finland* (Bloomington and London: Indiana University Press, 1976), pp. 32–4, 41–2.

58   Matti Klinge, '"Let Us Be Finns" – the Birth of Finland's National Culture" in Rosalind Mitchison (ed.), *The Roots of Nationalism. Studies in Northern Europe* (Edinburgh: John Donald, 1980), p. 74.

59   Seppo Zetterberg (ed.), *Suomen Historian Pikku Jättiläinen* (Porvoo, Helsinki, Juva: Werner Söderström Osakeyhtiö, 1995), p. 570.

60   Heikki Ylikangas, 'Über den gesellschaftlichen Hintergrund der finnischen nationalen Bewegung' in Tenho Takalo (ed.), *Finns and Hungarians between East and West* (Helsinki: Societas Historica Finlandiae, 1989), pp. 88–9.

61   Hannes Sihvo, 'Karelianism', in Olli Alho, Hildi Hawkins and Päivi Vallisaari (ed.), *Finland: A Cultural Encyclopedia* (Helsinki: Finnish Literature Society, 1997), pp. 173–4.

62   Lotte Tarkka, 'Karjalan kuvaus kansallisena retoriikkana' in Seppo Knuuttila and Pekka Laaksonen (ed.), *Runon ja rajan teillä* (Helsinki: Suomalaisen Kirjallisuuden Seura, 1989), pp. 243–4, 248.

63   Wilson, *Folklore and Nationalism in Modern Finland*, pp. 49, 62.

64   Wilson, *Folklore and Nationalism in Modern Finland*, pp. 183, 193.

65   William E. Simeone, 'Fascists and Folklorists in Italy', *Journal of American Folklore* vol. 91, no. 359 January–March 1978, p. 545.

66   Luigi M. Lombardi Satriani and Mariano Meligrana (eds), *Diritto egemone e diritto popolare*, 2nd edition (Vibo Valentia: Qualecultura/Jaca Book, 1995), p. 7.

67   Jean-Claude Lescure, 'Italie' in A. Guillaume, J.-C. Lescure and S. Michonneau, *L'Europe des nationalismes aux nations. Italie, Espagne, Irlande* (Paris: Sedes, 1996), p. 59.

68   Cirese, *Cultura egemonica e culture subalterne*, pp. 146, 161.

69   Lescure, 'Italie', pp. 9, 47 et seq.; Iniesta i Gonzàlez, *Els gabinets del món*, pp. 118–19; Lombardi Satriani and Meligrana, *Diritto egemone e diritto popolare*, pp. 7–8.

70   Lombardi Satriani and Meligrana, *Diritto egemone e diritto popolare*, pp. 24, 28 et seq., 46, 53, 59; Giovanni Battista Bronzini, '*Lares*' in Amiel, Piniès and Piniès, *Au miroir des revues*, p. 173.

71   Simeone, 'Fascists and Folklorists', pp. 546–47.

72   Simeone, 'Fascists and Folklorists', pp. 544, 546–51; Lombardi Satriani and Meligrana, *Diritto egemone e diritto popolare*, p. 59.

73   Simeone, 'Fascists and Folklorists', pp. 553–5.

74   The paragraphs which follow, with the exception of those on Catalonia, separately footnoted, are based on: the editor's chapter in the book of the same name, Ángel Aguirre Baztán (eds), *La antropología cultural en España. Un siglo de antropología* (Barcelona: P.P.U., 1986), pp. 15–56; Joan Prat, 'Historia' in Prat, Martínez, Contreras and Moreno, *Antropología de los pueblos de España*, pp. 13–30.

75   Llorenç Prats, *El mite de la tradició popular* (Barcelona: Edicions 62, 1988), p. 170.

76   Robert Hughes, *Barcelona* (London: Harvill, 1993), p. 348.

77   Prats, *El mite de la tradició popular*, pp. 103–4.

78   Llorenç Prats, 'Sobre el caràcter conservador de la cultura popular' in D. Llopart, J. Prat and Ll. Prats (ed.), *La cultura popular a debat* (Barcelona: Fundació Serveis de Cultura Popular Editorial Alta Fulla, 1985), pp. 76–7.

79   Josefina Romà Riu, 'Etnografía y folklore en Cataluña', pp. 161 et seq., and Aguirre Baztán, 'La antropología cultural en España. Un siglo de antropología', pp. 44–8: both in Aguirre Baztán, *La antropología cultural en España*.

80   Personal communication from Dr Dolors Llopart, director of the Museu d'Arts, Indústries i Tradicions Populars, 16 September, 1994.

81   Prat, 'Historia' in *Antropología de los pueblos de España*, pp. 20–30; Aguirre Baztán, 'La antropología cultural en España. Un siglo de antropología', p. 21.

82   Erixon, 'Ethnologie régionale ou folklore', p. 12; Hultkrantz, 'The Concept of "Folk" in Sigurd Erixon's Ethnological Theory', pp. 19–20.

83   Rehnberg, 'Folkloristiska inslag i olika tidevarvs idéströmningar kring det egna landet', pp. 23–5, 29–30; Burke, 'People's history or total history', p. 5.

84 Rehnberg, 'Folkloristiska inslag i olika tidevarvs idéströmningar kring det egna landet', pp. 25–6.

85 Löfgren, 'Rational and Sensitive', pp. 61–8.

86 Löfgren, 'Rational and Sensitive', pp. 57 et seq.

87 Ortiz, *A moderna tradição brasileira*, pp. 36–7. For Romero, see Cláudia Neiva de Matos, *A poesia popular na república das letras. Sílvio Romero folclorista* (Rio de Janeiro: Editora UFRJ and minC/FUNARTE, 1994). Freyre's most influential work was *Casa grande e senzala* (1933), later translated as *The Masters and the Slaves*. See also Bradford Burns, *A History of Brazil, passim*.

88 Luís Rodolfo Vilhena, *Projeto e missão. O movimento folclórico brasileiro 1947–1964* (Rio de Janeiro: Funarte, 1997), pp. 21, 24, 26, 31, 77, 94, 96, 104, 106, 139, 153.

89 João Gabriel de Lima, 'O limbo de Câmara Cascudo', *Veja*, 1 September, 1999, pp. 153–4.

90 Bradford Burns, *A History of Brazil*, p. 400.

91 Renato Ortiz, *Cultura brasileira e identidade nacional*, 5th edition (São Paulo: Editora Brasiliense, 1994), pp. 46, 48.

92 Ortiz, *Cultura brasileira e identidade nacional*, p. 56.

93 Vivian Schelling, *A presença do povo na cultura brasileira. Ensaio sobre o pensamento de Mário de Andrade e Paulo Freire*, trans. Federico Carotti (Campinas: Editora da UNICAMP, 1991), pp. 229–35. This is the Portuguese version of *Culture and Underdevelopment in Brazil, 1930–1968, Mário de Andrade and Paulo Freire*. The original was not available to me.

94 Roberto Schwarz, 'Culture and politics in Brazil, 1964–1969' (trans. John Gledson) in Schwarz, *Misplaced Ideas*, p. 134.

95 Paulo Freire, *Cultural Action for Freedom* (Harmondsworth: Penguin Books, 1972), pp. 59–60, 62–3.

96 Schwarz, 'Culture and politics in Brazil, 1964–1969', pp. 134–5.

97 Wolfgang Kaschuba, 'Historizing the Present? Construction and Deconstruction of the Past' in *Ethnologia Europaea* vol. 26, no.2 (1996), p. 124; Hannjost Lixfeld, 'Institutionalsierung und Instrumentalisierung der deutschen Volkskunde zu Beginn des dritten Reichs' in Wolfgang Jacobeit, Hannjost Lixfeld and Olaf Bockhorn (eds), *Völkische Wissenschaft. Gestalten und Tendenzen der deutschen und österreichischen Volkskunde in der ersten Hälfte des 20. Jahrhunderts* (Wien, Köln and Weimar: Böhlau Verlag, 1994), pp. 139–74; Christa Kamenetsky, 'Folklore as a Political Tool in Nazi Germany', *Journal of American Folklore* vol. 85, no. 337, July-September 1972, pp. 221–4, 226.

98 Jürgen Habermas, 'The Public Sphere' in Chandra Mukerji and Michael Schudson (eds), *Rethinking Popular Culture* (Berkeley, Los Angeles, Oxford: University of California Press, 1991), pp. 398–9.

99 See, for example, Arlette Farge, *Dire et mal dire. L'opinion publique au XVIIIe siècle* (Paris: Seuil, 1992); Luiz Beltrão, *Comunicação e folclore* (São Paulo: Edições Melhoramentos, 1971); Martín-Barbero, *Communication, Culture and Hegemony, passim*.

100 See Breandán Ó Buachalla, *Aisling Ghéar* (Dublin: An Clóchomhar, 1996), pp. 597 et seq.; Kevin Whelan, *The Tree of Liberty. Radicalism, Catholicism and the Construction of Irish Identity 1760–1830* (Cork: Cork University Press, 1996), pp. 61, 72, 75–6, 95; Croker, *Researches in the South of Ireland*, p. 329; Georges-Denis Zimmermann, *Songs of Irish Rebellion: Political Street Ballads and Rebel Songs 1780–1900* (Dublin: Allen Figgis, 1967), pp. 9–12, 20 et seq., 214–15, 273; Seamus Deane, 'Poetry and Song 1800–1890' in Seamus Deane (ed.), *The Field Day Anthology of Irish Writing* (Field Day Publications: Derry, 1991), vol. 2, p. 2.

101 Serge Ouaknine, 'Les rêves menacés de la transculturalité' in Jacques Langlais, Pierre Laplante and Joseph Levy (ed.), *Le Québec de demain et les communautés culturelles* (Montréal: Méridien, 1990), p. 218.

4: Irish Pioneers

1   Ó Danachair, 'The Progress of Irish Ethnology, 1783–1982', p. 4.
2   Leerssen, *Mere Irish and Fíor-Ghael*, p. 363.
3   Breandán Ó Buachalla, *I mBéal Feirste Cois Cuain* (Dublin: An Clóchomhar, 1968), pp. 69 et seq.
4   Leerssen, *Remembrance and Imagination*, pp. 3–4, 9–12, 61.
5   Leerssen, *Remembrance and Imagination*, pp. 70 et seq.
6   Ó Danachair, 'The Progress of Irish Ethnology', p. 4.
7   J.E. Caerwyn Williams and Máirín Ní Mhuiríosa, *Traidisiún Liteartha na nGael* (Dublin: An Clóchomhar Tta, 1979), pp. 317–18; Welch, *The Oxford Companion to Irish Literature*, p. 66; Leerssen, *Mere Irish and Fíor-Ghael*, pp. 363 et seq.
8   Leerssen, *Remembrance and Imagination*, pp. 31 et seq.
9   Ó Buachalla, *i mBéal Feirste Cois Cuain*, p. 31.
10   W.H. Crawford, 'The Belfast Middle Classes in the Late Eighteenth Century' in Dickson, Keogh and Whelan, *The United Irishmen*, pp. 62, 64.
11   Ó Buachalla, *i mBéal Feirste Cois Cuain*, pp. 14, 23–4.
12   Ó Buachalla, *I mBéal Feirste Cois Cuain*, pp. 14, 31 et seq., 49 et seq.; Breandán Breathnach, *Folkmusic and Dances of Ireland* (Dublin: Educational Company of Ireland, 1971), pp. 68–73; Welch, *The Oxford Companion to Irish Literature*, pp. 408–9.
13   Ó Buachalla, *I mBéal Feirste Cois Cuain*, p. 24.
14   Ó Buachalla, *I mBéal Feirste Cois Cuain*, pp. 23, 28–9, 37–44; Williams and Ní Mhuiríosa, *Traidisiún Liteartha na nGael*, p. 325.
15   Ó Buachalla, *I mBéal Feirste Cois Cuain*, pp. 69 et seq.
16   Ó Buachalla, *I mBéal Feirste Cois Cuain*, pp. 96, 100.
17   Fionnuala Williams, 'Six Hundred Gaelic Proverbs Collected in Ulster by Robert Mac Adam', *Proverbium* no. 12 (1995), pp. 343–51.
18   Leerssen, *Remembrance and Imagination*, p. 76.
19   Ó Danachair, 'The Progress of Irish Ethnology', p. 4.
20   Leerssen, *Remembrance and Imagination*, pp. 79 et seq.
21   Leerssen, *Remembrance and Imagination*, pp. 160 et seq.; see also Ó Danachair, 'The Progress of Irish Ethnology', p. 4.
22   T. Crofton Croker, *Researches in the South of Ireland. Illustrative of the Scenery, Architectural Remains and the Manners and Superstitions of the Peasantry with an Appendix containing a Private Narrative of the Rebellion of 1798* (Dublin: Irish Academic Press, 1981), pp. 12–14. I have found Cornelius G. Buttimer's close reading of Croker's *Researches* to be very helpful: see 'Remembering 1798', *Journal of the Cork Historical and Archaeological Society* vol. 103 (1998), pp. 1–26.
23   Richard M. Dorson, 'Foreword' to Seán O'Sullivan, *Folktales of Ireland*, pp. v–vii.
24   Neil C. Hultin and Warren U. Ober, 'An O'Connellite in Whitehall: Thomas Crofton Croker, 1798–1854', *Éire-Ireland* vol. xxvii, no. 3 (Fall 1993), pp. 65–86.
25   W.B. Yeats (ed.), *Fairy and Folk Tales of Ireland* (London: Picador, 1979), pp. 6–7. This edition combines *Fairy and Folk Tales of the Irish Peasantry* and *Irish Fairy Tales*.
26   Caoimhín Ó Danachair, 'Change in the Irish landscape', *Ulster Folklife* no. 8 (1962), pp. 65–6.
27   Joe Lee, 'An Gorta Mór agus Scríobh Stair na hÉireann' in Cathal Póirtéir (ed.), *Gnéithe an Ghorta* (Dublin: Coiscéim, 1995), pp. 19–21.
28   Leerssen, *Remembrance and Imagination*, p. 106.
29   Wilde, *Irish Popular Superstitions*, p. 24.
30   See Pádraig Ó Fiannachta (ed.), *Thaitin Sé le Peig. Iris na hOidhreachta* 1 (Baile an Fheirtéaraigh: Oidhreacht Chorca Dhuibhne, 1989).
31   Welch, *The Oxford Companion to Irish Literature*, pp. 608–9.

32   Mary Helen Thuente, *W.B. Yeats and Irish Folklore* (Dublin: Gill and Macmillan, 1980), pp. 34–5.

33   John Wilson Foster, *Fictions of the Irish Literary Revival. A Changeling Art* (Syracuse, New York: Syracuse University Press, 1987), pp. 205–6, 236.

34   Thuente, *W.B. Yeats and Irish Folklore*, pp. 1–2, 40–1.

35   The following paragraphs derive from Thuente, *W.B. Yeats and Irish Folklore*, pp. 4–6, 16, 24, 31, 74, 86, 92–3.

36   Zimmermann, *Songs of Irish Rebellion*, pp. 83–4.

37   W.B. Yeats (ed.), *Fairy and Folk Tales of Ireland* (London: Picador, 1979), pp. 5, 7, 301, 303.

38   Thuente, *W.B. Yeats and Irish Folklore*, pp. 124, 132, 139–40, 142.

39   Hyde, *Language, Lore and Lyrics*, p. 36.

40   Douglas Hyde, *Beside the Fire. A Collection of Gaelic Folk Stories* (London: David Nutt, 1910).

41   Hyde, *Beside the Fire*, pp. ix–l; Dorson 'Foreword' in O'Sullivan, *Folktales of Ireland*, p. xiv; Dubhglas de h-Íde, *An Sgeulaidhe Gaedhealach* (Dublin: Institiút Béaloideasa Éireann, 1933), pp. v–ix; Welch, *The Oxford Companion to Irish Literature*, pp. 254–6; Foster, *Fictions of the Irish Literary Revival*, pp. 221 et seq.

42   Mícheál Ó hAodha, 'Introduction' to Douglas Hyde, *Abhráin Grádh Chúige Connacht. Love Songs of Connacht* (Shannon: Irish University Press, 1969), p. vii.

43   Declan Kiberd, *Inventing Ireland. The Literature of the Modern Nation* (London: Vintage, 1996), pp. 155–6.

44   Kiberd, *Inventing Ireland*, pp. 84 et seq.

45   Quoted in Dorson, 'Foreword' in Sean O'Sullivan, *Folktales of Ireland*, p. xvii.

46   Lady Gregory, *Poets and Dreamers. Studies and Translations from the Irish* (Dublin and London: Hodges, Figgis, and Co., Ltd, and John Murray, 1903), p. 47.

47   Lady Gregory, *The Kiltartan History Book* (London: T. Fisher Unwin Ltd, 1926), pp. 152, 155.

48   See Patricia Lysaght, 'Perspectives on Narrative Communication and Gender: Lady Augusta Gregory's *Visions and Beliefs in the West of Ireland* (1920)' in *Fabula* vol. 39, nos. 3–4 (1998). This article was not available to me during the writing of this book.

49   Welch, *The Oxford Companion to Irish Literature*, p. 221.

50   Terence Brown, *Ireland: A Social and Cultural History 1922–1979* (Glasgow: Fontana, 1981), p. 93.

51   Williams and Ní Mhuiríosa, *Traidisiún Liteartha na nGael*, p. 358. The lines and paragraphs following derive from Declan Kiberd, *Synge and the Irish Language* (London and Basingstoke: Macmillan, 1979), pp. 155–6, 159, 161, 162, 245 et seq.

52   Mac Conghail, *The Blaskets*, pp. 132–5; Diarmuid Breathnach and Máire Ní Mhurchú, *1882–1982. Beathaisnéis a Ceathair* (Dublin: An Clóchomhar Tta, 1994), pp. 76–8.

53   Leerssen, *Remembrance and Imagination*, pp. 157 et seq., 190.

5: The Gaelicization of Folklore

1   Hyde, *Language, Lore and Lyrics*, pp. 153, 155, 157, 168–70.

2   Orvar Löfgren, 'The Cultural Grammar of Nation-Building' in Pertti J. Anttonen and Reimund Kvideland (eds), *Nordic Frontiers* (Turku: Nordic Institute of Folklore, 1993), pp. 217–18.

3   Nicholas Mansergh, *The Irish Question 1840–1921*, 2nd edition (London: George Allen and Unwin Ltd, 1965), pp. 75–82.

4   John Hutchinson, *The Dynamics of Cultural Nationalism. The Gaelic Revival and the Creation of the Irish Nation State* (London: Allen and Unwin, 1987), p. 222.

5   Roy Foster, *Modern Ireland* (London: Penguin Books, 1989), p. 438.
6   Tom Garvin, *Nationalist Revolutionaries in Ireland 1858–1928* (Oxford: Clarendon Press, 1987), pp. 102–6.
7   Lee, *The Modernisation of Irish Society 1848–1918*, pp. 139–40.
8   Williams and Ní Mhuiríosa, *Traidisiún Liteartha na nGael*, p. 346.
9   Breandán S. Mac Aodha, 'Was this a Social Revolution?' in Seán Ó Tuama (ed.), *The Gaelic League Idea* (Cork: Mercier Press, 1972), pp. 21–3.
10   Mac Aodha, 'Was this a Social Revolution?', pp. 21–3.
11   Tom Garvin, *The Evolution of Irish Nationalist Politics* (Dublin: Gill and Macmillan, 1981), p. 102.
12   Lee, *The Modernisation of Irish Society 1848–1918*, p. 89.
13   Garvin, *Nationalist Revolutionaries in Ireland: 1858–1928*, pp. 86–7. Catholics for long were under-represented in the professions: 75.4 per cent of the population in 1891 (73.86 per cent in 1911), they represented 41 per cent of barristers and solicitors (44 per cent in 1911), 39 per cent of the medical profession (48 per cent), 53 per cent of civil service officers and clerks (61 per cent), 62 per cent of schoolteachers (69 per cent) and 42 per cent of architects, accountants and civil engineers (46 per cent) – Hutchinson, *The Dynamics of Cultural Nationalism*, p. 262.
14   Tomás Ó Fiaich, 'The Great Controversy' in Ó Tuama, *The Gaelic League Idea*, pp. 63 et seq.
15   Garvin, *Nationalist Revolutionaries in Ireland: 1858–1928*, pp. 93–4.
16   Garvin, *Nationalist Revolutionaries in Ireland: 1858–1928*, p. 78.
17   Oliver MacDonagh, *States of Mind. A Study of Anglo-Irish Conflict 1780–1980* (London: George Allen and Unwin, 1983), pp. 104, 118–19.
18   Máirtín Ó Cadhain, 'Conradh na Gaeilge agus an Litríocht' in Ó Tuama, *The Gaelic League Idea*, pp. 53–6.
19   Philip O'Leary, *The Prose Literature of the Gaelic Revival, 1881–1921. Ideology and Innovation* (University Park, Pennsylvania: The Pennsylvania State University Press, 1994), p. 96.
20   Criostóir Mac Aonghusa, 'Mar a chuaigh an Conradh i bhfeidhm ar an nGaeltacht' in Ó Tuama, *The Gaelic League Idea*, p. 77.
21   Cited in O'Leary, *The Prose Literature of the Gaelic Revival*, p. 93.
22   Mac Aonghusa, 'Mar a chuaigh an Conradh i bhfeidhm ar an nGaeltacht', p. 78.
23   O'Leary, *The Prose Literature of the Gaelic Revival*, pp. 94–5.
24   Donncha Ó Súilleabháin, *Scéal an Oireachtais 1897–1924* (Dublin: An Clóchomhair Tta, 1984), pp. 90–2, 169, 171.
25   Ó Súilleabháin, *Scéal an Oireachtais*, chap. ix, *passim*.
26   Cathal Ó Háinle, 'Ó Chaint na nDaoine go dtí an Caighdeán Oifigiúil' in Kim McCone, et al. (eds), *Stair na Gaeilge* (Maynooth: Roinn na Sean-Ghaeilge, Coláiste Phádraig, 1994), pp. 756 et seq.; Williams and Ní Mhuiríosa, *Traidisiún Liteartha na nGael*, pp. 360–1; O'Leary, *The Prose Literature of the Gaelic Revival*, pp. 9–12.
27   O'Leary, *The Prose Literature of the Gaelic Revival*, pp. 102, 110–11.
28   Ó Súilleabháin, *Scéal an Oireachtais*, p. 63.
29   O'Leary, *The Prose Literature of the Gaelic Revival*, p. 112, 116, 139–40, 159.
30   Ole Munch-Pedersen (ed.), *Scéalta Mháirtín Neile* (Dublin: Comhairle Bhéaloideas Éireann, 1994).
31   See also Seán Ó Lúing, 'Lucht Léinn ón Iasacht' in Aogán Ó Muircheartaigh (ed.), *Oidhreacht an Bhlascaoid* (Dublin: Coiscéim, 1989), pp. 143–54.
32   See Muiris Mac Conghail, *The Blaskets. A Kerry Island Library* (Dublin: Country House, 1987), p. 127.
33   Mac Conghail, *The Blaskets*, p. 135.
34   Cited in Breathnach and Ní Mhurchú, *Beathaisnéis a Ceathair*, p. 76.

35 Mac Conghail, *The Blaskets*, pp. 137-9; Diarmuid Breathnach and Máire Ní Mhurchú, *1882-1982: Beathaisnéis a Trí* (Dublin: An Clóchomhar Tta, 1992), pp. 31-33.

36 Robin Flower, *The Western Island. Or The Great Blasket* (Oxford: Oxford University Press, 1978), p. 16.

37 Flower, *The Western Island*, pp. viii, 140-1.

38 Sims-Williams, 'The Medieval World of Robin Flower', p. 78.

39 Bo Almqvist, 'Bláithín agus an Béaloideas' in Mícheál de Mórdha (ed.), *Bláithín: Flower* (Dingle: An Sagart, 1998), pp. 97-116.

40 Mac Conghail, *The Blaskets*, pp. 139-40.

41 Mac Conghail, *The Blaskets*, p. 132.

42 Tomás Ó Criomhthain, *An t-Oileánach* (Dublin and Cork: Comhlacht Oideachais na hÉireann, Tta, 1929), p. 265.

43 Mac Conghail, *The Blaskets*, pp. 34-5.

44 Mac Conghail, *The Blaskets*, pp. 148-51.

45 See also Gösta Berg, 'Carl Wilhelm von Sydow (1878-1952)' in Dag Strömbäck (ed.), *Leading Folklorists of the North* (Oslo, Bergen, Tromsö: Universitetsforlaget, 1971), pp. 173, 175-6.

46 Bo Almqvist, 'Irländsk folklore med svenskt perspektiv' in Ingmar Jansson et al. (eds), *Irland: den gåtfulla ön* (Stockholm: Statens historiska museum, 1988), pp. 176-8. Some of von Sydow's photographs have been published in Tomás Ó Criomhthain, *Allagar na hInise*. 2nd edition (Dublin: Oifig an tSoláthair, 1977).

47 See his obituary, by T.K. Whittaker, in *The Irish Times*, 26 June, 1980; Breathnach and Ní Mhurchú, *Beathaisnéis a Cúig*, p. 163.

48 MacDonagh, *States of Mind*, pp. 116-18.

49 Diarmuid Breathnach and Máire Ní Mhurchú, *1882-1982 Beathaisnéis a hAon* (Dublin: An Clóchomhar, 1986), pp. 37-9.

50 Aindrias Ó Muimhneacháin, 'An Cumann le Béaloideas Éireann 1927-1977', *Béaloideas* nos 45-7 (1977-9), pp. 1-2.

51 Séamus Ó Duilearga, 'Volkskundliche Arbeit in Irland von 1850 bis zur Gegenwart mit besonderer Berücksichtigung der "Irischen Volkskunde-Kommission"', *Zeitschrift für Keltische Philologie und Volksvorschung* no. xxiii (1943), p. 8.

52 Séamus Ó Duilearga, 'Ó'n bhFear Eagair', *Béaloideas* vol. 1, no. 1 (1927), pp. 3-6.

53 Ó Muimhneacháin, 'An Cumann le Béaloideas Éireann', p. 3; Ó Danachair, 'The Progress of Irish Ethnology', p. 8.

54 Seán Ó Súilleabháin, 'Introduction' in Sean O'Sullivan, *Folktales of Ireland* (London: Routledge and Kegan Paul, 1966), p. xxxiii. Ó Súilleabháin and O'Sullivan are the same.

55 Ó Súilleabháin, 'Introduction', pp. xxxiv-xxxv.

56 Bo Almqvist, 'The Irish Folklore Commission: Achievement and Legacy', *Béaloideas* nos 45-7 (1977-9), p. 12.

57 Ó Súilleabháin, 'Introduction', p. xxxiv; Ó Duilearga, 'Volkskundliche Arbeit in Irland von 1850 bis zur Gegenwart', pp. 10-11.

58 Richard M. Dorson, 'Foreword' in O'Sullivan, *Folktales of Ireland*, pp. xxix-xxx.

59 Donncha Ó Cróinín, 'Seán Ó Cróinín (1915-1965): Bailitheoir Béaloideasa', *Béaloideas* no. 32 (1964), pp. 1-18.

60 Mícheál Briody, 'Mícheál Ó Gaoithín – Storyteller' in Folke Josephson (ed.), *Celts and Vikings. Proceedings of the Fourth Symposium of Societas Celtologica Nordica = Meijerbergs Arkiv för Svensk Ordforskning* 20 (Göteborgs Universitet: Göteborg, 1997), p. 160.

61 Ó Duilearga, 'Volkskundliche Arbeit in Irland von 1850 bis zur Gegenwart', p. 12.

62 Fionnuala Nic Suibhne, '"On the Straw" and Other Aspects of Pregnancy and Childbirth from the Oral Tradition of Women in Ulster', *Ulster Folklife* 38 (1992), p. 12.

63   Ó Danachair, 'The Progress of Irish Ethnology', p. 9.
64   *Irish Folklore and Tradition* (Department of Education, Dublin: 1937), p. 3. The authorship is not given, but the cover note states that the booklet was 'prepared by the Irish Folklore Commission'.
65   *Irish Folklore and Tradition*, p. 4.
66   Séamas Ó Catháin and Caitlín Uí Sheighin (ed.), *A Mhuintir Dhú Chaocháin, Labhraigí Feasta!* (Indreabhán, Co. Galway: Cló Chonamara, 1987), p. xviii.
67   Ó Súilleabháin, 'Introduction', p. xxxv.
68   Almqvist, 'The Irish Folklore Commission: Achievement and Legacy', p. 10.
69   Ó Súilleabháin, 'Introduction', p. xxxvi.
70   Ó Duilearga, 'Volkskundliche Arbeit in Irland von 1850 bis zur Gegenwart', pp 21–3, 30, 36.
71   J.H. Delargy, *The Gaelic Story-Teller: With some Notes on Gaelic Folk-Tales* (Chicago: University of Chicago Press, 1969), pp. 3, 9–10, 24, 30.
72   Delargy, *The Gaelic Story-Teller*, pp. 46–7.
73   Briody, 'Mícheál Ó Gaoithín – Storyteller', p. 155.
74   This is a dubious claim: see Seán Ó Coileáin, 'Oral or Literary: Some Strands of the Argument', *Studia Hibernica* (1977–8), pp. 7–35.
75   Séamus Ó Duilearga, *Leabhar Sheáin Í Chonaill* (Dublin: Comhairle Bhéaloideas Éireann, 1977), p. xxii.
76   Wilson Foster, *Fictions of the Irish Literary Revival*, p. 218.
77   See Clodagh Brennan Harvey, *Contemporary Irish Traditional Narrative. The English Language Tradition* (Berkeley, Los Angeles, Oxford: University of California Press, 1992), p. 37.

6: Folklore and Poverty

1   O'Leary, *The Prose Literature of the Gaelic Revival*, p. 122.
2   O'Leary, *The Prose Literature of the Gaelic Revival*, pp. 142–3.
3   Hyde, *Beside the Fire*, pp. ix–l.
4   Hyde, *An Sgeulaidhe Gaedhealach*, pp. v–ix.
5   Gregory, *Poets and Dreamers*, pp. 129–30.
6   Tim P. O'Neill, 'The Persistence of Famine in Ireland' in Cathal Póirtéir (ed.), *The Great Irish Famine* (Cork and Dublin: Mercier Press, 1995), pp. 204, 209.
7   Brighid Ní Mhóráin, *Thiar sa Mhainistir atá an Ghaeilge bhreá. Meath na Gaeilge in Uíbh Ráthach* (Dingle: An Sagart, 1997), p. 46.
8   Brown, *Ireland. A Social and Cultural History 1922–1979*, pp. 19–20.
9   D.P. Moran, *The Philosophy of Irish Ireland* (Dublin: James Duffy and Co., 1905), p. 10. Cited in Maurice Goldring, *Irlande. Idéologie d'une révolution nationale* (Paris: Éditions Sociales, 1975), p. 90.
10   Roger Bastide, 'Préfacio da Primeira Edição' in Souza Barros, *Arte, folclore, subdesenvolvimento* (Rio de Janeiro: Civilização Brasileira, 1977), pp. 13–14.
11   So said Joãozinho Trinta, 'the immensely creative stylist of the Beija-Flor Samba School of Nilópolis, Rio de Janeiro', referring to the carnival. Cited by Roberto DaMatta, 'For an Anthropology of the Brazilian Tradition or "A Virtude está no Meio"', in David J. Hess and Roberto A. DaMatta (eds), *The Brazilian Puzzle* (New York: Columbia University Press, 1995), p. 279.
12   Goldring, *Irlande. Idéologie d'une révolution nationale*, pp. 79–91.
13   See Goldring, *L'Irlande. Idéologie d'une révolution nationale*, p. 102; Conor Kostik, *Revolution in Ireland. Popular Militancy 1917 to 1923* ((London and Chicago: Pluto Press, 1996), p. 105.
14   Ó Crualaoich, 'The Primacy of Form: A "Folk Ideology" in de Valera's Politics', pp. 53–4.

15 Seán Ó Lúing, 'Seoirse Mac Tomáis – George Derwent Thomson' in Ó Lúing, *Saoir Theangan*, pp. 57 et seq.

16 Seoirse Mac Tomáis, *An Blascaod Mar a Bhí* (Maynooth: An Sagart, 1977), p. 24.

17 Mac Tomáis, *An Blascaod Mar a Bhí*, pp. 18, 23, 24–6.

18 Ó Lúing, 'Seoirse Mac Tomáis – George Derwent Thomson', pp. 76–91.

19 Garvin, *The Evolution of Irish Nationalist Politics*, p. 102; Garvin, *Nationalist Revolutionaries in Ireland: 1858–1928*, pp. 93–4.

20 An tSr. Bosco Costigan with Seán Ó Curraoin, *De Ghlaschloich an Oileáin. Beatha agus Saothar Mháirtín Uí Chadhain* (Béal an Daingin, Conamara: Cló Iar-Chonnachta, 1987), pp. 13–82.

21 Costigan, *De Ghlaschloich an Oileáin*, pp. 78–9.

22 The songs he collected in Connemara have been recently published: Ríonach Uí Ógáin and Seosamh Ó Cadhain (eds), *Faoi Rothaí na Gréine. Amhráin as Conamara a bhailigh Máirtín Ó Cadhain* (Dublin: Coiscéim, 1999).

23 Costigan, *De Ghlaschloich an Oileáin*, p. 90.

24 The following passages are taken from it. (Máirtín Ó Cadhain,)'An Chré' in Seán Ó Laighin (ed.), *Ó Cadhain i bhFeasta* (Dublin: Clódhanna Teoranta, 1990), pp. 129–30, 133, 138–9, 148–9, 152–4, 157, 165–6, 168. Quotations are all translated from the Irish.

25 Anne Showstack Sassoon, 'Gramsci's Life' in Showstack Sassoon (ed.), *Approaches to Gramsci* (London: Writers and Readers, 1982), p. 150.

26 Tom Nairn, 'Antonu Su Gobbu' in Showstack Sassoon, *Approaches to Gramsci*, pp. 160–1.

27 Showstack Sassoon, 'Gramsci's Life', *Approaches to Gramsci*, pp. 153–8.

28 Lombardi Satriani, *Antropologia culturale*, pp. 19–26.

29 Lombardi Satriani, *Antropologia culturale*, pp. 129–30.

30 In addition to Gramsci, *Selections from Prison Notebooks*, I have used Sassoon, *Approaches to Gramsci*, passim; Anne Showstack Sassoon, *Gramsci's Politics*, 2nd edition (London, Melbourne, Sydney, Auckland, Johannesburg: Hutchinson, 1987); Roger Simon, *Gramsci's Political Thought* (London: Lawrence and Wishart, 1982); Tony Bennett, Graham Martin, Colin Mercer and Janet Woolacott (ed.), *Culture, Ideology and Social Process* (London: Batsford/Open University Press, 1981): section 4 'Class, Culture and Hegemony', including Chantal Mouffe, 'Hegemony and Ideology in Gramsci'; James Joll, *Gramsci* (Glasgow: Fontana/Collins, 1977).

31 Néstor García Canclini, 'Gramsci e as culturas populares na América Latina' in Carlos Nelson Coutinho and Marco Aurélio Nogueira (ed. and trans.), *Gramsci e a América Latina*, 2nd edition (São Paulo and Rio de Janeiro: Paz e Terra, 1993), pp. 68–9.

32 David Forgacs, 'National-popular: genealogy of a concept' in Simon During (ed.), *The Cultural Studies Reader* (London and New York: Routledge, 1993), pp. 187–8.

33 García Canclini, 'Gramsci e as culturas populares na América Latina', p. 68.

34 Hall, 'Notes on deconstructing the popular', p. 226.

35 Gramsci, *Selections from Prison Notebooks*, p. 191.

36 Gramsci, *Selections from Prison Notebooks*, p. 3.

37 Alberto Maria [sic] Cirese, 'Gramsci's Observations on Folklore' in Sassoon, *Approaches to Gramsci*.

38 Lombardi Satriani, *Antropologia culturale*, p. 91.

39 Lombardi Satriani, *Antropologia culturale*, pp. 132–201.

40 Néstor García Canclini, *Transforming Modernity. Popular Culture in Mexico*, trans. Lidia Lozano (Austin: University of Texas Press, 1993), p. 26.

41 García Canclini, 'Gramsci e as culturas populares na América Latina', pp. 79–80.

42 García Canclini, 'Gramsci e as culturas populares na América Latina', pp. 80–1;

see Ernesto de Martino, *Sud e magia*, 10th edition (Milano: Feltrinelli, 1981) – cf. 'La destorificazione del negativo', pp. 77–81.

43   Paulo Freire, *Cultural Action for Freedom* (Harmondsworth: Penguin Books, 1972), pp. 59–60, 62–3.

44   Jack Zipes, *Breaking the Magic Spell. Radical Theories of Folk and Fairy Tales* (London: Heinemann, 1979), pp. 5–7, 29.

45   Claude Grignon and Jean-Claude Passeron, *Le savant et le populaire. Misérabilisme et populisme en sociologie et en littérature* (Paris: Seuil, 1989), pp. 65–70.

46   Ortiz, *Românticos e folcloristas*, p. 5.

47   Antonio Augusto Arantes, *O que é cultura popular*, 14th edition (São Paulo: Editora Brasiliense, 1990), pp. 7–8.

48   Néstor García Canclini, *Ideología, cultura y poder* (Buenos Aires: Oficina de Publicaciones Universidad de Buenos Aires, 1995), pp. 93–4; García Canclini, *Hybrid Cultures*, pp. 95, 102.

49   García Canclini, 'Gramsci e as culturas populares na América Latina', pp. 65–7, 71–3.

50   Roger D. Abrahams, 'The past in the presence: An overview of folkloristics in the late 20th century' in Reimund Kvideland (ed.), *Folklore Processed* (Helsinki 1992).

51   Lombardi Satriani, 'Premessa' to the new edition, *Antropologia culturale*, pp. 8–10.

7: From Folklore to Popular Culture . . . and Beyond?

1   Grignon and Passeron, *Le savant et le populaire*, pp. 9–10.

2   Wolfgang Kaschuba, 'Popular Culture and Workers' Culture as Symbolic Orders: Comments on the Debate about the History of Culture and Everyday Life' in Alf Lüdtke (ed.), *The History of Everyday Life*, trans. William Templar (Princeton University Press: Princeton, New Jersey, 1995), p. 172.

3   Goldring, *L'Irlande. Idéologie d'une révolution nationale*, p. 93.

4   Stuart Hall, 'Notes on deconstructing "the popular"' in Raphael Samuel (ed.), *People's History and Socialist Theory* (London, Boston and Henley: Routledge and Kegan Paul, 1981), p. 227.

5   Daniel J. Boorstin, *The Americans. The Democratic Experience* (London: Cardinal, 1988), pp. 91–2.

6   Williams, *Keywords*, pp. 192 et seq.

7   The preceeding paragraphs are based on Armand Mattelart, *The Invention of Communication*, trans. Susan Emanuel (Minneapolis and London: University of Minnesota Press, 1996), pp. 242–56 and Renato Ortiz, 'Cultura, comunicación y masa' in *Otro territorio*, pp. 93 et seq.

8   Luke Gibbons, *Transformations in Irish Culture* (Cork: Cork University Press, 1996), pp. 101–2.

9   Löfgren, 'The Cultural Grammar of Nation-building: The Nationalization of Nationalism', p. 227.

10 Søren Schou, 'Postwar Americanisation and the revitalisation of European culture' in Michael Skovmand and Kim Christian Schrøder, *Media Cultures. Reappraising Transnational Media* (Routledge: London and New York, 1992), p. 146.

11 Martín-Barbero, *Communication, Culture and Hegemony*, p. 159; García Canclini, 'Gramsci e as culturas populares na América Latina', pp. 68–9.

12 Löfgren, 'The Cultural Grammar of Nation-Building', p. 227.

13 Umberto Eco, *Apocalittici e integrati*, 7th edition (Milano: Bompiani, 1988), p. 9.

14 Kirsten Drotner, 'Modernity and media panics' in Skovmand and Schrøder, *Media Cultures. Reappraising Transnational Media*, pp. 42, 46–7, 57.

15 Cited in Seán Ó Lúing, *Saoir Theangan*, p. 86; see also Béla Gunda, 'America in Hungarian Folk Tradition' in Béla Gunda, *Ethnographica Carpatho-Balcanica*

(Budapest: Akadémiai Kiadó, 1979), pp. 381–92; Reimund Kvideland, 'Slaraf-fenlandet som motiv i emigrantvisene' in Brittmari Wikström (ed.), *Flykten från vardagen. Meddelanden från Ålands Högskola* nr 6, Mariehamn, 1995, pp. 49–59.

16   See Ralph Willett, *The Americanization of Germany, 1945–1949* (London and New York: Routledge, 1989) and Silvio Lanaro, *L'Italia nuova. Identità e sviluppo 1861–1988* (Torino: Einaudi, 1988), pp. 81–8 ('Il sogno americano').

17   Martín-Barbero, *Communication, Culture and Hegemony*, p. 37; Eco, *Apocalittici e integrati*, pp. 3–4; Ortiz, 'Cultura, comunicación y masa', pp. 102 et seq.; Theodor W. Adorno and Max Horkheimer, 'The Culture Industry: Enlightenment as Mass Deception' in Adorno and Horkheimer, *Dialectic of Enlightenment*, trans. John Cumming (London and New York: Verso, 1997); Walter Benjamin, 'The Work of Art in the Age of Mechanical Reproduction' in Benjamin, *Illuminations*, trans. Harry Zohn (London: Fontana Press, 1992), pp. 211–44.

18   Zipes, *Breaking the Magic Spell*, p. 103.

19   David Harvey, *The Condition of Postmodernity* (Cambridge MA and Oxford UK: Blackwell, 1990), pp. 240, 272; Eric Hobsbawm and Terence Ranger (eds), *The Invention of Tradition* (Cambridge: Cambridge University Press, 1983).

20   Timothy W. Luke, 'Identity, Meaning and Globalization: Detraditionalization in Postmodern Space-time Compression' in Paul Heelas, Scott Lash and Paul Morris (eds), *Detraditionalization. Critical Reflections on Authority and Identity* (Cambridge, Massachusetts, USA and Oxford, England: Blackwell, 1996), pp. 126–7.

21   Hans Magnus Enzensberger cited in Ulrich Beck and Elisabeth Beck-Gernsheim, 'Individualization and "Precarious Freedoms": Perspectives and Controversies of a Subject-orientated Sociology' in Heelas, Lash and Morris, *Detraditionalization*, p. 39.

22   Ulf Hannerz, 'Stockholm: Doubly Creolizing' in Åke Daun, Billy Ehn and Barbro Klein (eds), *To Make the World Safe for Diversity* (Tumba and Stockholm: The Swedish Immigration Institute and Museum and The Ethnology Institute, Stockholm University, 1992), p. 91.

23   Ulf Hannerz, *Cultural Complexity* (New York: Columbia University Press, 1992), p. 218.

24   Helmut Hartwig, 'Youth culture – forever?' in *Young. Nordic Journal of Youth Research*, vol. 1, no. 3 (September, 1993), pp. 13–14; see also Jürgen Habermas, *Identidades nacionales y posnacionales* (Madrid: Tecnos, 1989), p. 89.

25   Zygmunt Bauman, 'Modernity and Ambivalence' in Mike Featherstone (ed.), *Global Culture* (London, Newbury Park, New Delhi: Sage, 1990), pp. 167–8.

26   Renato Ortiz, *Mundialización y cultura*, trans. Elsa Noya (Buenos Aires and Madrid: Alianza Editorial, 1997), pp. 173, 177, 190.

27   Edmund Leach, 'Tribal Ethnography: past, present, future' in Elizabeth Tonkin, Maryon McDonald and Malcolm Chapman (eds), *History and Ethnicity* (London and New York: Routledge, 1989), pp. 37, 42–3.

28   Sims-Williams, 'The Medieval World of Robin Flower', p. 78.

29   Paul Heelas, 'Introduction: Detraditionalization and its Rivals' in Heelas, Lash and Morris, *Detraditionalization*, pp. 7–9.

30   Kearney, *Reconceptualizing the Peasantry*, pp. 3–4, 9.

31   Luke, 'Identity, Meaning and Globalization' in Heelas, Lash and Morris, *Detraditionalization*, pp. 113, 114, 122–3.

32   Honko, 'Studies on tradition and cultural identity: An introduction', pp. 9–11.

33   Lauri Honko, 'The Folklore Process' in *Folklore Fellows' Summer School Programme* (Turku: FFSS, 1991), p. 34.

34   Richard Handler, *Nationalism and the Politics of Culture in Quebec* (Madison: University of Wisconsin Press, 1988), p. 55.

35   Honko, 'The Folklore process', p. 43.

36   Beate Sydhoff, 'The Unknown Folk Art', trans. Angela Adegren, in Gunnar Arnborg et al., *Folkkonsten – All tradition är förändring* (Stockholm: Kulturhuset, 1992), p. 185.
37   García Canclini, *Hybrid Cultures*, pp. 2, 5–6, 16–17, 153, 157.
38   Pierre Bourdieu, *The Logic of Practice*, trans. Richard Nice (Cambridge: Polity Press, 1990), p. 125; Pierre Bourdieu, *Sociology in Question*, trans. Richard Nice (London, Thousand Oaks, New Delhi: Sage, 1993), pp. 1–5, 33–4.
39   Harvey, *The Condition of Postmodernity*, pp. 173 et seq.
40   García Canclini, *Hybrid Cultures*, pp. 16–17, 58, 100; Pierre Bourdieu, 'The Market of Symbolic Goods' in Pierre Bourdieu, *The Field of Cultural Production* (Cambridge: Polity Press, 1993), pp. 112–41.
41   Kaschuba, 'Historizing the Present?', pp. 123–4.
42   Henri Mendras, *La fin des paysans* (Arles: Babel, 1984), p. 365.
43   Kearney, *Reconceptualizing the Peasantry*, pp. 2–4, 9, 62.
44   See, for example, Frantz Fanon, *The Wretched of the Earth*, trans. Constance Farrington (London: Penguin, 1967) and Albert Memmi, *The Colonizer and the Colonized*, new edition, trans. Howard Greenfeld (London: Earthscan Publications, 1990).
45   *Independent on Sunday* magazine 8 February, 1998.
46   Abrahams, 'The past in the presence: An overview of folkloristics in the late 20th century', p. 34.
47   The most challenging Irish readings have been by Angela Bourke. See her *The Burning of Bridget Cleary* (London: Pimlico, 1999).
48   Brennan Harvey, *Contemporary Irish Traditional Narrative*, p. 48.
49   Claire R. Farrer (ed.), *Women and Folklore* (Austin and London: University of Texas Press, 1975), p. xi. This previously appeared as *Journal of American Folklore* vol. 88, no. 347 (Jan.-March 1975).
50   Henrietta L. Moore, *Feminism and Anthropology* (Cambridge: Polity Press, 1988), pp. 1–2.
51   The seminal texts include the following: Alan Dundes, 'Texture, Text and Context' in *Southern Folklore Quarterly* no. 28 (1964), pp. 251–65; Roger D. Abrahams, 'Introductory Remarks to a Rhetorical Theory of Folklore' in *Journal of American Folklore* no. 81 (1968), pp. 143–58; Roger D. Abrahams, 'The Complex Relations of Simple Forms' in *Genre* no. 2 (1969), pp. 104–28; Dan Ben-Amos, 'Towards a Definition of Folklore in Context' in *Journal of American Folklore* no. 84 (1971), pp. 3–15.
52   Kaschuba, 'Historizing the Present?', p. 126.
53   Kearney, *Reconceptualizing the Peasantry*, pp. 34 et seq.
54   Gustavo Esteva, 'Development', in Wolfgang Sachs, *The Development Dictionary* (Johannesburg, London and New Jersey: Witwatersrand University Press/Zed Books, 1992), pp. 6–7.
55   Majid Rahnema, 'Poverty' in Sachs, *The Development Dictionary*, pp. 169–72.
56   Lauri Honko, 'The Final Text of the Recommendation for the Safeguarding of Folklore', *NIF Newsletter* 2–3 (1989), pp. 3, 6–7, 8.

Select Bibliography

Aarne, Antti and Thompson, Stith, *The Types of the Folktale. A Classification and Bibliography*. FF Communications no. 184 (Helsinki: Academia Scientiarum Fennica, 1973).

Abrahams, Roger D., 'Introductory Remarks to a Rhetorical Theory of Folklore' in *Journal of American Folklore*, no. 81 (1968).

Abrahams, Roger D., 'The Complex Relations of Simple Forms', in *Genre*, no. 2 (1969).

Abrahams, Roger D., 'The past in the presence: An overview of folkloristics in the late 20th century' in Reimund Kvideland (ed.), *Folklore Processed* (Helsinki: Suomalaisen Kirjallisuuden Seura, 1992).

Adorno, Theodor W. and Horkheimer, Max, 'The Culture Industry: Enlightenment as Mass Deception' in Adorno and Horkheimer, *Dialectic of Enlightenment*, trans. John Cumming (London and New York: Verso, 1997).

Aguirre Baztán, Ángel (ed.), *La antropologia cultural en España* (Barcelona: P.P.U., 1986).

Alter, Peter, *Nationalism*, trans. Stuart McKinnon-Evans (London, New York, Melbourne, Auckland: Edward Arnold, 1989).

Almqvist, Bo, 'The Irish Folklore Commission: Achievement and Legacy', *Béaloideas* 45–47 (1977–79).

Almqvist, Bo, 'Irländsk folklore med svenskt perspektiv' in Ingmar Jansson et al. (eds), *Irland. Den gåtfulla ön* (Stockholm: Statens historiska museum, 1988).

Almqvist, Bo, 'Bláithín agus an Béaloideas' in Mícheál de Mórdha (ed.), *Bláithín: Flower* (Dingle: An Sagart, 1998).

Amiel, Christiane, Piniès, Jean-Pierre and Piniès, René (eds), *Au miroir des revues. Ethnologie de l'Europe du Sud* (Carcassonne and Paris: Garae/Hesiode and Ent're-vues, 1991).

Anderson, Benedict, *Imagined Communities* (London and New York: Verso, 1983).

Anderson, Bonnie and Zinsser, Judith, 'Women in the Salons' in Stuart Hall and Bram Gieben (eds), *Formations of Modernity* (Cambridge: Polity Press, 1992).

Anttonen, Pertti J., 'Profiles of Folkore 2: Department of European Ethnology Lund University, Sweden', *NIF Newsletter* (Turku: Nordic Institute of Folklore) no. 2, 1993.

Anttonen, Pertti J., 'Nationalism, Ethnicity and the Making of Antiquities as a Strategy in Cultural Representation', *Suomen Antropologi. Journal of the Finnish Anthropological Society* no. 1 (1994).

Anttonen, Pertti J. and Kvideland, Reimund (eds), *Nordic Trontiers* (Turku: Nordic Institute of Folklore) no. 2, 1993.

Arantes, Antonio Augusto, *O que é cultura popular*, 14th edition (São Paulo: Editora Brasiliense, 1990).

Arnold, Matthew, *On the Study of Celtic Literature* (London: Smith, Elder and Co., 1867).

Bakhtin, Mikhail, *Rabelais and his World*, trans. Hélène Iswolsky (Bloomington: Indiana University Press, 1984).

Balakrishnan, Gopal (ed.), *Mapping the Nation* (London and New York: Verso, 1996).

Bann, Stephen, 'Romanticism in France' in Roy Porter and Mikuláš Teich (eds), *Romanticism in National Context* (Cambridge: Cambridge University Press 1988).

Barth, Fredrik, *Ethnic Groups and Boundaries. The Social Organization of Cultural Difference* (Bergen-Oslo/London: Universitets Forlaget/George Allen and Unwin, 1969).

Bastide, Roger, 'Préfacio da Primeira Edição' in Souza Barros, *Arte, folclore, subdesenvolvimento* (Rio de Janeiro: Civilização Brasileira, 1977).

Bauman, Zygmunt, 'Modernity and Ambivalence' in Mike Featherstone (ed.), *Global Culture* (London, Newbury Park, New Delhi: Sage, 1990).

Bausinger, Hermann, *Volkskunde ou l'ethnologie allemande*, trans. Dominique Lassaigne and Pascale Godenir (Paris: Éditions de la Maison des sciences de l'homme, 1993).

Belmont, Nicole, *Aux sources de l'ethnologie française. L'Académie celtique* (Paris: Éditions du Comité des Travaux Historiques Scientifiques, 1995).

Benjamin, Walter, 'The Work of Art in the Age of Mechanical Reproduction' in Walter Benjamin, *Illuminations*, trans. Harry Zohn (London: Fontana Press, 1992).

Bennett, Tony, *The Birth of the Museum: History, Theory, Politics* (London and New York: Routledge, 1995).

Bennett, Tony, Martin, Graham, Mercer, Colin and Woolacott, Janet (eds), *Culture, Ideology and Social Process* (London: Batsford/Open University Press, 1981).

Berg, Gösta, 'Carl Wilhelm von Sydow (1878–1952)' in Dag Strömbäck (ed.), *Leading Folklorists of the North* (Oslo, Bergen, Tromsö: Universitetsforlaget, 1971).

Berlin, Isaiah, *Vico and Herder. Two Studies in the History of Ideas* (London: The Hoggarth Press, 1976).

Blyn-LaDrew, Roslyn, 'Geoffrey Keating, William Thoms, Raymond Williams, and the Terminology of Folklore: '"*Béaloideas*" as a "Keyword"', *Folklore Forum* vol. 27, no. 2.

Boorstin, Daniel J., *The Americans. The Democratic Experience* (London: Cardinal, 1988).

Bourdieu, Pierre, *The Logic of Practice*, trans. Richard Nice (Cambridge: Polity Press, 1990).

Bourdieu, Pierre, *Sociology in Question*, trans. Richard Nice (London, Thousand Oaks, New Delhi: Sage, 1993).

Bourdieu, Pierre, 'The Market of Symbolic Goods' in Pierre Bourdieu, *The Field of Cultural Production* (Cambridge: Polity Press, 1993).

Boyce, D. George, *Nationalism in Ireland*, 2nd edition (London and New York: Routledge, 1991).

Brady, Philip, 'Volk or Proletariat? Folklore and Agitprop' in Venetia J. Newall (ed.), *Folklore Studies in the Twentieth Century. Proceedings of the Centenary Conference of the Folklore Society* (Woodbridge, Suffolk/Totowa, N.J.: Boydell and Brewer Ltd/ Rowman and Littlefield, 1978/1980).

Breathnach, Breandán, *Folkmusic and Dances of Ireland* ([Dublin]: Educational Company of Ireland, 1971).

Breathnach, Diarmuid and Ní Mhurchú, Máire, *1882–1982: Beathaisnéis*, 5 vols. (Dublin: An Clóchomhar Tta, 1986, 1990, 1992, 1994, 1997).

Brennan Harvey, Clodagh, *Contemporary Irish Traditional Narrative. The English language Tradition* = Folklore and Mythology Studies Vol. 35 (Berkeley, Los Angeles, Oxford: University of California Press, 1992).

Briody, Mícheál, 'Mícheál Ó Gaoithín – Storyteller' in Folke Josephson (ed.), *Celts and Vikings. Proceedings of the Fourth Symposium of Societas Celtologica Nordica* =

Meijerbergs Arkiv för Svensk Ordforskning 20 (Göteborgs Universitet: Göteborg, 1997).

Brown, Terence, *Ireland. A Social and Cultural History 1922–1979* (Glasgow: Fontana, 1981).

Brückner, Wolfgang, 'Histoire de la Volkskunde. Tentative d'une approche à l'usage des Français' in Isac Chiva and Utz Jeggle (eds), *Ethnologies en Miroir. La France et les pays de langue allemande* (Paris: Éditions de la Maison des sciences de l'homme, 1987).

Brunner, José Joaquín, *Cartografías de la modernidad* (Santiago [de Chile]: Dolmen Ediciones, n.d.).

Burke, Peter, *Popular Culture in Early Modern Europe*, revised edition (Aldershot: Scolar Press, 1994).

Burns, E. Bradford, *A History of Brazil*, 3rd edition (New York: Columbia University Press, 1993).

Buttimer, Cornelius G., 'Remembering 1798', *Journal of the Cork Historical and Archaeological Society* vol. 103 (1998).

Caro Baroja, Julio, *La aurora del pensamiento antropológico* (Madrid: Consejo Superior de Investigaciones Científicas, 1983).

Céitinn, Seathrún, *Forus Feasa ar Éirinn* I (London: Irish Texts Society, 1902).

Céitinn, Seathrún, *Forus Feasa ar Éirinn* II (London: Irish Texts Society, 1908).

Chapman, Malcolm, *The Celts. The Construction of a Myth* (New York: St Martin's Press, 1992).

Chatterjee, Partra, 'Whose Imagined Community?' in Gopal Balakrishnan (ed.), *Mapping the Nation* (London and New York: Verso, 1996).

Chesnutt, Michael (ed.), *Telling Reality. Folklore Studies in Memory of Bengt Holbek* (Copenhagen and Turku: Dept of Folklore, University of Copenhagen and Nordic Institute of Folklore, 1993).

Chiva, Isac and Joggle, Utz (eds), *Ethnologies en Miroir. La France et les pays de langue allemande* (Paris: Editions de la Maison des sciences de l'homme, 1987).

Cirese, Alberto M., *Folklore e antropologia* (Palermo: Palumbo, 1972).

Cirese, Alberto M., *Cultura egemonica e culture subalterne*, 2nd edition (Palermo: Palumbo, 1979).

Clifford, James, *The Predicament of Culture. Twentieth-Century Ethnography, Literature, and Art* (Cambridge, Mass. and London, England: Harvard University Press, 1988).

Cocchiara, Giuseppe, *Storia del folklore in Europa* (Torino: Boringhieri, 1971).

Cocchiara, Giuseppe, *Storia del folklore in Italia* (Palermo: Sellerio, 1981).

Connolly, S.J. (ed.), *The Oxford Companion to Irish History* (Oxford: Oxford University Press, 1998).

Costigan, An tSr. Bosco with Ó Curraoin, Seán, *De Ghlaschloich an Oileáin. Beatha agus Saothar Mháirtín Uí Chadhain* (Béal an Daingin, Conamara: Cló Iar-Chonnachta, 1987).

Crawford, W.H., 'The Belfast Middle Classes in the Late Eighteenth Century' in David Dickson, Dáire Keogh and Kevin Whelan (eds), *The United Irishmen: Republicanism, Radicalism and Rebellion* (Dublin: The Lilliput Press, 1993).

Croker, T. Crofton, *Researches in the South of Ireland. Illustrative of the Scenery, Architectural Remains and the Manners and Superstitions of the Peasantry with an Appendix containing a Private Narrative of the Rebellion of 1798* (Dublin: Irish Academic Press, 1981).

Cuche, Denys, *La noción de cultura en las ciencias sociales*, trans. Paula Mahler (Buenos Aires: Ediciones Nueva Visión, 1999).

Cuisenier, Jean and Segalen, Martine, *Ethnologie de la France* (Paris: Presses Universitaires de France, 1986).

Curtin, Chris, Donnan, Hastings and Wilson, Thomas M. (eds), *Irish Urban Cultures* (Belfast: Institute of Irish Studies, The Queen's University of Belfast, 1993).

DaMatta, Roberto, 'For an Anthropology of the Brazilian Tradition or "A Virtude está no Meio"', in David J. Hess and Roberto A. DaMatta (eds), *The Brazilian Puzzle* (New York: Columbia University Press, 1995).

Deane, Seamus (ed.), *The Field Day Anthology of Irish Writing*, vol. 2 (Field Day Publications: Derry, 1991).

De Certeau, Michel, Julia, Dominique and Revel, Jacques, 'La beauté du mort' in Michel de Certeau, *La culture au pluriel* (Paris: Seuil, 1993).

de h-Íde, Dubhglas, *An Sgeulaidhe Gaedhealach* (Dublin: Institiút Béaloideasa Éireann, 1933).

Delargy, J.H., *The Gaelic Story-Teller. With some Notes on Gaelic Folk-Tales* (Chicago: University of Chicago Press, 1969).

de Martino, Ernesto, *Sud e magia*, 10th edition (Milano: Feltrinelli, 1981).

de Mórdha, Mícheál (ed.), *Bláithín: Flower* (Dingle: An Sagart, 1998).

Denvir, Gearóid, *Litríocht agus Pobal. Cnuasach Aistí* (Indreabhán, Conamara: Cló Iar-Chonnachta, 1997).

Dickson, David, Keogh, Dáire and Whelan, Kevin (eds), *The United Irishmen. Republicanism, Radicalism and Rebellion* (Dublin: The Lilliput Press, 1993).

Donnelly, J.S. and Miller, Kerby A. (eds), *Irish Popular Culture 1650–1850* (Dublin: Irish Academic Press, 1998).

Dorson, Richard, *The British Folklorists* (London: Routledge and Kegan Paul, 1968).

Dorson, Richard M., *Folklore and Folklife. An Introduction* (Chicago and London: University of Chicago Press, 1972).

Dorson, Richard M., *Folklore and Fakelore* (Cambridge, Massachusetts and London, England: Harvard University Press, 1976).

Dostal, Walter, 'Silence in the darkness: German Ethnology in the National Socialist Period', *Social Anthropology* vol. 2, part 3, October 1994.

Dundes, Alan, 'Texture, Text and Context' in *Southern Folklore Quarterly* no. 28 (1964).

Dundes, Alan, *The Study of Folklore* (Englewood Cliffs, NJ: Prentice Hall, 1968).

Dundes, Alan, *Analytic Essays in Folklore* (The Hague, Paris and New York: Mouton, 1975).

Dundes, Alan, 'Nationalistic Inferiority Complexes and the Fabrication of Folklore: A Reconsideration of Ossian, the *Kinder- und Hausmärchen*, the *Kalevala*, and Paul Bunyan' in Reimund Kvideland and Torunn Selberg (eds), *Papers 1: The 8th Congress for the International Society for Folk Narrative Research* (Bergen: no publisher, 1984).

Dunne, Tom, 'Haunted by History: Irish Romantic writing 1800–1850' in Roy Porter and Mikuláš Teich (eds), *Romanticism in National Context* (Cambridge: Cambridge University Press, 1988).

Eco, Umberto, *Apocalittici e integrati*, 7th edition (Milano: Bompiani, 1988).

Ehn, Billy, Frykman, Jonas, Löfgren, Orvar, *Försvenskningen av Sverige* (Stockholm: Natur och Kultur, 1993).

Elias, Norbert, *The Civilizing Process*, trans. Edmund Jephcott (Oxford UK and Cambridge USA: Blackwell, 1994).

Erixon, Sigurd, 'Ethnologie régionale ou folklore' in *Laos* no. I (1951).

Erixon, Sigurd, 'The Position of Regional Ethnology and Folklore at the European Universities: An International Inquiry' in *Laos* no. III (1955).

Evans Wentz, W.Y., *The Fairy Faith in Celtic Countries* (Colin Smythe/Humanities Press: Gerards Cross/Atlantic Highlands 1977).

Fabian, Johannes, *Time and the Other. How Anthropology makes its object* (New York: Columbia University Press, 1983).

Fanon, Frantz, 'On National Culture' in *The Wretched of the Earth*, trans. Constance Farrington (London: Penguin Books, 1967).

Farfán, Rafael, 'F. Tönnies: la crítica a la modernidad a partir de la comunidad' in Gina Zabludovsky (ed.), *Teoría sociológica y modernidad* (México: Plaza y Valdés, 1998).

Farrer, Claire R. (ed.), *Women and Folklore* (Austin and London: University of Texas Press, 1975).

Ferguson, C.A., 'Diglossia' in Pier Paolo Giglioli (ed.), *Language and Social Context* (Harmondsworth: Penguin, 1972).

Flower, Robin, *The Western Island. Or The Great Blasket* (Oxford: Oxford University Press, 1978).

Foley, Tadhg and Ryder, Seán (eds), *Ideology and Ireland in the Nineteenth Century* (Dublin: Four Courts Press, 1998).

Forgacs, David, 'National-popular: genealogy of a concept' in Simon During (ed.), *The Cultural Studies Reader* (London and New York: Routledge, 1993).

Foster, John Wilson, *Fictions of the Irish Literary Revival. A Changeling Art* (Syracuse, New York: Syracuse University Press, 1987).

Foster, Roy, *Modern Ireland* (London: Penguin Books, 1989).

Fox, Jennifer, 'The Creator Gods: Romantic Nationalism and the En-genderment of Women in Folklore' in *Journal of American Folkore* no. 100 (1987).

Freire, Paulo, *Pedagogy of the Oppressed*, trans. Myra Bergman Ramos (Harmondsworth: Penguin Books, 1972).

Freire, Paulo, *Cultural Action for Freedom*, (Harmondsworth: Penguin Books, 1972).

Friel, Brian, John Andrews and Kevin Barry, 'Translations and A Paper Landscape: Between Fiction and History', *The Crane Bag* vol. 7, no. 2 (1983).

Frykman, Jonas and Löfgren, Orvar, *Culture Builders. A Historical Anthropology of Middle-Class Life*, trans. Alan Crozier (New Brunswick and London: Rutgers University Press, 1987).

Gailey, Alan (ed.), *Ethnological Mapping in Ireland. A Document for discussion towards an ethnological atlas of Ireland* ([Cultra, Co. Down:] Ulster Folk and Transport Museum, 1974).

Gailey, Alan, 'Folk-life Study and the Ordnance Survey Memoirs' in Alan Gailey and Dáithí Ó hÓgáin (eds), *Gold Under the Furze. Studies in Folk Tradition* (Dublin: The Glendale Press, 1982)

Gailey, Alan and Ó Danachair, Caoimhín, 'Ethnological Mapping in Ireland', *Ethnologia Europaea* vol. IX, no. 1 (1976).

García Canclini, Néstor, 'Gramsci e as culturas populares na América Latina' in Carlos Nelson Coutinho and Marco Aurélio Nogueira (ed. and trans.), *Gramsci e a América Latina*, 2nd edition (São Paulo and Rio de Janeiro: Paz e Terra, 1993).

García Canclini, Néstor, *Transforming Modernity. Popular Culture in Mexico*, trans. Lidia Lozano (Austin: University of Texas Press, 1993).

García Canclini, Néstor, *Ideología, cultura y poder* (Buenos Aires: Oficina de Publicaciones Universidad de Buenos Aires, 1995).

García Canclini, Néstor, *Hybrid Cultures. Strategies for Entering and Leaving Modernity*, trans. Christopher L. Chiappari and Silvia L. López (Minneapolis and London: University of Minnesota, 1995).

Garvin, Tom, *The Evolution of Irish Nationalist Politics* (Dublin: Gill and Macmillan, 1981).

Garvin, Tom, *Nationalist Revolutionaries in Ireland: 1858–1928* (New York: Doubleday, 1987).

Gellner, Ernest, *Nations and Nationalism* (Oxford UK and Cambridge USA: Blackwell, 1983).

Gellner, Ernest, 'The Coming of Nationalism and its Interpretation: The Myths of Nation and Class' in Gopal Balakrishnan (ed.), *Mapping the Nation* (London and New York: Verso, 1996).

Gibbons, Luke, *Transformations in Irish Culture* (Cork: Cork University Press, 1996).

Giddens, Anthony, *Durkheim* (Glasgow: Fontana/Collins, 1978).

Giddens, Anthony, *Sociology* (Cambridge: Polity Press, 1989).

Girola, Lidia, 'Durkheim y el diagnóstico de la modernidad' in Gina Zabludovsky (ed.), *Teoía sociológica y modernidad* (México: Plaza y Valdés, 1998).

Glassie, Henry, *Passing the Time. Folklore and History of an Ulster Community* (Dublin: The O'Brien Press, 1982).

Goldring, Maurice, *Irlande. Idéologie d'une révolution nationale* (Paris: Éditions Sociales, 1975).

Gramsci, Antonio, *Selections from Prison Notebooks*, ed. and trans. Quintin Hoare and Geoffrey Nowell Smith (London: Lawrence and Wishart, 1971).

Gramsci, Antonio, *Letteratura e vita nazionale* (Roma: Editori Riuniti, 1991).

Gregory, Lady Augusta, *Poets and Dreamers. Studies and Translations from the Irish* (Dublin and London: Hodges, Figgis, and Co., Ltd, and John Murray, 1903).

Gregory, Lady Augusta, *The Kiltartan History Book* (London: T. Fisher Unwin Ltd, 1926).

Grignon, Claude and Passeron, Jean-Claude, *Le savant et le populaire. Misérabilisme et populisme en sociologie et en littérature* (Paris: Seuil, 1989).

Gross, David, *The Past in Ruins. Tradition and the Critique of Modernity* (Amherst: University of Massachusetts Press, 1992).

Gulliver, Marilyn and Gulliver, P.H. (eds), *Approaching the Past: Historical Anthropology through Irish Case Studies* (New York: Columbia University Press, 1992).

Gunda, Béla (ed.), *Ethnographica Carpatho-Balcanica* (Budapest: Akadémiai Kiadó, 1979).

Habermas, Jürgen, *Identidades nacionales y posnacionales*, trans. Manuel Jiménez Redondo (Madrid: Tecnos, 1989).

Habermas, Jürgen, 'The Public Sphere' in Chandra Mukerji and Michael Schudson (eds), *Rethinking Popular Culture* (Berkeley, Los Angeles, Oxford: University of California Press, 1991).

Habermas, Jürgen, 'The European Nation-State – Its Achievements and its Limits' in Gopal Balakrishnan (ed.), *Mapping the Nation* (London and New York: Verso, 1996).

Hall, Stuart and Gieben, Bram (eds), *Formations of Modernity* (Cambridge: Polity Press, 1992).

Handler, Richard, *Nationalism and the Politics of Culture in Quebec* (Madison: University of Wisconsin Press, 1988).

Hannerz, Ulf, 'Stockholm: Doubly Creolizing' in Åke Daun, Billy Ehn and Barbro Klein (eds), *To Make the World Safe for Diversity* (Tumba and Stockholm: The Swedish Immigration Institute and Museum and The Ethnology Institute, Stockholm University, 1992).

Hannerz, Ulf, *Cultural Complexity* (New York: Columbia University Press, 1992).

Hartwig, Helmut, 'Youth culture – forever?' in *Young. Nordic Journal of Youth Research*, vol. 1, no. 3 (September, 1993).

Harvey, David, *The Condition of Postmodernity* (Cambridge MA and Oxford UK: Blackwell, 1990).

Hautala, Jouko, *Finnish Folklore Research 1828–1918* (Helsinki: Finnish Society of Sciences, 1968).

Hechter, Michael, *Internal Colonialism* (London and Henley: Routledge and Kegan Paul, 1975).

Heelas, Paul, Lash, Scott and Morris, Paul (eds), *Detraditionalization. Critical Reflections on Authority and Identity* (Cambridge, Massachusetts, USA and Oxford, England: Blackwell, 1996).

Held, David, 'The Development of the Modern State' in Stuart Hall and Bram Gieben (eds), *Formations of Modernity* (Cambridge: Polity Press, 1992).

Hermet, Guy, *Histoire des nations et du nationalisme en Europe* (Paris: Éditions du Seuil, 1996).

Herzfeld, Michael, *Ours Once More. Folklore, Ideology, and the Making of Modern Greece* (Austin: University of Texas Press, 1982).

Hettne, Björn, *Development Theory and the Three Worlds*, 2nd edition (London: Longman, 1994).

Hindley, Reg, *The Death of the Irish Language. A Qualified Obituary* (London: Routledge, 1990).

Hobsbawm, Eric and Ranger, Terence (eds), *The Invention of Tradition* (Cambridge: Cambridge University Press, 1983).

Holbek, Bengt, *On the Comparative Method in Folklore Research. NIF Papers no. 3* (Turku: Nordic Institute of Folklore, 1992).

Honko, Lauri (ed.), *Folklore och Nationsbyggande i Norden* (Åbo: Nordiska Institutet för Folkdiktning, 1980).

Honko, Lauri, 'Studies on tradition and cultural identity. An introduction' in Honko (ed.), *Tradition and Cultural Identity* (Turku: Nordic Institute of Folklore, 1988).

Honko, Lauri, 'The Final Text of the Recommendation for the Safeguarding of Folklore', *NIF Newsletter* nos 2–3 (1989).

Honko, Lauri, 'The Folklore Process' in Folklore Fellows' Summer School *Programme* (Turku: FFSS, 1991).

Hroch, Miroslav, 'From National Movement to Fully-formed Nation: The Nation-building Process in Europe' in Gopal Balakrishnan (ed.), *Mapping the Nation* (London and New York: Verso, 1996).

Hughes, Robert, *Barcelona* (London: Harvill, 1993).

Hultin, Neil C. and Ober, Warren U., 'An O'Connellite in Whitehall: Thomas Crofton Croker, 1798–1854', *Éire-Ireland* vol. xxvii, no. 3 (Fall 1993).

Hultkranz, Åke, 'The Concept of "Folk" in Sigurd Erixon's Ethnological Theory' in Hermanna W.M. Plattenburg (ed.), *Erixoniana Contributions to the Study of European Ethnology in memory of Sigurd Erixon* (Arnhem: Rijksmuseum voor Volkskunde "Het Nederlands Open-lucht-museum", 1970).

Hutchinson, John, *The Dynamics of Cultural Nationalism. The Gaelic Revival and the Creation of the Irish Nation State* (London: Allen and Unwin, 1987).

Hyde, Douglas, *Beside the Fire. A Collection of Gaelic Folk Stories* (London: David Nutt, 1910).

Hyde, Douglas, *Language, Lore and Lyrics. Essays and Lectures*, ed. with a preface and introduction Breandán Ó Conaire (Dublin: Irish Academic Press, 1986).

Iniesta i González, Montserrat, *Els gabinets del món. Antropologia, museus i museologies* (Lleida: Pagès, 1994).

[Irish Folklore Commission], *Irish Folklore and Tradition* (Department of Education, Dublin: 1937).

Joll, James, *Gramsci* (Glasgow: Fontana/Collins, 1977).

Josephson, Folke (ed.), *Celts and Vikings: Proceedings of the Fourth Symposium of Societas Celtologica Nordica* (Göteborg: Göteborgs Universitet, 1997).

Kamenetsky, Christa, 'Folklore as a Political Tool in Nazi Germany', *Journal of American Folklore* vol. 85, no. 337, (July–Sept., 1972).

Kanike, Anu, '"Rahvuslik" rahvakultuur/"National" Folk Culture', *Pro Ethnologia* no. 2 (1994).

Karp, Ivan and Lavine, Stephen D. (eds), *Exhibiting Cultures: The Poetics and Politics of Museum Display* (Washington and London: Smithsonian Institution Press, 1991).

Kaschuba, Wolfgang, 'Popular Culture and Workers' Culture as Symbolic Orders: Comments on the Debate about the History of Culture and Everyday Life' in Alf

Lüdtke (ed.), *The History of Everyday Life*, trans. William Templar (Princeton University Press: Princeton, New Jersey, 1995).

Kaschuba, Wolfgang, 'Historizing the Present? Construction and Deconstruction of the Past' in *Ethnologia Europaea* vol. 26, no. 2 (1996).

Kearney, Michael, *Reconceptualizing the Peasantry. Anthropology in Global Perspective* (Boulder, Colorado and Oxford: Westview Press, 1996).

Kiberd, Declan, *Synge and the Irish Language* (London and Basingstoke: Macmillan, 1979).

Kiberd, Declan, *Inventing Ireland. The Literature of the Modern Nation* (London: Vintage, 1996).

Kirby, David, *The Baltic World 1772–1993. Europe's Northern Periphery in an Age of Change* (London and New York: Longman, 1995).

Kirshenblatt-Gimblett, Barbara, 'Objects of Ethnography' in Ivan Karp and Stephen D. Lavine (eds), *Exhibiting Cultures. The Poetics and Politics of Museum Display* (Washington and London: Smithsonian Institution Press, 1991).

Klinge, Matti, '"Let Us Be Finns" – the Birth of Finland's National Culture' in Rosalind Mitchison (ed.), *The Roots of Nationalism. Studies in Northern Europe* (Edinburgh: John Donald, 1980).

Köngäs-Maranda, Elli Kaija, 'Ethnologie, Folklore et l'Indépendence des majorités minorisées' in *Travaux et Inédits de Elli Kaija Köngäs-Maranda. Cahiers du CELAT* 1 (1983).

Kristeva, Julia, *Étrangers à nous-mêmes* (Paris: Gallimard, 1988).

Kvideland, Reimund, 'Slaraffenlandet som motiv i emigrantvisene' in Brittmari Wikström (ed.), *Flykten från vardagen* Meddelanden från Ålands Högskola nr 6, Mariehamn 1995.

Laar, Mart, Vahtre, Lauri and Valk, Heiki, *Kodu lugu 1* (Tallinn: Loomingu Raamatukogu 40/41, 1989).

Laclau, Ernesto, *Politics and Ideology in Marxist Theory* (London: NLB, 1977).

Lanaro, Silvio, *L'Italia nuova. Identità e sviluppo 1861–1988* (Torino: Einaudi, 1988).

Langlais, Jacques, Laplante, Pierre and Levy, Joseph (eds), *Le Québec de demain et les communautés culturelles* (Montréal: Méridien, 1990).

Laugaste, Eduard, *Eesti rahvaluule*, 3rd edition (Tallinn: Valgus, 1986).

Leach, Edmund, 'Tribal Ethnography: past, present, future' in Elizabeth Tonkin, Maryon McDonald and Malcolm Chapman (eds), *History and Ethnicity* (London and New York: Routledge, 1989).

Lee, Joseph, *The Modernisation of Irish Society 1848–1918* (Dublin: Gill and Macmillan, 1989).

Lee, Joe, 'An Gorta Mór agus Scríobh Stair na hÉireann' in Cathal Póirtéir (ed.), *Gnéithe an Ghorta* (Dublin: Coiscéim, 1995).

Leerssen, Joep, *Mere Irish and Fíor-Ghael. Studies in the Idea of Irish Nationality, its Development and Literary Expression prior to the Nineteenth Century*, 2nd edition (Cork: Cork University Press, 1996).

Leerssen, Joep, *Remembrance and Imagination* (Cork: Cork University Press, 1996).

Lescure, Jean-Claude, 'Italie' in A. Guillaume, J.-C. Lescure and S. Michonneau, *L'Europe des nationalismes aux nations. Italie, Espagne, Irlande* (Paris: Sedes, 1996).

Lévi-Strauss, Claude, *Structural Anthropology 2*, trans. Monique Layton (Harmondsworth: Penguin, 1978).

Lévy Zumwalt, Rosemary, *American Folklore Scholarship: A Dialogue of Dissent* (Bloomington and Indianapolis: Indiana University Press, 1988).

Lewis, I.M., *Social Anthropology in Perspective* (Harmondsworth: Penguin Books, 1976).

Lisón Tolosana, Carmelo, *Ensayos de antropología social* (Madrid: Ayuso, 1978).

Lixfeld, Hannjost, 'Institutionalsierung und Instrumentalisierung der deutschen Volkskunde zu Beginn des dritten Reichs' in Wolfgang Jacobeit, Hannjost Lixfeld and

Olaf Bockhorn (eds), *Völkische Wissenschaft. Gestalten und Tendenzen der deutschen und österreichischen Volkskunde in der ersten Hälfte des 20. Jahrhunderts* (Wien, Köln and Weimar: Böhlau Verlag, 1994).

Llopart, D., Prats, J. and Prats, Ll. (eds), *La cultura popular a debat* (Barcelona: Fundació Serveis de Cultura Popular Editorial Alta Fulla, 1985).

Löfgren, Orvar, 'The Cultural Grammar of Nation-building: The Nationalization of Nationalism' in Pertti J. Anttonen and Reimund Kvideland (eds), *Nordic Frontiers* (Turku: Nordic Institute of Folklore, 1993).

Loit, Aleksander (ed.), *National Movements in the Baltic Countries during the 19th Century. Studia Baltica Stockholmiensia* 2 (Stockholm: Centre for Baltic Studies, 1985).

Lombardi Satriani, Luigi M. and Meligrana, Mariano (eds), *Diritto egemone e diritto popolare*, 2nd edition (Vibo Valentia: Qualecultura/Jaca Book, 1995).

Lombardi Satriani, Luigi M., *Antropologia culturale e analisi della cultura subalterna*, 2nd edition (Milano: Biblioteca Universale Rizzoli, 1997).

Loorits, Oskar, 'Eesti rahvaluuleteaduse tänapäev', *Õpetatud Eesti Seltsi Kirjad* 1. *Vanavara vallast* (Tartu: Õpetatud Eesti Selts, 1932).

Lotman, Ju. M., 'On the Metalanguage of a Typological Description of Culture', *Semiotica* vol. 14, no. 2 (1975).

Lotman, Ju. M., 'The Dynamic Model of a Semiotic System', *Semiotica* vol. 21, nos 3/4 (1977).

Lucas, A.T., 'The National Folk Life Collection' in Patricia Lysaght, Anne O'Dowd and Bairbre O'Flynn (eds), *A Folk Museum for Ireland* (Dublin: [no publisher], 1984).

Lysaght, Patricia, Anne O'Dowd and Bairbre O'Flynn (eds), *A Folk Museum for Ireland* (Dublin: [no publisher], 1984).

MacAodha, Breandán S., 'Was this a Social Revolution?' in Seán Ó Tuama (ed.), *The Gaelic League Idea* (Cork: Mercier Press, 1972).

McCone, Kim, McManus, Damian, Ó Háinle, Cathal, Williams, Nicholas, Breatnach, Liam (eds), *Stair na Gaeilge* (Maynooth: Roinn na Sean-Ghaeilge, Coláiste Phádraig, 1994).

Mac Conghail, Muiris, *The Blaskets. A Kerry Island Library* (Dublin: Country House, 1987).

MacDonagh, Oliver, *States of Mind. A Study of Anglo-Irish Conflict 1780–1980* (London: George Allen and Unwin, 1983).

Mączak, Antoni, *Viaggi e viaggiatori nell'Europa moderna*, trans. Renzo Panzone and Andrzei Litwornia (Roma-Bari: Editori Laterza, 1994).

Mair, Lucy, *An Introduction to Social Anthropology*, 2nd edition (Oxford: Clarendon Press, 1972).

Mansergh, Nicholas, *The Irish Question 1840–1921*, 2nd edition (London: George Allen and Unwin Ltd, 1965).

Martín-Barbero, Jesús, *Communication, Culture and Hegemony*, trans. Elizabeth Fox and Robert A. White (London, Newbury Park, New Delhi: Sage, 1993).

Marx, Karl and Engels, Frederick, *Selected Works*, vol. 1 (Moscow and London: Foreign Language Publishing House and Lawrence and Wishart Ltd, 1951).

Masing, Uku, 'Esten' in Kurt Ranke (ed.), *Enzyklopädie des Märchens* 4 (Berlin and New York: Walter de Gruyter, 1984).

Mattelart, Armand, *The Invention of Communication*, trans. Susan Emanuel (Minneapolis and London: University of Minnesota Press, 1996).

Maxwell, Constantia, *The Stranger in Ireland. From the Reign of Elizabeth to the Great Famine* (Dublin: Gill and Macmillan, 1979).

Memmi, Albert, *The Colonizer and the Colonized*, new edition, trans. Howard Greenfeld (London: Earthscan Publications, 1990).

Mendras, Henri, *La fin des paysans* (Arles: Babel, 1984).

Miller, David, *Anarchism* (London and Melbourne: J.M. Dent, 1984).

Moore, Henrietta L., *Feminism and Anthropology* (Cambridge: Polity Press, 1988).

Morash, Christopher, 'Introduction' in W.M. Thackeray, *The Irish Sketchbook* (Dublin: Gill and Macmillan, 1990).

Moser-Rath, Elfriede, 'Deutschland' in Kurt Ranke (ed.), *Enzyklopädie des Märchens* Band 3 (Berlin and New York: Walter de Gruyter, 1981).

Muchembled, Robert, *Culture populaire et culture des élites dans la France moderne (XVe–XVIIIe siècle)*, 2nd edition (Paris: Flammarion, 1991).

Munch-Pedersen, Ole (ed.), *Scéalta Mháirtín Neile* (Dublin: Comhairle Bhéaloideas Éireann, 1994).

Ngũgĩ wa Thiong'o, *Decolonising the Mind. The Politics of Language in African Literature* (London, Nairobi and Portsmouth N.H.: James Currey/EAEP/Heinemann, 1986).

Nic Craith, Máiréad, *An tOileánach Léannta* (Dublin: An Clóchomhar, 1988).

Nic Suibhne, Fionnuala, '"On the Straw" and Other Aspects of Pregnancy and Child-birth from the Oral Tradition of Women in Ulster', *Ulster Folklife* no. 38 (1992).

Ní Mhóráin, Brighid, *Thiar sa Mhainistir atá an Ghaeilge bhreá: Meath na Gaeilge in Uíbh Ráthach* (Dingle: An Sagart, 1997).

Nimni, Ephraim, *Marxism and Nationalism* (London and Boulder, Colorado: Pluto Press, 1991).

Ó Buachalla, Breandán, *I mBéal Feirste Cois Cuain* (Dublin: An Clóchomhar, 1968).

Ó Buachalla, Breandán, *Aisling Ghéar* (Dublin: An Clóchomhar, 1996).

O'Carroll, J.P. and Murphy, John A. (eds), *De Valera and His Times* (Cork: Cork University Press, 1986).

Ó Catháin, Séamas and Uí Sheighin, Caitlín (eds), *A Mhuintir Dhú Chaocháin, Labhraigí Feasta!* (Indreabhán: Cló Chonamara, 1987).

Ó Ciosáin, Niall, *Print and Popular Culture in Ireland, 1750–1850* (London: Macmillan, 1997).

Ó Ciosáin, Niall, 'Boccoughs and God's Poor: Deserving and Undeserving Poor in Irish Popular Culture' in Tadhg Foley and Seán Ryder (eds), *Ideology and Ireland in the Nineteenth Century* (Dublin: Four Courts Press, 1998).

Ó Coileáin, Seán, 'Oral or Literary: Some Strands of the Argument', *Studia Hibernica* 1977–78.

Ó Conghaile, Micheál, *Gnéithe d'Amhráin Chonamara Ár Linne* (Indreabhán, Conamara: Cló Iar-Chonnachta, 1993).

Ó Criomhthain, Tomás, *An t-Oileánach* (Dublin and Cork: Comhlacht Oideachais na hÉireann, Tta, 1929).

Ó Cróinín, Donncha, 'Seán Ó Cróinín (1915–1965): Bailitheoir Béaloideasa', *Béaloideas* no. xxxii (1964).

Ó Crualaoich, Gearóid, 'The Primacy of Form: A "Folk Ideology" in de Valera's Politics' in J.P. O'Carroll and John A. Murphy (eds), *De Valera and His Times* (Cork: Cork University Press, 1986).

Ó Crualaoich, Gearóid, 'The "Merry Wake"' in J.S. Donnelly and Kerby A. Miller (eds), *Irish Popular Culture 1650–1850* (Dublin: Irish Academic Press, 1998).

Ó Danachair, Caoimhín, 'Change in the Irish landscape', *Ulster Folklife* no. 8 (1962).

Ó Danachair, Caoimhín, 'Cottier and Landlord in Pre-Famine Ireland', *Béaloideas* nos. 48–49 (1980–1).

Ó Danachair, Caoimhín, 'The Progress of Irish Ethnology, 1783–1982', *Ulster Folklife* vol. 29 (1983).

Ó Duilearga, Séamus, 'Ó'n bhFear Eagair', *Béaloideas* vol. 1, no. 1 (1927).

Ó Duilearga, Séamus, 'Volkskundliche Arbeit in Irland von 1850 bis zur Gegenwart mit besonderer Berücksichtigung der "Irischen Volkskunde–Kommission"', *Zeitschrift für Keltische Philologie und Volksvorschung* no. xxiii (1943).

Ó Duilearga, Séamus, *Leabhar Sheáin Í Chonaill*, new edition (Dublin: Comhairle Bhéaloideas Éireann, 1977).

Ó Fiannachta, Pádraig (ed.), *Thaitin Sé le Peig. Iris na hOidhreachta* 1 (Baile an Fheirtéaraigh: Oidhreacht Chorca Dhuibhne, 1989).

Ó Giolláin, Diarmuid, 'Myth and History. Exotic Foreigners in Folk-belief', *Temenos. Studies in Comparative Religion presented by Scholars in Denmark, Finland, Norway and Sweden* vol. 23 (1987).

Ó Giolláin, Diarmuid, 'Colonialism in the Eastern Baltic? The Estonian and Finnish Cases'. Unpublished paper given to the Conference of the Anthropology Association of Ireland, St Patrick's College, Maynooth, 1996.

Ó Giolláin, Diarmuid, 'The Pattern' in J.S. Donnelly and Kerby A. Miller (eds), *Irish Popular Culture 1650–1850* (Dublin: Irish Academic Press, 1998).

Ó Háinle, Cathal, 'Ó Chaint na nDaoine go dtí an Caighdeán Oifigiúil' in Kim McCone, Damian McManus, Cathal Ó Háinle, Nicholas Williams, Liam Breatnach (eds), *Stair na Gaeilge* (Maynooth: Roinn na Sean-Ghaeilge, Coláiste Phádraig, 1994).

O'Halloran, Claire, 'Irish Re-creations of the Gaelic Past: The Challenge of Macpherson's Ossian', *Past and Present* no. 124, August 1989.

Ó hAodha, Mícheál, 'Introduction' to Douglas Hyde, *Abhráin Grádh Chúige Connacht. Love Songs of Connacht* (Shannon: Irish University Press, 1969).

Ó Laighin, Seán (ed.), *Ó Cadhain i bhFeasta* (Dublin: Clódhanna Teoranta, 1990).

O'Leary, Philip, *The Prose Literature of the Gaelic Revival, 1881–1921. Ideology and Innovation* (University Park, Pennsylvania: The Pennsylvania State University Press, 1994).

Ó Lúing, Seán, 'Lucht Léinn ón Iasacht' in Aogán Ó Muircheartaigh (ed.), *Oidhreacht an Bhlascaoid* (Dublin: Coiscéim, 1989).

Ó Muimhneacháin, Aindrias, 'An Cumann le Béaloideas Éireann 1927–1977', *Béaloideas* 45–47 (1977–1979).

O'Neill, Patrick, 'Ossian's Return: The German Factor in the Irish literary Revival' in Wolfgang Zach and Heinz Kosok (eds), *Literary Interrelations: Ireland, England and the World 2. Comparison and Impact* (Tübingen: Gunter Narr Verlag, 1987).

O'Neill, Tim P., 'The Persistence of Famine in Ireland' in Cathal Póirtéir (ed.), *The Great Irish Famine* (Cork and Dublin: Mercier Press, 1995)

Ong, Walter J., *Orality and Literacy. The Technologizing of the Word* (London and New York: Methuen, 1982).

Ortiz, Renato, *Românticos e folcloristas* (São Paulo: Olho d'Água, 1992).

Ortiz, Renato, *Cultura brasileira e identidade nacional*, 5th edition (São Paulo: Editora Brasiliense, 1994).

Ortiz, Renato, *A moderna tradição brasileira*, 5th edition (São Paulo: Editorial Brasiliense, 1994).

Ortiz, Renato, *Otro territorio. Ensayos sobre el mundo contempóraneo*, trans. Ada Solari (Buenos Aires: Universidad Nacional de Quilmes, 1996).

Ortiz, Renato, *Mundialización y cultura*, trans. Elsa Noya (Buenos Aires and Madrid: Alianza Editorial, 1997).

Ó Súilleabháin, Donncha, *Scéal an Oireachtais 1897–1924* (Dublin: An Clóchomhar Tta, 1984).

O'Sullivan, Sean (ed. and trans.), *Folktales of Ireland* (London: Routledge and Kegan Paul, 1966).

Ó Tuama, Seán (ed.), *The Gaelic League Idea* (Cork: Mercier Press, 1972).

Ouaknine, Serge, 'Les rêves menacés de la transculturalité' in Jacques Langlais, Pierre Laplante and Joseph Levy (eds), *Le Québec de demain et les communautés culturelles* (Montréal: Méridien, 1990).

Panoff, Michel and Perrin, Michel, *Dictionnaire de l'ethnologie* (Paris: Payot, 1973).

Plettenburg, Hermanna W.M. (ed.), *Erixoniana. Contributions to the Study of European Ethnology in memory of Sigurd Erixon* 1 (Arnhem: Rijksmuseum voor Volkskunde 'Het Nedelands Openluchtmuseum', 1970).

Poirier, Jean, *Histoire de l'ethnologie*, 2nd edition (Paris: Presses Universitaires de France, 1974).

Polanyi, Karl, *Origins of Our Time. The Great Transformation* (London: Victor Gollancz Ltd, 1945).

Porter, Roy and Teich, Mikuláš (eds), *Romanticism in National Context* (Cambridge: Cambridge University Press, 1988).

Prat, Joan, 'Historia' in Joan Prat, Ubaldo Martínez, Jesús Contreras and Isodoro Moreno (eds), *Antropología de los Pueblos de España* (Madrid: Taurus Universitaria, 1991).

Prats, Llorenç, 'Sobre el caràcter conservador de la cultura popular' in D. Llopart, J. Prat and Ll. Prats (eds), *La cultura popular a debat* (Barcelona: Fundació Serveis de Cultura Popular Editorial Alta Fulla, 1985).

Prats, Llorenç, *El mite de la tradició popular* (Barcelona: Edicions 62, 1988).

Rafroidi, Patrick, *L'Irlande et le romantisme* (Paris: Éditions Universitaires, 1972).

Ranke, Kurt (ed.), *Enzyklopädie des Märchens* (Berlin and New York: Walter de Gruyter, 1977).

Raun, Toivo, 'The Estonians and the Russian Empire, 1905–1917', *Journal of Baltic Studies* vol. XV, nos 2/3 (1984).

Redfield, Robert, *The Little Community / Peasant Society and Culture* (Chicago and London: University of Chicago Press, 1960).

Rehnberg, Mats, 'Folkloristiska inslag i olika tidevarvs idéströmningar kring det egna landet' in Lauri Honko (ed.), *Folklore och Nationsbyggande i Norden* (Åbo: Nordiska Institutet för Folkdiktning, 1980).

Renan, Ernest, *The Poetry of the Celtic Races, and other Studies*, trans. with introduction and notes William G. Hutchison (London: Walter Scott, Ltd: n.d.).

Renan, Ernest, 'What is a Nation?' in Omar Dahbour and Micheline R. Ishay (eds), *The Nationalism Reader* (New Jersey: Humanities Press, 1995).

Revel, Jacques, *A invenção da sociedade*, trans. Vanda Anastácio (Lisboa and Rio de Janeiro: Difel and Bertrand Brasil, 1990).

Roth, Klaus, 'European Ethnology and Intercultural Communication' in *Ethnologia Europaea* vol. 2, no. 1 (1996), pp. 3–16.

Saagpakk, Paul F., *Eesti-Inglise Sõnaraamat/Estonian-English Dictionary*, 2nd edition (Tallinn: Koolibri, 1992).

Sachs, Wolfgang, *The Development Dictionary* (Johannesburg/London and New Jersey: Witwatersrand University Press/Zed Books, 1992).

Samuel, Raphael (ed.), *People's History and Socialist Theory* (London, Boston and Henley, Routledge and Kegan Paul, 1981).

Schelling, Vivian, *A presença do povo na cultura brasileira. Ensaio sobre o pensamento de Mário de Andrade e Paulo Freire*, trans. Federico Carotti (Campinas: Editora da UNICAMP, 1991).

Schenk, H.G., *The Mind of the European Romantics* (Oxford, New York, Toronto and Melbourne: Oxford University Press, 1979).

Schaer, Roland, *L'invention des musées* (Paris: Gallimard/Réunion des Musées Nationaux, 1993).

Schwarz, Roberto, 'Brazilian Culture: Nationalism by Elimination', trans. Linda Briggs, in Roberto Schwarz, *Misplaced Ideas. Essays on Brazilian Culture* (London and New York: Verso, 1992).

Sebreli, Juan José, *El asedio a la modernidad*, 8th edition (Buenos Aires: Editorial Sudamericana, 1995).

Showstack Sassoon, Anne (ed.), *Approaches to Gramsci* (London: Writers and Readers, 1982).

Showstack Sassoon, Anne, *Gramsci's Politics*, 2nd edition (London, Melbourne, Sydney, Auckland, Johannesburg: Hutchinson, 1987).

Sihvo, Hannes, 'Karelianism', in Olli Alho, Hildi Hawkins and Päivi Vallisaari (eds), *Finland. A Cultural Encyclopedia* (Helsinki: Finnish Literature Society, 1997).

Simeone, William E., 'Fascists and Folklorists in Italy', *Journal of American Folklore* vol. 91, no. 359 (Jan.–March, 1978).

Simon, Roger, *Gramsci's Political Thought* (London: Lawrence and Wishart, 1982).

Simonsen, Michèle, *Le conte populaire français* (Paris: Presses Universitaires de France, 1981).

Simms-Williams, Patrick, 'The Medieval World of Robin Flower in Mícheál de Mórdha (ed.), *Bláithín: Flower. Ceiliúradh an Bhlascaoid* I (Dingle: An Sagart, 1988).

Skovmand, Michael and Schrøder, Kim Christian (eds), *Media Cultures. Reappraising Transnational Media* (London and New York: Routledge, 1992).

Smith, Anthony D., *National Identity* (London: Penguin, 1991).

Stocking, George W. Jr., *Race, Culture, and Evolution. Essays in the History of Anthropology* (Chicago and London: University of Chicago Press, 1982).

Stocking, George W. Jr, *After Tylor. British Social Anthropology 1888–1951* (London: The Athlone Press, 1996).

Stocklund, Bjarne, 'How the Peasant House Became a National Symbol. A Chapter in the History of Museums and Nation-Building' in *Ethnologia Europaea* vol. 29, no. 1 (1999).

Sydhoff, Beate, 'The Unknown Folk Art', trans. Angela Adegren, in Gunnar Arnborg et al., *Folkkonsten – All tradition är förändring* (Stockholm: Kulturhuset, 1992).

Synge, J.M., *The Aran Islands* (Oxford: Oxford University Press, 1979).

Talve, Ilmar, *Suomen kansankulttuuri* (Helsinki: Suomalainen Kirjallisuuden Seura, 1980).

Tarkka, Lotte, 'Karjalan kuvaus kansallisena rctoriikkana' in Seppo Knuuttila and Pekka Laaksonen (eds), *Runon ja rajan teillä* (Helsinki: Suomalaisen Kirjallisuuden Seura, 1989).

Thackeray, W.M., *The Irish Sketchbook* (Dublin: Gill and Macmillan, 1990).

Therborn, Göran, *European Modernity and Beyond. The Trajectory of European Societies 1945–2000* (London, Thousand Oaks and New Delhi 1995).

Thompson, Stith, *The Folktale* (Bekeley, Los Angeles and London 1971: University of California Press, 1971).

Thuente, Mary Helen, *W.B. Yeats and Irish Folklore* (Dublin: Gill and Macmillan, 1980).

Todd, Emmanuel, *L'Invention de l'Europe*, new edition (Paris: Seuil, 1996).

Todorov, Tzvetan, *Les morales de l'histoire* (Paris: Bernard Grasset, 1991).

Tönnies, Ferdinand, *Community and Association*, trans. and supp. Charles P. Loomis (London: Routledge and Kegan Paul Ltd, 1955).

Tylor, Edward B., *Primitive Culture. Researches into the Development of Mythology, Philosophy, Religion, Art, and Custom* (London: John Murray, 1871).

Viidalepp, Richard, *Valimik muistendeid Koolide Kogumisvõistluselt 1939. Eesti Rahvaluule Arhiivi Toimetused* no. 10 (1939).

Viidalepp, Richard, 'Auhindadest ja auhindamisest', *Rahvapärimuste Selgitaja* II nr. 1 (8 [1940]).

Vilhena, Luís Rodolfo, *Projeto e missão. O movimento folclórico brasileiro 1947–1964* (Rio de Janeiro: Funarte, 1997).

Weber, Eugen, *Peasants into Frenchmen. The Modernization of Rural France 1870–1914* (London: Chatto and Windus, 1977).

Welch, Robert (ed.), *The Oxford Companion to Irish Literature* (Oxford: Clarendon Press, 1996).

Whelan, Kevin, *The Tree of Liberty. Radicalism, Catholicism and the Construction of Irish Identity 1760–1830* (Cork: Cork University Press, 1996).

Wikström, Brittmari (ed.), *Flykten från vardagen*. Meddelanden från Ålands Högskola nr 6, Mariehamn, 1995.

Wilde, William R., *Irish Popular Superstitions* (Dublin: Irish Academic Press, 1979 [1852]).

Willett, Ralph, The *Americanization of Germany, 1945–1949* (London and New York: Routledge, 1989).

Williams, Fionnuala, 'Six Hundred Gaelic Proverbs Collected in Ulster by Robert Mac Adam', *Proverbium* no. 12 (1995).

Williams, J.E. Caerwyn and Ní Mhuiríosa, Máirín, *Traidisiún Liteartha na nGael* (Dublin: An Clóchomhar Tta, 1979).

Williams, Raymond, *Keywords*, revised and expanded edition (London: Fontana, 1988).

Wilson, William A., *Folklore and Nationalism in Modern Finland* (Bloomington and London: Indiana University Press, 1976).

Wolf, Eric R., *Peasants* (Englewood Cliffs, New Jersey: Prentice Hall, Inc., 1966).

Yeats, W.B. (ed.), *Fairy and Folk Tales of Ireland* (London: Picador, 1979).

Ylikangas, Heikki, 'Über den gesellschaftlichen Hintergrund der finnischen nationalen Bewegung' in Tenho Takalo (ed.), *Finns and Hungarians between East and West* (Helsinki: Societas Historica Finlandiae, 1989).

Yoder, Don (ed.), *American Folklife* (Austin and London: University of Texas Press, 1976).

Zabludovsky, Gina (ed.), *Teoría sociológica y modernidad* (México: Plaza y Valdés, 1998).

Zetterberg, Seppo (ed.), *Suomen Historian Pikku Jättiläinen* (Porvoo, Helsinki, Juva: Werner Söderström Osakeyhtiö, 1995).

Zimmermann, Georges-Denis, *Songs of Irish Rebellion. Political Street Ballads and Rebel Songs 1780–1900* (Dublin: Allen Figgis, 1967).

Zipes, Jack, *Fairy tales and the Art of Subversion. The classical genre for children and the process of civilization* (London: Heinemann, 1983).

Index